FRIEDRICH NIETZSCHE

Daybreak

Thoughts on the prejudices of morality

EDITED BY

MAUDEMARIE CLARK
Colgate University, New York

BRIAN LEITER
University of Texas, Austin

TRANSLATED BY

R. J. HOLLINGDALE

CAMBRIDGE
UNIVERSITY PRESS

PUBLISHED BY THE PRESS SYNDICATE OF THE UNIVERSITY OF CAMBRIDGE
The Pitt Building, Trumpington Street, Cambridge, United Kingdom

CAMBRIDGE UNIVERSITY PRESS
The Edinburgh Building, Cambridge CB2 2RU, UK
40 West 20th Street, New York, NY 10011–4211, USA
477 Williamstown Road, Port Melbourne, VIC 3207, Australia
Ruiz de Alarcón 13, 28014 Madrid, Spain
Dock House, The Waterfront, Cape Town 8001, South Africa

http://www.cambridge.org

First published 1997
Ninth printing 2006

Printed in the United Kingdom at the University Press, Cambridge

Typeset in New Baskerville

A catalogue record for this book is available from the British Library

Library of Congress Cataloguing in Publication data
Nietzche, Friedrich Wilhelm, 1844–1900.
[Morgenröthe. English]
Daybreak: thoughts on the prejudices of morality / Friedrich Nietzsche:
edited by Maudemarie Clark, Brian Leiter; translated by R. J. Hollingdale.
p.   cm. – (Cambridge texts in the history of philosophy)
Includes bibliographical references and index.
ISBN 0 521 59050 7 (hardback). – ISBN 0 521 59963 6 (paperback)
1. Prejudices.   I. Clark, Maudemarie.   II. Leiter, Brian.
III. Title.   IV. Series.
B3313.M73E5   1997
193 – dc21   97–8910 CIP

ISBN 0 521 59050 7 hardback
ISBN 0 521 59963 6 paperback

Contents

Introduction

The place of *Daybreak* in the Nietzschean corpus

Nietzsche began compiling the notes that would comprise *Daybreak* in January of 1880, finishing the book by May of the following year. Like all of Nietzsche's books, it sold poorly (fewer than 250 copies in the first five years, according to William Schaberg). Unlike most of his other works, however, it has been sadly neglected during the Nietzsche renaissance of the past three decades. *Daybreak* post-dates his famous, polemical study of classical literature, *The Birth of Tragedy* (1872) – the book that, at the time, destroyed Nietzsche's professional reputation in classical philology (the subject he taught at the University of Basel, until ill health forced his retirement in 1879). *Daybreak* also post-dates a somewhat less-neglected prior volume, *Human, All Too Human: A Book for Free Spirits* (1878–80), the book often said to constitute the highwater mark of Nietzsche's "positivist" phase (in which he accepted, somewhat uncritically, that science was the paradigm of all genuine knowledge).

Daybreak's relative obscurity, however, is due more to his subsequent writings, which have overshadowed it in both the classroom and the secondary literature: *The Gay Science* (1882), the four books of *Thus Spoke Zarathustra* (1883–84), *Beyond Good and Evil* (1886), *On the Genealogy of Morality* (1887), and, to a lesser extent, the works of his last sane year (1888): *Twilight of the Idols*, *The Antichrist*, and *Ecce Homo*. Even the compilation made (against Nietzsche's wishes) from his notebooks after his mental collapse (in January 1889) and subsequently published as *The Will to Power* (first German edition, 1901) has received more scholarly scrutiny than *Daybreak* – a book Nietzsche intended to publish, and one that he pronounced (in late 1888) the "book [in which] my campaign against morality begins" (*Ecce Homo*, "Why I Write Such Good Books," sub-section 1 of section on *Daybreak*).[1]

This last observation is of crucial importance: for as he goes on to tell us in the same passage, *Daybreak* "seeks [a] new morning...[i]n a *revaluation of all values*, in a liberation from all moral values." The book, in short, marks the beginning of Nietzsche's central philosophical project: a revaluation of all values, a thorough-going critique of morality itself. It is the book that broaches "[t]he question concerning the origin of moral values" (*ibid.*), the question he returns to in *Beyond Good and Evil* (esp. Section 260) and, most famously, in the *Genealogy*. More importantly, it is the book that first develops in a substantial way themes that mark the "mature" Nietzsche: for example, his critique of the conventional view of human agency, as well as his development of a "naturalistic" conception of persons.

That it is a serious mistake to neglect *Daybreak*, and that this new edition presents a splendid opportunity for students and scholars to reconsider its central place in the corpus, we hope will become apparent in the following pages. We also hope to demonstrate how wrong-headed is the following common view of *Daybreak*, most recently expressed by the editors of *The Cambridge Companion to Nietzsche*: "Nietzsche seems bent [in *Daybreak*] on conveying a particular type of experience in thinking to his readers, much more than he is concerned to persuade his readers to adopt any particular point of view." Nietzsche's ambitions are, we will show, far more philosophically substantial, as would befit the book in which Nietzsche's "campaign against morality" begins. First, however, we must set the intellectual stage on which *Daybreak* enters.

Nietzsche and Nietzsche's Germany

The widespread pedagogic practice of treating Nietzsche as a figure of "nineteenth-century philosophy," along with Hegel and Marx, actually does considerable violence to the real intellectual

---

[1] We will generally refer to Nietzsche's texts by their standard English-language acronyms: D=*Daybreak*; HA=*Human, All Too Human*; BGE=*Beyond Good and Evil*; GM=*On the Genealogy of Morality*; EH=*Ecce Homo*. Roman numerals refer to major parts or chapters; Arabic numerals refer to sections, not pages.

history of Germany. While Hegel did dominate German philosophical life in the first quarter of the century, by 1830 his influence was waning seriously. By the 1840s and 1850s, Hegel's critics – Karl Marx, Arthur Schopenhauer, and Ludwig Feuerbach, among others – were both better known and more widely read than Hegel. By the time Nietzsche (born 1844) was being educated at the post-secondary level, it was not Hegel's Idealism that dominated the intellectual landscape, but rather Schopenhauer's own more Kantian metaphysical system, as well as the broad-based intellectual movement known as "German Materialism," of which Feuerbach was an early figure. (There is no evidence, however, that Nietzsche ever read Marx, who was not himself part of the "Materialist" movement at issue here.) For purposes of understanding Nietzsche, the key German figures are really Kant, Schopenhauer, and the Materialists.

Nietzsche, of course, was trained not in philosophy *per se*, but in classical philology, the exacting study of the texts and cultures of the ancient world. Unlike contemporary literary theorists, nineteenth-century German classicists viewed the interpretation of texts as a *science*, whose aim was to discover what texts *really mean* through an exhaustive study of language, culture and context. Nietzsche proved a brilliant student, and was awarded a professorship in 1869, even before earning his doctorate. Yet Nietzsche was always ill-at-ease with the narrow academic horizons of professional philology. He sought to do more than solve mere scholarly "puzzles"; he wanted to connect the study of classical civilization to his far more pressing concern with the state of contemporary German culture. It was this project he undertook in *The Birth of Tragedy*, a book that was, not surprisingly, poorly received by his academic peers.

Evidence of Nietzsche's classical training and his admiration of classical civilization abounds throughout *Daybreak*. Two themes, in particular, recur. First, Nietzsche embraced the "realism" of the Sophists and Presocratics, philosophers who had the courage, in Nietzsche's view, to look reality in the eye, and report things as they really are, without euphemism or sentimentality. Nietzsche saw, with good reason, the great Greek historian Thucydides as the embodiment of this perspective on human nature and human affairs, noting that in Thucydides, "that *culture of the most impartial knowledge of the world* finds its last glorious flower: that culture which had in Sophocles its poet, in Pericles its statesman, in Hippocrates its

physician, in Democritus its natural philosopher; which deserves to
be baptized with the name of its teachers, the Sophists..." (168).
Nietzsche himself strives to imitate Thucydides' realistic appraisal of
human motivations, for example, when he observes that "egoistic"
actions "have hitherto been by far the most frequent actions, and
will continue to be so for all future time" (148).

Second, Nietzsche defends the "empiricism" of the Presocratics
against the "idealism" of Plato; indeed he sees as fundamental to
the whole history of philosophy the dispute between those who
accept as the only reality what the "senses" reveal about the world
and those who claim that the "real" world exists beyond the sensible world. It is clear where Nietzsche stands on this question. He
rejects the "dialectic" method as a way of getting behind "the veil
of appearance" – a project he attributes to Plato and Schopenhauer
– noting that "For that to which they want to show us the way does
not *exist*" (474). Elsewhere in *Daybreak*, he observes: "Thus did
Plato flee from reality and desire to see things only in pallid mental pictures; he was full of sensibility and knew how easily the
waves of his sensibility could close over his reason" (448; cf. 43).
Here we see a characteristic Nietzschean move (to which we will
return shortly): to explain a particular philosophical position
(e.g. Plato's view that the "real" world is the world of "Forms" or
"Ideas," that are inaccessible to the senses) in terms of facts
about the person who advances the position (e.g. Plato's excessive
sensitivity).

These critical remarks about Plato must be balanced with
Nietzsche's admiration for Plato's "genius" (497). Thus, in a remark
that remains apt today, Nietzsche contrasts the "Platonic dialogue" in which "souls were filled with drunkenness at the rigorous and sober game of concept, generalization, refutation, limitation" with "how philosophy is done today" in which philosophers
"want to be 'artistic natures'" and to enjoy "the divine privilege of
being incomprehensible" (544).

Nietzsche's engagement with the classical world marks just one
of the three important intellectual influences on his philosophical
writing. The other two were the philosophy of Schopenhauer and
the German Materialist movement of the 1850s and 1860s. We
shall discuss Schopenhauer's impact on Nietzsche in detail below
in the context of *Daybreak*'s central theme, the critique of morality.
Here we introduce some of the main themes of German
Materialism.

x

German Materialism had its origins in Feuerbach's work of the late 1830s and early 1840s, but it really exploded on to the cultural scene in the 1850s, under the impetus of the startling new discoveries about human beings made by the burgeoning science of physiology. The medical doctor Ludwig Büchner summed up the Materialist point of view well in his 1855 best-seller *Force and Matter*, the book that became the "Bible" of Materialism. "The researches and discoveries of modern times," he wrote in the preface to the eighth edition, "can no longer allow us to doubt that man, with all he has and possesses, be it mental or corporeal, is a *natural product* like all other organic beings." Our evidence of Nietzsche's familiarity with the Materialists is extensive. For one thing, it is impossible that a literate young person in Germany at the time could have been *unfamiliar* with the Materialists. As one critic wrote in 1856: "A new world view is settling into the minds of men. It goes about like a virus. Every young mind of the generation now living is affected by it" (quoted in Gregory, *Scientific Materialism*, p. 10). More concretely, we do know that Nietzsche read (with great enthusiasm) Friedrich Lange's *History of Materialism* (published 1866), a book which mounted an extensive (but sympathetic) NeoKantian critique of the Materialists. In fact, in a letter of February 1868 (quoted in Stack, *Lange and Nietzsche*, p. 13), Nietzsche called Lange's book "a real treasure-house," mentioning, among other things, Lange's discussion of the "materialist movement of our times," including the work of Feuerbach, Büchner, and the physiologists Jacob Moleschott and Herman von Helmholtz. From Lange, Nietzsche would have learned of the Materialist view that "The nature of man is...only a special case of universal physiology, as thought is only a special case in the chain of the physical processes of life." Indeed, that he took the lesson to heart is suggested in his autobiography, *Ecce Homo*, where he tells us (in his discussion of *Human, All Too Human*) that in the late 1870s, "A truly burning thirst took hold of me: henceforth I really pursued nothing *more* than physiology, medicine and natural science." A bit earlier in the same work (II: 2), he complains of the "blunder" that he "became a philologist – why not at least a physician or something else that opens one's eyes?"

Yet the most compelling evidence of the Materialist impact on Nietzsche is the extent to which Materialist themes appear in Nietzsche's work, including *Daybreak*. The Materialists embraced the idea that human beings were essentially *bodily* organisms, whose attitudes, beliefs, and values were explicable by reference to *physiological* facts about them. Spiritual, religious, and moral explanations of human beings were to be supplanted by purely physical or physiological explanations.

Thus, Moleschott's 1850 work *The Physiology of Food* contained 500 pages of detailed information about the physical and chemical properties of food and human digestion, while his popular companion volume, *The Theory of Food: For the People*, spelled out the implications of this research in terms of the different diets that different types of people need to flourish. In reviewing Moleschott's book, Feuerbach expressed the core idea as follows: "If you want to improve the people then give them better food instead of declamations against sin. Man is what he eats" (quoted in Gregory, *Scientific Materialism*, p. 92). Büchner's *Force and Matter* took a related tack, seeking to explain human character and belief systems in physiological terms. So, for example, he suggested that "A copious secretion of bile has, as is well known, a powerful influence on the mental disposition" and arguing elsewhere in the same work that it was, "Newton's atrophied brain [that] caused him in old age to become interested in studying the...Bible."

With figures like Moleschott and Büchner ascendant on the intellectual scene, it is hardly surprising to find Nietzsche writing as follows in *Daybreak*:

> Whatever proceeds from the stomach, the intestines, the beating of the heart, the nerves, the bile, the semen – all those distempers, debilitations, excitations, the whole chance operation of the machine of which we still know so little! – had to be seen by a Christian such as Pascal as a moral and religious phenomenon, and he had to ask whether God or Devil, good or evil, salvation or damnation was to be discovered in them! Oh what an unhappy interpreter. (86; cf. 83)

Like the Materialists, Nietzsche replaces "moral" or "religious" explanations for phenomena with *naturalistic* explanations, particularly explanations couched in physiological or quasi-physiological language. Thus, he suggests that "Three-quarters of all the evil done in the world happens out of timidity: and this [is] above all a physiological phenomenon" (538), and that "our moral judgments and evaluations...are only images and fantasies based on a physiological process unknown to us" (119). Indeed, he endorses, as a general explanatory scruple, the view that "all the products of [a person's] thinking are bound to reflect the condition he is in" (42), noting, accordingly, that any particular philosophy "translate[s] as it were into reason" what amounts to a "personal diet" (553).

The critique of morality

The central theme of *Daybreak* is its attack on morality. The attack proceeds essentially along two fronts. First, Nietzsche takes tradi- tional morality to involve *false* presuppositions: for example, a *false* picture of human agency (roughly, the view that human beings act autonomously or freely, and thus are morally responsible for what they do). He attacks this picture of agency from the perspec- tive of a *naturalistic* view of persons as *determined* in their actions by the fundamental physiological and psychological facts about them. Second, he takes traditional morality to be inhospitable to certain types of human flourishing. This second theme, which is less prominent than the first, is voiced at various points in *Daybreak*: for example, when Nietzsche complains that morality entails "a fundamental remoulding, indeed weakening and aboli- tion of the individual" (132), a result of the fact that "morality is nothing other...than obedience to customs" (9), and thus is incompatible with a "free human being...[who] is *determined* to depend upon himself and not upon a tradition" (9). A variation on this criticism is also apparent when he observes (*contra* Rousseau) that "Our weak unmanly, social concepts of good and evil and their tremendous ascendancy over body and soul have finally weakened all bodies and souls and snapped the self-reliant, independent, unprejudiced men, the pillars of a *strong* civiliza- tion..." (164). The view that morality poses a special threat to human *excellence* or *greatness* is one that will become more promi- nent in Nietzsche's later works, though it remains visible in this early book as well.

Yet the crux of the argument in *Daybreak* is directed at the prob- lematic presuppositions of morality. As he writes in an important passage on two different ways of "denying" morality:

> "To deny morality" – this can mean, *first*: to deny that the moral motives which men *claim* have inspired their actions really have done so – it is thus the assertion that morality consists of words and is among the coarser or more subtle deceptions (especially self-deceptions) which men practise... *Then* it can mean: to deny that moral judgments are based on truths. Here it is admitted that

they really are motives of action, but that in this way it is *errors* which, as the basis of all moral judgment, impel men to their moral actions. This is *my* point of view: though I should be the last to deny that *in very many cases* there is some ground for suspicion that the other point of view – that is to say, the point of view of La Rochefoucauld and others who think like him – may also be justified and in any event of great general application.

Thus I deny morality as I deny alchemy, that is, I deny their presuppositions [*die Voraussetzungen*, which might also be translated "premises"]: *not* that countless people *feel* themselves to be immoral, but there is any *true* reason so to feel. It goes without saying that I do not deny – unless I am a fool – that many actions called...moral ought to be done and encouraged – but I think the one should be encouraged and the other avoided *for other reasons than hitherto*. We have to *learn to think differently* – in order at last, perhaps very late on, to attain even more: *to feel differently*. (D, 103)

This important passage is of great value in understanding the argument of *Daybreak*, and we shall have more to say about it, below. Note now, however, the crucial analogy Nietzsche draws between his attack on "morality" and a comparable attack on alchemy. When we deny *alchemy* we don't deny that "countless people" believed themselves to be alchemists, that is, believed themselves to be engaged in the process of transforming the base metals into gold. Rather, we deny a presupposition of their undertaking: namely (to put it in modern terms) the presupposition that the application of forces to the macro-properties of substances can effect a transformation in their micro-properties (i.e. their molecular constitution). So to "deny" morality in a similar fashion is not to deny that people act for *moral* reasons or that they take *morality* seriously, but to "deny" that the reasons for which they do so are sound: the *presuppositions* of morality are as wrong-headed as the presuppositions of alchemy.

We return, below, to the crucial question of what are the "presuppositions" of morality in Nietzsche's sense. Before we do so, however, we will sketch those features of the moral philosophies of Kant and Schopenhauer against the background of which Nietzsche came to understand morality as having false presuppositions.

Kant and Schopenhauer on morality

According to Kant and Schopenhauer, actions are praiseworthy from the viewpoint of morality only when done from a moral motive. But these philosophers disagree about the character of moral motivation and therefore about which actions have the special kind of value they both call "moral worth" (or "ethical significance," as Schopenhauer sometimes says).

Kant and Schopenhauer agree that an action is devoid of moral worth if it is motivated purely by a desire for the agent's own happiness. But Kant goes further, claiming that desiring the happiness of others "stands on the same footing as other inclinations" and cannot therefore give moral worth to actions (G 398/66).[2] His reasoning seems to be that the desire for the happiness of another cannot give an action moral worth if the desire for one's own happiness clearly does not. Inclinations and desires may deserve praise and encouragement, but never esteem, the mark of the moral.

Kant considers duty to be the only reasonable alternative to desire or inclination as the source of moral worth. To have moral worth an action must be done from the motive of duty. This means that it is done because one recognizes that one ought to perform the action and that the action is "objectively necessary in itself" regardless of one's own desires or ends (G 414/82). The action is thus motivated by the recognition of a categorical imperative.

If one recognizes an ought statement as a hypothetical imperative, in contrast, one recognizes only a conditioned necessity, the necessity of an action for the achievement of some further end. The shopkeeper recognizes that he ought not cheat his customers because they will buy from his competitors if he does. The necessity he recognizes is thus conditioned by his own end or desire: to run a successful business. In this case, the necessity of the commanded action can be escaped if he abandons the end or purpose, whereas this is not so in the case of a categorical imperative – the necessity it formulates is not dependent on any of the agent's purposes. There is one purpose Kant thinks we cannot

---

[2] Kant's *Grundlegung zur Metaphysic der Sitten* is cited as "G" followed by the page number in the Academy edition and the page number in H. J. Paton's translation: *The Moral Law: Kant's Groundwork of the Metaphysic of Morals* (London: Hutchinson and Co., 1958).

abandon, for "we can assume with certainty that all *do* have [it] by natural necessity": our own happiness. Yet imperatives that affirm the practical necessity of an action as a means to the furtherance of happiness – imperatives of prudence – still count as hypothetical rather than categorical: "an action is commended not absolutely, but only as a means to a further purpose" (G 416/83). To act from the motive of duty, according to Kant, is to act out of reverence for the law: to be motivated sufficiently to perform an action by the recognition of its objective or unconditioned necessity.

Schopenhauer denies that Kant's idea of "objective necessity" adds to our understanding of morality, calling it "nothing but a cleverly concealed and very forced paraphrase of the word *ought*" (BM 67).[3] Arguing that "every *ought* derives all sense and meaning simply and solely in reference to threatened punishment or promised reward" (BM 55), he further denies that the recognition of an ought ever involves "unconditioned necessity." The Kantian notions of absolute obligation, law, and duty are derived from theology, he claims, and have no sense or content at all apart from the assumption of a God who gives the law (BM 68). For we simply can make no sense of the idea of law, and thus of how a law could confer on us duties or obligations, unless we regard obedience as promising reward and disobedience as threatening punishment. Even if we assume that God has laid down a law, Schopenhauer would refuse it moral status. Because even a divine command would acquire the status of law only by being able to promise reward and threaten punishment, it could only be a hypothetical imperative. "Obedience to it is, of course, wise or foolish according to circumstances; yet it will always be selfish, and consequently without moral value" (BM 55).

According to Schopenhauer, then, an ought statement never counts as a categorical imperative or moral judgment, but can only be what Kant would have called a "judgment of prudence." An action performed for the sake of duty, simply because one recognizes that one ought to do it, is selfish rather than morally

---

[3] Schopenhauer's *Die beiden Grundprobleme der Ethik* is cited as "BM," followed by the page number in the translation by E. F. J. Payne: *On the Basis of Morality* (Indianapolis: Bobbs-Merrill, 1965). Schopenhauer's *Die Welt als Wille und Vorstellung* is cited as "WW," followed by the volume and page number in the translation by E. F. J. Payne: *The World as Will and Representation* (New York: Dover, 1966).

motivated. Schopenhauer thus argues against Kant within the latter's own terms. If Kant accepted Schopenhauer's motivational claim – which he in fact explicitly rejects – that "nothing can induce us to obey except *fear* of the evil consequences of *disobedience*" (BM 142), he would have to admit either that there are no morally motivated actions, or that he had characterized them incorrectly.

The latter choice seemed obvious to Schopenhauer, who believed that few "are not convinced from their own experience that a man often acts justly, simply and solely that no wrong or injustice may be done to another," and that many of us help others with no intention in our hearts other than helping those whose distress we see (BM 138–39). It is to such actions, he claims, that we attribute "real *moral worth*," and they are motivated not by what Kant called "duty," but by compassion, "the immediate *participation*, independent of all ulterior considerations, primarily in the *suffering* of another, and thus in the prevention or elimination of it" (BM 144).

The "ulterior considerations" Schopenhauer regards as incompatible with compassion, and thus with moral worth, are egoistic concerns, concerns for one's own well-being. Schopenhauer agrees with Kant that if an action "has as its motive an egoistic aim, it cannot have any moral worth" (BM 141). Unlike Kant, he does not infer from this that concern for another's happiness cannot give actions moral worth. From the premise that "*egoism* and the *moral* worth of an action absolutely exclude each other," he infers instead that "the moral significance of an action can only lie in its reference to others" (BM 142). He draws this conclusion by way of the claim that the will is moved only by considerations of well-being or suffering. If moral worth does not belong to actions motivated by a concern for one's own well-being or suffering, it must belong to actions motivated by a concern for the well-being and suffering of others.

How then would Schopenhauer answer Kant's implied question as to how concern for others' well-being can give an action moral worth when concern for one's own well-being does not? He could not claim that the sphere of other-regarding behavior simply is the sphere of morality, and thus that only other-regarding behavior is properly called "moral." Neither Schopenhauer nor Kant can regard the issue about moral worth that separates them to be simply a matter of what something is called. Both philosophers assume that moral worth is a higher kind of worth – than, say, intellectual worth, aesthetic worth, or prudential value – and Kant describes moral worth as "that pre-eminent good which we call moral" (G 401/69). Schopenhauer claims not simply that we *call* acting for another's sake "moral," but that so acting has a higher value than acting for one's own sake. To answer Kant's question he must therefore show that there is a difference between these two kinds of motives that justifies the claim that one is of a higher value than the other. Though Schopenhauer never explicitly tries to answer this question, the kind of answer provided by his theory seems clear: it would be given in terms of his conception of the thing-in-itself.

The distinction between appearances (the "phenomenal" or "sensible" world) and the thing-in-itself (the "noumenal" world) – that is, the distinction between the world as it appears to us and the world as it really is "in-itself" – plays an important role in the moral theories of both Kant and Schopenhauer. In each case, the motive claimed to give moral worth to actions is also claimed to have its source in the noumenal world.

For Kant, all inclinations and desires belong to the phenomenal world – they are the "appearances" in terms of which human actions, insofar as we encounter them in the "sensible world," the world accessible to sense observation, are explained and made intelligible. If human beings belonged solely to the world of appearances, all of their actions "would have to be taken as in complete conformity with the laws of nature governing desires and inclinations" (G 453/121).

Kant's claim that concern for the happiness of others "stands on the same footing as other inclinations" therefore means that it belongs to the world of appearances, that actions motivated by it are merely natural, that they are fully explicable in terms of our status as natural creatures, members of the phenomenal world. That this seems sufficient for Kant to dismiss it as a moral motive suggests that Schopenhauer was right to attribute to him the view he attributed to most philosophers:

> It is undeniably recognized by all nations, ages, and creeds, and even by all philosophers (with the exception of the materialists proper), that the ethical significance of human conduct is meta-physical, in other words, that it reaches beyond this phenomenal existence and touches eternity. (BM 54)

This is why Schopenhauer rejects Kant's view of moral worth: if recognizing that one ought to perform an action is always conditioned by fear of punishment or the desire for reward, acting from duty has no metaphysical significance, and therefore no moral worth. Kant would have to agree if he agreed about the role of reward and punishment in the recognition of duty – for he accepts the same principle: whatever belongs only to the phenomenal world cannot be the source of moral worth. That is why he rejects moral theories like Schopenhauer's that locate the source of moral worth in sympathetic concern for others: he regards such concern as rooted in natural inclination, and therefore as devoid of metaphysical significance.

Acting out of reverence for the law, in contrast, does have metaphysical significance for Kant – for it involves recognizing as law the commands of the noumenal self. Although Kant denies that we can have knowledge of the thing-in-itself, he argues that we can make sense of morality only if we take human beings as they are "in-themselves" as autonomous, as legislators of universal law. To act morally is to act out of reverence for the law legislated by the noumenal self – the "true self," one is tempted to say. For Kant the noumenal source of the motive of duty bestows on actions an incomparably higher worth than could come from mere inclination (or anything else that belongs only to the phenomenal or natural world).

Schopenhauer had his own ideas regarding the thing-in-itself with which to counter Kant's suggestion that concern for others is of no more value than other inclinations. He believed that Kant had already shown that time and space do not belong to the thing-in-itself, and therefore that individuality and plurality are foreign to the "true essence of the world" (BM 207). Individuality is only the appearance in time and space of the thing-in-itself, which, in complete opposition to Kant, Schopenhauer took to be blindly striving will (the forerunner, perhaps, of Freud's id). To the extent that we fail to recognize our individuality as mere appearance, we are moved to action only by egoistic concerns. We see the world completely in terms of how it affects our own well-being. If we care about the welfare of others, this is due not to our natural inclinations, but only to the recognition in others of something that lies beyond nature, of our "own self," our "own true inner nature" (BM 209). Schopenhauer again stays within Kant's own terms: compassion, immediate concern for the welfare of another, possesses a higher worth than egoistic inclinations because, rather than being part of our natural equipment, it is a sign of our connection to a reality that goes beyond the phenomenal or natural world. This is basically the same claim Kant makes about the motive of duty. To have moral worth, Schopenhauer and Kant thus agree, actions must be motivated by something of higher value than egoistic concern, something that is rooted in a realm beyond the natural world. They disagree about moral worth because they hold very different views about which human motive is rooted in the noumenal world.

From *Human, All Too Human* to *Daybreak*

In *Human, All Too Human*, the work preceding *Daybreak*, Nietzsche began a long effort to free morality from the metaphysical world to which Kant and Schopenhauer had connected it. He set out to show that one need not posit the existence of such a world to explain the so-called "higher" activities – art, religion, and morality – which are often taken as signs of human participation in a higher or metaphysical realm (HA 10). He wanted to explain these "higher" things in terms of the "lower," the merely human. The book's title, he writes in *Ecce Homo*, meant: "'where you see ideal things, I see what is – human, alas, all-too-human!' – I know man better."

In this book, Nietzsche continues,

> you discover a merciless spirit that knows all the hideouts where the ideal is at home... One error after another is coolly placed on ice; the ideal is not refuted – it *freezes* to death. – Here, for example, "the genius" freezes to death; at the next corner, "the saint"; under a huge icicle, "the hero"; in the end, "faith," so-called "conviction"; "pity" also cools down considerably – and almost everywhere "the thing in itself" freezes to death. (EH III: HA 1)

The ideals Nietzsche places on ice are idealizations, beliefs that certain kinds of persons, activities, or states of mind exceed the standard of the merely human. "The saint" counts as an ideal because saints have been thought to represent "something that exceeded the human standard of goodness and wisdom" (HA 143). Nietzsche places this ideal on ice by showing it to involve an error. He isolates the characteristics regarded as elevating saints above the human standard and explains them as expressions of egoistic drives to which no one would attribute an ideal character. For instance, he explains their self-denial and asceticism in such terms as the lust for power and the desire to excite an exhausted nervous system (HA 135–42).

Applying the same method of "psychological observation" or "reflection on the human, all-too-human" (HA 35) throughout the book, Nietzsche explains many other idealized activities or types in terms of psychological needs that he considers egoistic and merely human. The ultimate effect of this procedure, he says, may be to lay an axe "to the root of the human 'metaphysical need'" (HA 37). Even though "there might be a metaphysical world" (HA 9), if we can explain the so-called higher aspects of human life without positing anything beyond the natural world, "the strongest interest in the purely theoretical problem of the 'thing in itself' and the 'appearance' will cease" (HA 10). If the human world can be explained without the assumption of a metaphysical world, the latter will be of no cognitive interest to us. We can say of it only that it is other than our world – an inaccessible, incomprehensible "being-other,…a thing with negative qualities" (HA 9).

In view of the importance of the noumenal world to the moral theories of Kant and Schopenhauer, we should expect Nietzsche's attack on ideals in *Human, All Too Human* to involve a rejection of both. Kant does not play much of a role, however, for, as the following passage suggests, Nietzsche had accepted his "great teacher" (GM: P5) Schopenhauer's criticism of Kant's theory.

> For there is no longer any *ought*; for morality, insofar as it was an *ought*, has been just as much annihilated by our mode of thinking as has religion. Knowledge can allow as motives only pleasure and pain, utility and injury. (HA 34)

Nietzsche presumably bases this denial of moral *oughts* on Schopenhauer's argument against Kant's categorical imperative – that a command or rule receives its force as an ought only from an egoistic concern with one's own pleasure or pain, advantage or injury. Schopenhauer's view entails that a belief in *moral* oughts depends on misunderstanding the way in which rules and commands affect behavior. If we realized that people feel obliged to obey them only because of egoistic concerns, we would not think of them as having a kind of *moral* force and thereby misinterpret them as *moral* oughts or categorical imperatives. Following out this line of argument and reflecting on the self-serving origins of just actions, Nietzsche writes (HA 92): "How little moral would the world appear without forgetfulness!" Because *Human, All Too Human* attempts to exhibit the egoistic concerns lying behind our feelings of being obliged to do something, Nietzsche could expect it to undermine our sense that oughts have *moral* force and lead us to agree with Schopenhauer, that obedience to them can only be judged as either "wise or foolish," according to the circumstances.

Schopenhauer had used this argument to support his own view of moral motivation and worth – that compassion, the one non-egoistic motive, rather than Kant's motive of duty, gives moral worth to actions. Nietzsche turns the same kind of argument against Schopenhauer in *Human, All Too Human*. Compassion[4] too can be explained in terms of what is egoistic, or human, all too human:

> For it conceals within itself at least two (perhaps many more) elements of personal pleasure, and is to that extent self-enjoyment: first as the pleasure of emotion, which is the kind represented by pity in tragedy, and then, when it eventuates in action, as the pleasure of gratification in the exercise of power. If, in addition to this, a suffering person is very close to us, we rid ourselves of our own suffering by performing an act of pity [or: through compassionate actions]. Apart from a few philosophers, human beings have always placed pity very low on the scale of moral feelings – and rightly so. (HA 103)

The opposition Nietzsche accepts between the moral and the egoistic should actually lead him to a more radical conclusion: that there are no moral actions. For he claims:

> No one has ever done anything that was solely for the sake of another and without a personal motive. How indeed *could* he do anything that was not related to himself, thus without an inner necessity (which simply must have its basis in a personal need)? How could the *ego* act without *ego*? (HA 133)

Nietzsche's rhetorical question combined with his claim in the same passage that the whole idea of an "unegoistic action" vanishes upon "close examination," suggests that he considers the whole idea of an unegoistic action unintelligible. That Nietzsche's

[4] In the following passage, the German word *Mitleid* has been translated as "pity," following the normal practice among translators of Nietzsche, but this is the same word translators of Schopenhauer render as "compassion."

position is in any case a form of psychological egoism becomes even more obvious when he goes on to quote with approval Lichtenberg and La Rochefoucauld to the effect that we do not really love others – "neither father, nor mother, nor wife, nor child" – but only "the pleasant feelings they cause us" (HA 133). We do not even love others, much less act solely for their sake. As we love only the satisfaction of our own interests, we always act for our own sake. If so, and if, as Nietzsche and Schopenhauer agree, actions cannot be both moral and egoistic, there are no moral actions.

Recall that Schopenhauer views the moral significance of conduct as "metaphysical" in the sense that it "reaches beyond this phenomenal existence" and "directly touch[es] the thing-in-itself" (WW I: 422). Because egoistic motives are fully comprehensible in terms of the phenomenal world, they have no moral worth. Unegoistic motives, in contrast, spring from "the immediate knowledge of the numerical identity of the inner nature of all living things" (WW II: 609) – an identity which is completely inaccessible to empirical knowledge and is therefore not to be found in the phenomenal world. Moral worth attaches to such motives precisely because they point beyond the phenomenal world to the thing-in-itself.

Schopenhauer's assumption of the "numerical identity" of all living things is among the metaphysical assumptions Nietzsche wanted to show we could dispense with in *Human, All Too Human*. This book began his task of "translat[ing] human beings back into nature" (BG 230), and his first problem was to show that so-called "unegoistic" actions could be so translated. But Schopenhauer's world-view (unlike Kant's) had no room for a natural unegoistic action: actions done for the sake of another have moral significance, which they could not have if they were comprehensible in terms of a natural relation between individuals, which would belong only to the phenomenal world. Schopenhauer recognizes only two kinds of motivation – the egoistic motivation human beings have insofar as they act as individuals, hence as members of the phenomenal or natural world, and the motivation they acquire by seeing through the natural or phenomenal world to the metaphysical unity underlying it. Under Schopenhauer's influence, Nietzsche assumed that explaining human behavior naturalistically (i.e., non-metaphysically) meant explaining it egoistically. Accepting Schopenhauer's account of the natural or phenomenal world, he simply denied that it had any connection to a metaphysical world. *Human, All Too Human*'s psychological egoism amounts to a claim that we can explain human behavior without appeal to a reality lying beyond the natural or phenomenal world, combined with Schopenhauer's assumption that all motivation in the latter world is egoistic.

Looking back on *Human, All Too Human*, Nietzsche claimed to find in it a more important issue than the existence of unegoistic actions. This issue "was the *value* of morality."

> In particular the issue was the *value* of the unegoistic, of the instincts of compassion, self-denial, self-sacrifice, which Schopenhauer had gilded, deified, and made otherworldly until finally they alone were left for him as "values in themselves," on the basis of which he *said No* to life, also to himself. (GM: P5)

Nietzsche claims to have seen in the unegoistic instincts Schopenhauer had deified "the great danger to humanity... the will turning itself against life, the last sickness gently and melancholically announcing itself." If such a challenge to Schopenhauer's values is present in *Human, All Too Human*, however, it is well hidden. On the surface, it appears that Nietzsche rejects Schopenhauer's view that unegoistic actions exist, but completely agrees with him about their higher value.

Consider that the book's basic strategy for exhibiting the error involved in attributing a higher value to certain types of behavior is to explain them in egoistic terms. These explanations can seem to reveal the error involved in such judgments only if one assumes that a belief in the higher value of a type of behavior depends on interpreting it as unegoistic. Yet Nietzsche offers no reason to think that it does, and never questions why unegoistic behavior should be so highly valued. He seems simply to take for granted that the unegoistic is of high value, the egoistic of low value, and therefore that demonstrating an action's egoistic nature undermines its claim to high value. Rather than challenging Schopenhauer on the value of unegoistic actions, *Human, All Too Human* seems to argue that nothing possessing the higher value that an unegoistic action would have actually makes its appearance in the human world.

In *Daybreak*, by contrast, we can begin to see the shift in Nietzsche's strategy: he explicitly raises the question about the *value* of unegoistic actions, at the same time that he begins to move away from the psychological egoism of *Human, All Too Human*. Thus, while still conceding (in the spirit of *Human, All Too Human*) that egoistic actions "have hitherto been by far the most frequent actions, and will continue to be for all future time," he suggests – contrary to Kant and Schopenhauer – that we should "restore to these actions their *value*" and thus "*deprive them of their bad conscience*" (D 148). As he explains later, the *value* of "*ideal selfishness*" (as he calls it) is a matter of its role in human flourishing: "continually to watch over and care for and to keep our soul still, so that our fruitfulness shall *come to a happy fulfillment*" (D 552). And he now treats the fact that "men today feel the sympathetic, disinterested, generally useful social actions to be the *moral* actions" as a mere artifact of Christianity, "a residuum of Christian states of mind" (D 132).

Daybreak's repudiation of the thoroughgoing psychological egoism of *Human, All Too Human* is clearest in the important passage on "two ways of denying morality" (D 103), quoted earlier. As we saw, the denial of morality Nietzsche endorses in this passage differs from one "in the spirit of La Rochefoucauld" because Nietzsche admits that human beings do sometimes act from moral motives. In citing La Rochefoucauld, Nietzsche clearly alludes to the egoism of *Human, All Too Human* (see HA 133) which, by way of the equivalence between "moral" and "unegoistic," had implied the non-existence of moral motives. The passage (D 103) thus functions to separate Nietzsche's new position from his earlier one: he no longer denies the existence of morally motivated actions, but claims instead that these actions, when they occur, are based on erroneous presuppositions. In admitting that a suspicion in accord with La Rochefoucauld's way of denying morality is called for "*in very many cases*," the passage also indicates that Nietzsche continues to hold that morally motivated actions cannot be egoistic. Because he now wants to admit that people are sometimes morally motivated, he evidently must also admit that their actions can be in some sense unegoistic.

That *Human, All Too Human* and *Daybreak* thus involve two different ways of denying morality allows us to understand why Nietzsche calls *Daybreak* the beginning of his "campaign against morality." On the topic of morality, *Daybreak* can seem very similar to its predecessor, and Nietzsche's interpreters have seen little difference between them. The claims of HA 39–40, that morality is an "error" and a "lie," sound similar to the denial of morality

xxv

announced in D 103. Yet, as D 103 also suggests, there is a crucial difference. *Human, All Too Human* labels as "lie" and "error" not morality, but the belief that human beings act from moral motives. It directs its polemic against this belief – and, ultimately, against a world it perceived as "human, alas, all-too-human." Only when *Daybreak* admits the existence of moral motivation can Nietzsche begin his actual campaign against morality. Rather than denying that morally motivated actions exist, he now claims that the presuppositions of such actions are erroneous.

Morality's false presuppositions I
A false picture of agency

But what are these presuppositions? *Daybreak* suggests that they are of two types: first, a certain picture of human agents as free and morally responsible (a *logical* presupposition, as it were of morality and moral judgment); second, false beliefs (or superstitions) that explain the *moral* regard with which ancient practices and customs were regarded and that function as *causal* presuppositions of people's "moral" feelings in the present. We shall briefly illustrate both themes in *Daybreak*.

Recall Nietzsche's analogy between the denial of morality and alchemy (103). Nietzsche develops the same analogy several years later in *Beyond Good and Evil*, where he writes that:

> morality in the traditional sense, the morality of intentions, was a prejudice, precipitate and perhaps provisional – something on the order of astrology and alchemy... [T]he decisive value of an action lies precisely in what is *unintentional* in it, while everything that is intentional, everything about it that can be seen, known, "conscious," still belongs to its surface and skin – which, like every skin, betrays something but *conceals* even more. (32)

Here Nietzsche agrees with one premise of the "morality of intentions" – the premise that "the origin of an action...allows [one] to decide its value" (*id.*) – but is denying the premise that the origin is to be found in the conscious intention: what people do is determined by *non-conscious* factors (psychological and physiological), rather than the conscious motives of which we are aware. Insofar as people assess the moral value of an action in terms of its conscious motives – as both Kant and Schopenhauer would have us do – they make moral judgments based on a false presupposition:

the supposition that the conscious motive is the *cause* of the action.

Nietzsche makes this point several times in *Daybreak* (cf. 115, 116, 119, 129, 130). For example, he notes that,

> The primeval delusion still lives on that one knows, and knows quite precisely in every case, *how human action is brought about*... "I know what I want, what I have done, I am free and responsible for it, I hold others responsible, I can call by its name every moral possibility and every inner motion which precedes action..." – that is how everyone formerly thought, that is how almost everyone still thinks... Actions are *never* what they appear to us to be! We have expended so much labour on learning that external things are not as they appear to us to be – very well! the case is the same with the inner world! Moral actions are in reality "something other than that" – more we cannot say: and all actions are essentially unknown. (116)

But if moral judgment requires that we know how human action *is* brought about, then the impossibility of doing that means that our practice of moral judgment is predicated on an error: we believe we can assess the "morality" of our own and others' actions, but in fact we cannot, because we are ignorant as to their true causes.

Yet why, for Nietzsche, is it so difficult to understand what causes us to do what we do? In this regard, it is important to appreciate Nietzsche's picture of human agency, one that very much anticipates the picture later developed with great precision by Freud. As Nietzsche writes:

> However far a man may go in self-knowledge, nothing however can be more incomplete than his image of the totality of *drives* which constitute his being. He can scarcely name even the cruder ones: their number and strength, their ebb and flood, their play and counterplay among one another and above all the laws of their *nutriment* remain wholly unknown to him. (119)

Who we are is a "totality of drives" and what we do is a function of "their play and counterplay." But these drives are so various, so deeply seated, and their triggers (their "nutriments") so poorly understood that who we are and why we do what we do must remain largely mysterious to us. That this is Nietzsche's view is strikingly apparent a few sections earlier in his discussion of the different ways in which a person might attain "mastery" of a drive or instinct (e.g. a particularly strong sex drive). After reviewing six possible "methods" for conquering such a drive, he comments as follows:

> [T]hat one *desires* to combat the vehemence of a drive at all, how-
> ever, does not stand within our own power; nor does the choice of
> any particular method; nor does the success or failure of this
> method. What is clearly the case is that in this entire procedure our
> intellect is only the blind instrument of *another drive* which is a *rival*
> of the drive whose vehemence is tormenting us: whether it be the
> drive to restfulness, or the fear of disgrace and other evil conse-
> quences, or love. While "we" believe we are complaining about the
> vehemence of a drive, at bottom it is one drive *which is complaining
> about another*, that is to say: for us to become aware that we are suf-
> fering from the *vehemence* of a drive presupposes the existence of
> another equally vehement or even more vehement drive, and that
> a *struggle* is in prospect in which our intellect is going to have to
> take sides. (109)

Whereas the conventional "moralist" believes that we freely choose our actions, that the motives for which we choose these actions are known, and that, accordingly, the moral worth of our actions can be assessed, Nietzsche suggests that this entire picture of action is a false one: we do not freely choose our action (we are mere "spectators" on the struggle between drives); we do not know the "motives" for which we act (what determines our actions are the underlying drives and the outcome of their "struggle"); and thus, insofar as moral worth depends on this (discredited) picture of action, the presuppositions of morality are false. This is not to deny that there might be good reasons to condemn those who, e.g., murder (cf. 103); Nietzsche's point is just that con-demning them because they freely chose to act on the basis of an immoral motive is *not* a good reason, supposing as it does an utterly fictitious picture of human action.

Morality's false presuppositions II
The morality of custom

There is another way, though, in which the "presuppositions" of morality are errors, one somewhat more complex than the first. This also marks the new element in *Daybreak*. In *Human, All Too Human*, Nietzsche had already denied that human agents are free and morally responsible, and had taken this to undermine judgments of moral worth (HA 39, 107). But recall that he had also denied that anyone is ever morally motivated, and that *Daybreak*'s new "denial of morality" is predicated upon his changing his mind on this issue. He now admits that human beings are sometimes morally motivated, but insists that when they are, errors move them to their actions (D 103). The key to understanding Nietzsche's new view is to appreciate the important role he now finds for "custom" (*Sitte*) in the phenomenon of morality. Early on in *Daybreak*, he broaches this theme:

> In comparison with the mode of life of whole millennia we present-day men live in a very immoral [*unsittlich*] age: the power of custom [*Sitte*] is astonishingly enfeebled and the sense of morality [*Sittlichkeit*] so rarefied and lofty it may be described as having more or less evaporated. This is why the fundamental insights into the origins of morality [*Moral*] are so difficult for us late-comers... This is, for example, already the case with the *chief proposition*: morality [*Sittlichkeit*] is nothing other (therefore *no more!*) than obedience to customs [*Sitten*], of whatever kind they may be; customs, however, are the *traditional* way of behaving and evaluating. In things in which no tradition commands there is no morality...
>
> The free human being is immoral because in all things he *is determined* to depend upon himself and not upon a tradition... Judged by the standards of these conditions, if an action is performed *not* because tradition commands it, but for other motives (because of its usefulness to the individual, for instance)...it is called immoral and felt to be so by the individual who performed it...
>
> What is tradition? A higher authority which one obeys, not because it commands what is *useful* to us, but simply because it *commands*. – What distinguishes this feeling in the presence of tradition from the feeling of fear in general? It is fear in the presence of a higher intellect which here commands, of an incomprehensible, indefinite power, of something more than personal – there is *superstition* in this fear. (D 9)

Here we have an account of the origin of morality (*Moral*) inspired by the etymological connection between "*Sittlichkeit*" (morality) and "*Sitte*" (custom). This connection suggests to Nietzsche the plausible hypothesis that customs constituted the first morality, that traditional ways of acting played the same role during early human life that "rarefied and lofty" moral codes, rules, and principles play today: that is, they provided the criteria for moral right and wrong. But being moral, Nietzsche emphasizes, required acting from a specific motive: the motive of "obedience to tradition."

There is a striking resonance here with Kant's notion that actions possessing moral worth are done out of respect or reverence for the moral law:

> What I recognize immediately as law for me, I recognize with reverence, which means merely *subordination* of my will to a law without mediation of external influences on my senses. Immediate determination by the law and consciousness of this determination is called "*reverence*"... Reverence is properly awareness of a value that demolishes my self-love. Hence there is something which is regarded neither as an object of inclination nor as an object of fear, though it has at the same time some analogy with both... All moral *interest*, so-called, consists solely in reverence for the law. (G 401/69)

Despite a slight difference in terminology, Nietzsche's description of the most primitive form of moral motivation closely follows Kant's description of reverence. Kant's "reverence for the law" in effect becomes "obedience to tradition," while Kant's "immediate determination by" and "subordination of my will to a law without mediation" becomes obedience to "a higher authority ... not because it commands what it would be *useful* for one to do, but simply because it commands." The difference in terminology, importantly, is traceable to Schopenhauer's critique of Kant. For among Schopenhauer's many formulations of his basic objection to Kant's account of moral worth, we find the complaint that what Kant calls "reverence" [*Achtung*] is in German called "obedience" [*Gehorsam*], and the claim that only fear can induce human beings "to obey some absolute command that comes from an admittedly unknown but obviously superior authority" (BM 67, 142). In these terms Schopenhauer had already stripped Kant's reverence for the law of its metaphysical connections. That Nietzsche uses almost exactly the same terms to describe what he takes to be the earliest form of moral motivation provides overwhelming evidence that he is taking Kant's conception of morality and, as it were, *naturalizing* it, so that he can tell a story about the origin of morality *without* invoking a "noumenal" world or any other suspect metaphysical categories. Morality consists, in effect, of "categorical imperatives" – imperatives that apply regardless of the agent's particular ends – but these imperatives are originally found, Nietzsche thinks, in the customary practices and obedience to a "higher authority" that constitute a tradition.[5]

But why does Nietzsche claim that the presuppositions of the morality of custom are false? On his picture, an imperative commanded by "tradition" has "categorical" or "moral" force only for those persons who have a suitably reverent or submissive attitude toward the tradition. The question then is: what sustains such an attitude? In D 9, Nietzsche suggests it is a certain sort of superstitious "fear" – not the fear of specific punishment that Schopenhauer imagines to lie at the root of all imperatives, but perhaps something more like the "irresistible fear" that Freud claims maintains both primitive taboos and the obsessional prohibitions of neurotics: "No external threat of punishment is required, for there is an internal certainty, a moral conviction, that any violation will lead to intolerable disaster." If the individual is able to articulate anything about this disaster, Freud adds, it is at most "the undefined feeling that some particular person in his environment will be injured as a result of the violation."[6] In D 9, Nietzsche similarly remarks that in a morality of custom, "punishment for breaches of custom will fall before all on the community: that supernatural punishment whose forms of expression and limitations are so hard to comprehend and are explored with so much superstitious fear."

Importantly, Nietzsche continues in the very next passage (D 10) by observing that:

In the same measure as the sense for causality increases, the extent of the domain of morality [*Sittlichkeit*] decreases: for each time one has understood the necessary effects and has learned how to segregate them from all the accidental effects and incidental consequences (*post hoc*), one has destroyed a countless number of *imaginary causalities* hitherto believed in as the foundation of customs – the real world is much smaller than the imaginary – and each time

---

[5] Notice that this naturalization of Kant leads Nietzsche to part company with Schopenhauer's critique of Kant. For Schopenhauer, as we saw earlier, claimed that the real motive for obedience to an imperative was always egoistic, e.g., fear of punishment. Yet in the "morality of custom" (as described in D 9), moral behavior involves obedience to custom; it is precisely the *egoist*, from this perspective, who is *immoral*, who acts not out of "reverence" for the tradition but based on considerations of "usefulness to the individual." So Nietzsche's naturalized version of Kant's reverence for the law is *not* an egoistic motive, contrary to Schopenhauer.

[6] Sigmund Freud, *Totem and Taboo: Some Points of Agreement between the Mental Lives of Savages and Neurotics*, James Strachey, tr. (New York: W. W. Norton and Company, 1950), pp. 26–27.

a piece of anxiety and constraint has vanished from the world, each time too a piece of respect [*Achtung*] for the authority of custom; morality as a whole has suffered a diminution. Whoever wants to increase it must know how to prevent the results from being *subject to control.* (D 10)

Nietzsche thus claims that "respect for the authority of customs" is maintained by a belief in "*imaginary causalities*" – an irrational belief or superstition, as in the case of Freud's obsessional neurotics, that something bad will happen if customs are not followed, unaccompanied by any specific idea of what will happen or how it is related to the violation of custom. Reverence for the authority of customs depends on a belief in supernatural connections, on the "outcome of an action [being] not a consequence but a free supplement – [ultimately] God's... The action and its outcome had to be worked at separately, with quite different means and practices!" (D 12)

But once the natural causal connection between a proscribed action and its result is discovered, the proscription loses its higher authority. If the individual recognizes that an action is to be avoided because of a harmful consequence, the latter is regarded as the action's own result, rather than something added on to it by a supernatural power. In that case, Nietzsche agrees with Schopenhauer that the agent acts from an egoistic fear of consequences, not from a moral motive. No longer regarded as the command of a higher power, the custom has lost it moral force, and the agent no longer acts from the moral motive that Kant called "reverence," which, on Nietzsche's account, is a superstitious fear not of specific consequences, but of a higher power that controls all consequences. The false presuppositions of this "morality of custom," then, are beliefs in imaginary causalities and supernatural powers which confer on customs "moral" or "categorical" status by inducing a feeling of reverence toward them: so morality depends, *causally* as it were, on these psychological facts about human beings (i.e., their being in the grip of superstitious beliefs and fears).

But does Nietzsche believe that such superstitious beliefs have anything to do with the "rarefied and lofty" version of the "moral sense" we find today? Much suggests that he does. Since he claims that the morality of custom is the origin of our more "lofty" morality, he must think that some kind of continuity exists between them. One possibility is that current morality is structurally similar to the morality of custom, but that more "lofty" authorities have replaced tradition as the source of its higher authority: while some maintain a moral or reverent attitude toward traditional practices, the more "enlightened" substitute the authority of God, conscience, or the noumenal self for that of tradition, which now becomes "mere custom." Nietzsche may well think that these new commanding authorities are also maintained as such by a belief in "imaginary causalities." That seems a plausible inference to draw from his claim that the "logic of feelings" has changed little since the morality of custom (D 18), and from his focus on a particular "imaginary causality," which certainly exists beyond the morality of custom – namely, the alleged connection between guilt and suffering, which is equivalent to the conception of suffering as a punishment. In a section on *"the re-education of the human race,"* he pleads with us to help "in this one work: to take the concept of punishment which has overrun the whole world and root it out! There exists no more noxious weed" (D 13). A later section confirms that the tendency to take natural effects as punishments is central to *Daybreak*'s understanding of current morality: "And in *summa*: what is it you really want changed? We want to cease making causes into sinners and consequences into executioners" (D 208). It would hardly be strange for Nietzsche to think that the "imaginary causality" of guilt plays a role in the modern moral conscience – for Schopenhauer, who did not even believe in God, did believe that *all* suffering results from guilt (e.g., WW II, 603–05). Accordingly, Nietzsche might well think that our perception of suffering as following from guilt induces us to experience the dictates of conscience with a primitive feeling of dread or reverence, and that this gives our judgments of right and wrong their moral or categorical force.

But how can he explain the authority many people still grant morality even though they reject any causality that is not scientifically respectable, including that of guilt? Nietzsche provides an answer shortly before he explains his "denial of morality": *"Wherein we are all irrational.* – We still draw conclusions from judgments we consider false, from teachings in which we no longer believe – through our feelings" (D 99). This explains the ending of the passage on the denial of morality: "We have to *learn to think differently* – in order at least, perhaps very late on, to achieve even more: *to feel differently* (D 103). Nietzsche presumably believes that even those who no longer accept superstitious or unscientific beliefs retain *feelings* of reverence that were originally produced by these erroneous beliefs, which therefore function even now as *causal* presuppositions of people's "moral" feelings. Learning thus to think differently, to recognize our moral feelings as results of beliefs we no longer hold, Nietzsche seems to suppose, will eventually free us from these feelings, and free us to take seriously other values, as he himself was beginning to do in *Daybreak*.

Conclusion

Daybreak's "denial of morality" is very far from Nietzsche's last word on the subject. His later works, especially *On the Genealogy of Morality*, replace *Daybreak*'s account of the origins of morality with a much more sophisticated and complex one, and his "denial of morality" undergoes a corresponding transformation. Too often paired with *Human, All Too Human*, *Daybreak* has been too little appreciated as the real beginning of Nietzsche's own path on the topic of morality. *Human, All Too Human* lies too much under the shadow of Schopenhauer's values; only in *Daybreak* does Nietzsche break free and begin to raise his characteristic questions about the value of the unegoistic and, ultimately, of morality. The means he found to do so, his naturalized Kantian interpretation of the morality of custom, did not in fact satisfy him for long (see GM II, 1–3 for his later account), and it is worth trying to figure out why as one reads *Daybreak*. For Nietzsche himself reached the perspective of his *Genealogy* only by overcoming the account of the origins of morality offered here. *Daybreak*'s importance to him lay in the fact that it gave him an initial set of hypotheses about the origins of morality as a phenomenon of nature that he could then go on to revise and refine. *Daybreak*'s importance to us may lie primarily in its ability to show that his later genealogy of morality did not emerge from thin air nor spring full-blown from Nietzsche's head, but was the product of a serious and sustained effort to understand what morality is and how it could have arisen on the assumption that it is a purely natural phenomenon.

Chronology

highest task and truly metaphysical activity of this life"; devastating reviews follow.

1873 Publishes "David Strauss, the Confessor and the Writer," the first of his *Untimely Meditations*; begins taking books on natural science out of the Basel library, whereas he had previously confined himself largely to books on philological matters.

1874 Publishes two more *Meditations*, "The Uses and Disadvantages of History for Life" and "Schopenhauer as Educator."

1876 Publishes the fourth *Meditation*, "Richard Wagner in Bayreuth," which already bears subtle signs of his movement away from Wagner.

1878 Publishes *Human, All Too Human* (dedicated to the memory of Voltaire); it praises science over art as the mark of high culture and thus marks a decisive turn away from Wagner.

1879 Terrible health problems force him to resign his chair at Basel (with a small pension); publishes "Assorted Opinions and Maxims," the first part of Vol. 2 of *Human, All Too Human*; begins living alone in Swiss and Italian boarding houses.

1880 Publishes "The Wanderer and his Shadow," which becomes the second part of Volume 2 of *Human, All Too Human*.

1881 Publishes *Daybreak*.

1882 Publishes *Idylls of Messina* (eight poems) in a monthly magazine; publishes *The Gay Science*; friendship with Paul Ree and Lou Salomé ends badly, leaving Nietzsche devastated.

1883 Publishes the first two parts of *Thus Spoke Zarathustra*; learns of Wagner's death just after mailing Part One to the publisher.

1884 Publishes the third part of *Thus Spoke Zarathustra*.

1885 Publishes the fourth part of *Zarathustra* for private circulation only.

1886 Publishes *Beyond Good and Evil*; writes prefaces for new releases of: *The Birth of Tragedy*, *Human, All Too Human*, Vol. 1 and Vol. 2, and *Daybreak*.

1887 Publishes expanded edition of *The Gay Science* with a new preface, a fifth part, and an appendix of poems; publishes *Hymn to Life*, a musical work for chorus and orchestra; publishes *On the Genealogy of Morality*.

1888   Publishes *The Case of Wagner*, composes a collection of poems, *Dionysian Dithyrambs*, and four short books: *Twilight of the Idols*, *The Antichrist*, *Ecce Homo*, and *Nietzsche contra Wagner*.

1889   Collapses physically and mentally in Turin on 3 January; writes a few lucid notes but never recovers sanity; is briefly institutionalized; spends remainder of his life as an invalid, living with his mother and then his sister, who also gains control of his literary estate.

1900   Dies in Weimar on 25 August.

Further reading

Unlike many philosophers, Nietzsche tended not to offer a systematic exposition of his views in a single place; his books were often culled from the various notebooks he kept. (The publication history of Nietzsche's books is discussed in great detail by William Schaberg in *The Nietzsche Canon* (University of Chicago Press, 1995).) One result is that themes broached in one work often receive important development in other works. A good place to start in Nietzsche with regard to the main themes of *Daybreak* is *On the Genealogy of Morality*. There are several editions of this work that can be recommended: by M. Clark and A. Swensen (Indianapolis: Hackett, 1997); by K. Ansell-Pearson and C. Diethe (Cambridge University Press, 1994); and by W. Kaufmann and R. J. Hollingdale (Vintage Books/Random House, 1967). The Hackett edition has the most extensive critical apparatus. Also fruitfully read in conjunction with *Daybreak* are the chapters "Natural History of Morals," "Our Virtues," and "What Is Noble" in *Beyond Good and Evil,* translated by W. Kaufmann (Vintage Books/Random House, 1966), and the chapters "Morality as Anti-Nature" and "The Four Great Errors," in *Twilight of the Idols,* which appears in *The Portable Nietzsche,* edited and translated by W. Kaufmann (Penguin Books, 1954).

There is a voluminous secondary literature on Nietzsche, but nothing that can be recommended on *Daybreak* itself and only a little of philosophical interest on the main themes broached in *Daybreak.* For an introduction to the major themes of Nietzsche's philosophy and their development, see the "Nietzsche" entry by Maudemarie Clark in E. Craig (ed.), *The Routledge Encyclopedia of*

Philosophy (1998). A valuable and more detailed overview of Nietzsche's thought as a whole is provided by Richard Schacht, *Nietzsche* (London: Routledge, 1983). John Richardson, *Nietzsche's System* (Oxford University Press, 1996) offers a more philosophically ambitious and systematic account of Nietzsche's thought; its picture of Nietzsche differs in several respects from the one developed in the Introduction here.

Useful additional readings on the particular themes broached in the "Introduction" include the following:

Intellectual context and background: The discipline of nineteenth-century classical philology, in which Nietzsche was trained, is helpfully described in M. S. Silk and J. P. Stern, *Nietzsche on Tragedy* (Cambridge University Press, 1981), pp. 9–14, 22–24. An illuminating commentary on Nietzsche's own classical scholarship is Jonathan Barnes, "Nietzsche and Diogenes Laertius," *Nietzsche-Studien* 15 (1986), pp. 16–40. Difficulties presented by the failure of recent commentators to heed Nietzsche's philological training are discussed in Brian Leiter, "Nietzsche and Aestheticism," *Journal of the History of Philosophy* 30 (1992), pp. 275–80 (esp. at 276–80).

An excellent introduction to philosophically important themes in Thucydides (and to Sophistic culture more generally) is Paul Woodruff, *Thucydides on Justice, Power and Human Nature* (Indianapolis: Hackett, 1993). Also useful is W. K. C. Guthrie's classic work, *The Sophists* (Cambridge University Press, 1971), esp. Chapters IV and VII.

A splendid, short introduction to Schopenhauer's views is Christopher Janaway, *Schopenhauer* (Oxford University Press, 1994), which also contains helpful pointers to the rest of the Schopenhauer literature. Maudemarie Clark discusses Schopenhauer's influence on Nietzsche's metaphysics and epistemology in *Nietzsche on Truth and Philosophy* (Cambridge University Press, 1990), esp. Chapters 3 and 5, and also in her contribution to C. Janaway (ed.), *Willing and Nothingness: Schopenhauer as Nietzsche's Educator* (Oxford University Press, 1998). In this same volume, Brian Leiter considers Schopenhauer's influence on Nietzsche's conception of human agency in "The Paradox of Fatalism and Self-Creation in Nietzsche." An interesting, if unusual, account of Schopenhauer's influence on Nietzsche's theory of aesthetic value is Julian Young, *Nietzsche's Philosophy of Art* (Cambridge University Press, 1992). Kant's moral philosophy is helpfully introduced in the essays by

Onora O'Neill and J. B. Schneewind in P. Guyer (ed.), *The Cambridge Companion to Kant* (1992). A detailed study of Nietzsche's critique of Kant's moral philosophy has yet to be written.

A useful overview of the "materialist" movement in Germany can be found in Frederick Gregory, *Scientific Materialism in Nineteenth Century Germany* (Dordrecht: D. Reidel, 1977). Some of the influence of German materialism on Nietzsche – via Friedrich Lange, the nineteenth-century critic of, yet sympathizer with, materialism – is discussed in George Stack, *Lange and Nietzsche* (Berlin: de Gruyter, 1983), though Stack systematically overstates Nietzsche's indebtedness to Lange. Interested readers might also look at the book Nietzsche himself studied with some care: Lange's *History of Materialism*, translated by E. C. Thomas (New York: Humanities Press, 1950), especially the Second Book. Nietzsche's naturalism is both defined and examined in Leiter, "The Paradox of Fatalism and Self-Creation in Nietzsche." Other helpful discussions of naturalistic themes in Nietzsche include Schacht, *Nietzsche* (see the index entries for "naturalism"); Ken Gemes, "Nietzsche's Critique of Truth," *Philosophy & Phenomenological Research* 52 (1992), pp. 47–65; Peter Poellner, *Nietzsche and Metaphysics* (Oxford: Clarendon Press, 1995), pp. 138–49.

Nietzsche on morality: For two contrasting views of Nietzsche's critique of morality, see Maudemarie Clark, "Nietzsche's Immoralism and the Concept of Morality," in R. Schacht (ed.), *Nietzsche, Genealogy, Morality* (Berkeley: University of California Press, 1994), pp. 15–34, and Brian Leiter, "Morality in the Pejorative Sense: On the Logic of Nietzsche's Critique of Morality," *British Journal for the History of Philosophy* 3 (1995), pp. 113–45. Also useful are: Frithjof Bergmann, "Nietzsche's Critique of Morality," in R. C. Solomon & K. M. Higgins (eds.), *Reading Nietzsche* (Oxford University Press, 1988); Maudemarie Clark's introduction to the Hackett edition of the *Genealogy*; Philippa Foot, "Nietzsche: The Revaluation of Values," in R. C. Solomon (ed.), *Nietzsche: A Collection of Critical Essays* (University of Notre Dame Press, 1973), pp. 156–68; Brian Leiter, "Beyond Good and Evil," *History of Philosophy Quarterly* 10 (1993), pp. 261–70; Alexander Nehamas, *Nietzsche: Life as Literature* (Cambridge, Mass.: Harvard University Press, 1985), chapter 7 ("Beyond Good and Evil"). Nietzsche's views in ethics are considered in the light of contemporary philosophical concerns in Lester Hunt, *Nietzsche and the Origin of Virtue* (London:

Routledge, 1991) and Brian Leiter, "Nietzsche and the Morality Critics," *Ethics* 107 (1997), pp. 250–85.

Nietzsche on human action: In addition to the relevant portions of Schacht, *Nietzsche* (chapter v) and Richardson, *Nietzsche's System* (Sections 1.4–1.5, 2.5, 3.1, 3.5.2), detailed discussions of aspects of Nietzsche's theory of mind and agency may be found in Leiter, "The Paradox of Fatalism and Self-Creation in Nietzsche"; and Poellner, *Nietzsche and Metaphysics* pp. 213–29.

Editors' note

The editors prepared the introduction, chronology, and essay on further reading, and have overseen the preparation of the index and notes. The notes are primarily the work of Saul Laureles, with assistance from Joshua Brysk and Stefan Sciaraffa. We have also benefited from the advice of Professor Stephen A. White of the Department of Classics at the University of Texas at Austin.

DAYBREAK

THOUGHTS ON THE PREJUDICES OF MORALITY

'There are so many days that have not yet broken.' *Rig Veda*

PREFACE

1

In this book you will discover a 'subterranean man' at work, one who tunnels and mines and undermines. You will see him – presupposing you have eyes capable of seeing this work in the depths – going forward slowly, cautiously, gently inexorable, without betraying very much of the distress which any protracted deprivation of light and air must entail; you might even call him contented, working there in the dark. Does it not seem as though some faith were leading him on, some consolation offering him compensation? As though he perhaps desires this prolonged obscurity, desires to be incomprehensible, concealed, enigmatic, because he knows what he will thereby also acquire: his own morning, his own redemption, his own *daybreak?* . . . He will return, that is certain: do not ask him what he is looking for down there, he will tell you himself of his own accord, this seeming Trophonius and subterranean, as soon as he has 'become a man' again. Being silent is something one completely unlearns if, like him, one has been for so long a solitary mole – – –

2

And indeed, my patient friends, I shall now tell you what I was after down there – here in this late preface which could easily have become a funeral oration: for I have returned and, believe it or not, returned safe and sound. Do not think for a moment that I intend to invite you to the same hazardous enterprise! Or even only to the same solitude! For he who proceeds on his own path in this fashion encounters no one: that is inherent in 'proceeding on one's own path'. No one comes along to help him: all the perils, accidents, malice and bad weather which assail him he has to tackle by himself. For his path is *his alone* – as is, of course, the bitterness and occasional ill-humour he feels at this 'his alone': among which is included, for instance, the knowledge that even his friends are unable to divine where he is or whither he is going, that they will sometimes ask themselves: 'what? is he going at all? does he still have – a path?' – At that time I undertook something not everyone may undertake: I

1

descended into the depths, I tunnelled into the foundations, I commenced an investigation and digging out of an ancient *faith*, one upon which we philosophers have for a couple of millennia been accustomed to build as if upon the firmest of all foundations – and have continued to do so even though every building hitherto erected on them has fallen down: I commenced to undermine our *faith in morality*. But you do not understand me?

3

Hitherto, the subject reflected on least adequately has been good and evil: it was too dangerous a subject. Conscience, reputation, Hell, sometimes even the police have permitted and continue to permit no impartiality; in the presence of morality, as in the face of any authority, one is not *allowed* to think, far less to express an opinion: here one has to – *obey*! As long as the world has existed no authority has yet been willing to let itself become the object of criticism; and to criticise morality itself, to regard morality as a problem, as problematic: what? has that not been – *is* that not – immoral? – But morality does not merely have at its command every kind of means of frightening off critical hands and torture-instruments: its security reposes far more in a certain art of enchantment it has at its disposal – it knows how to 'inspire'. With this art it succeeds, often with no more than a single glance, in paralysing the critical will and even in enticing it over to its own side; there are even cases in which morality has been able to turn the critical will against itself, so that, like the scorpion, it drives its sting into its own body. For morality has from of old been master of every diabolical nuance of the art of persuasion: there is no orator, even today, who does not have recourse to its assistance (listen, for example, even to our anarchists: how morally they speak when they want to persuade! In the end they even go so far as to call themselves 'the good and the just'.) For as long as there has been speech and persuasion on earth, morality has shown itself to be the greatest of all mistresses of seduction – and, so far as we philosophers are concerned, the actual *Circe of the philosophers*. Why is it that from Plato onwards every philosophical architect in Europe has built in vain? That everything they themselves in all sober seriousness regarded as *aere perennius* is threatening to collapse or already lies in ruins? Oh how false is the answer which even today is reserved in readiness for this question: 'because they had all neglected the presupposition for such an undertaking, the testing of the foundations, a critique of reason as a whole' – that fateful answer of Kant's which has certainly not lured us

modern philosophers on to any firmer or less treacherous ground!
(– and, come to think of it, was it not somewhat peculiar to demand
of an instrument that it should criticise its own usefulness and
suitability? that the intellect itself should 'know' its own value, its
own capacity, its own limitations? was it not even a little absurd? –).
The correct answer would rather have been that all philosophers
were building under the seduction of morality, even Kant – that they
were apparently aiming at certainty, at 'truth', but in reality at
'majestic moral structures': to employ once again the innocent language
of Kant, who describes his own 'not so glittering yet not undeserving'
task and labour as 'to level and make firm the ground for these
majestic moral structures' (*Critique of Pure Reason* II, p.257). Alas, we
have to admit today that he did not succeed in doing that, quite the
contrary! Kant was, with such an enthusiastic intention, the true son
of his century, which before any other can be called the century of
enthusiasm: as he fortunately remained also in regard to its more
valuable aspects (for example in the good portion of sensism he took
over into his theory of knowledge). He too had been bitten by the
moral tarantula Rousseau, he too harboured in the depths of his soul
the idea of that moral fanaticism whose executor another disciple of
Rousseau felt and confessed himself to be, namely Robespierre, '*de
fonder sur la terre l'empire de la sagesse, de la justice et de la vertu*' (speech of 7
June 1794). On the other hand, with such a French fanaticism in
one's heart, one could not have gone to work in a less French fashion,
more thoroughly, more in a German fashion – if the word 'German'
is still permitted today in this sense – than Kant did: to create
room for *his* 'moral realm' he saw himself obliged to posit an
undemonstrable world, a logical 'Beyond' – it was for precisely
that that he had need of his critique of pure reason! In other
words: *he would not have had need of it* if one thing had not been
more vital to him than anything else: to render the 'moral realm'
unassailable, even better incomprehensible to reason – for he
felt that a moral order of things was only too assailable by
reason! In the face of nature and history, in the face of the
thorough *immorality* of nature and history, Kant was, like every
good German of the old stamp, a pessimist; he believed in morality,
not because it is demonstrated in nature and history, but in spite of
the fact that nature and history continually contradict it. To
understand this 'in spite of', one might perhaps recall something
similar in Luther, that other great pessimist who, with all the
audacity native to him, once admonished his friends: 'if we could
grasp by reason who the God who shows so much wrath and malice

can be just and merciful, what need would we have of *faith?*' For nothing has from the beginning made a more profound impression on the German soul, nothing has 'tempted' it more, than this most perilous of all conclusions, which to every true Roman is a sin against the spirit: *credo quia absurdum est*: – it was with this conclusion that German logic first entered the history of Christian dogma: but even today, a millennium later, we Germans of today, late Germans in every respect, still sense something of truth, of the *possibility* of truth behind the celebrated dialectical principle with which in his day Hegel assisted the German spirit to conquer Europe – 'Contradiction moves the world, all things contradict themselves' –: for we are, even in the realm of logic, pessimists.

4

But *logical* evaluations are not the deepest or most fundamental to which our audacious mistrust can descend: faith in reason, with which the validity of these judgments must stand or fall, is, as faith, a *moral* phenomenon . . . Perhaps German pessimism still has one last step to take? Perhaps it has once again to set beside one another in fearful fashion its *credo* and its *absurdum?* And if *this* book is pessimistic even into the realm of morality, even to the point of going beyond faith in morality – should it not for this very reason be a German book? For it does in fact exhibit a contradiction and is not afraid of it: in this book faith in morality is withdrawn – but why? *Out of morality!* Or what else should we call that which informs it – and *us?* for our taste is for more modest expressions. But there is no doubt that a 'thou shalt' still speaks to us too, that we too still obey a stern law set over us – and this is the last moral law which can make itself audible even to us, which even we know how to *live*, in this if in anything we too are still *men of conscience*: namely, in that we do not want to return to that which we consider outlived and decayed, to anything 'unworthy of belief', be it called God, virtue, truth, justice, charity; that we do not permit ourselves any bridges-of-lies to ancient ideals; that we are hostile from the heart to everything that wants to mediate and mix with us; hostile to every kind of faith and Christianness existing today; hostile to the half-and-halfness of all romanticism and fatherland-worship; hostile, too, towards the pleasure-seeking and lack of conscience of the artists which would like to persuade us to worship where we no longer believe – for we are artists; hostile, in short, to the whole of European *feminism* (or idealism, if you prefer that word), which is for ever 'drawing us

4

upward' and precisely thereby for ever 'bringing us down': – it is only as men of *this* conscience that we still feel ourselves related to the German integrity and piety of millennia, even if as its most questionable and final descendants, we immoralists, we godless men of today, indeed in a certain sense as its heirs, as the executors of its innermost will – a pessimistic will, as aforesaid, which does not draw back from denying itself because it denies with *joy*! In us there is accomplished – supposing you want a formula – the *self-sublimation of morality*. – –

5

– Finally, however: why should we have to say what we are and what we want and do not want so loudly and with such fervour? Let us view it more coldly, more distantly, more prudently, from a greater height; let us say it, as it is fitting it should be said between ourselves, so secretly that no one hears it, that no one hears *us*! Above all let us say it *slowly* . . . This preface is late but not too late – what, after all, do five or six years matter? A book like this, a problem like this, is in no hurry; we both, I just as much as my book, are friends of *lento*. It is not for nothing that I have been a philologist, perhaps I am a philologist still, that is to say, a teacher of slow reading: – in the end I also write slowly. Nowadays it is not only my habit, it is also to my taste – a malicious taste, perhaps? – no longer to write anything which does not reduce to despair every sort of man who is 'in a hurry'. For philology is that venerable art which demands of its votaries one thing above all: to go aside, to take time, to become still, to become slow – it is a goldsmith's art and connoisseurship of the *word* which has nothing but delicate, cautious work to do and achieves nothing if it does not achieve it *lento*. But for precisely this reason it is more necessary than ever today, by precisely this means does it entice and enchant us the most, in the midst of an age of 'work', that is to say, of hurry, of indecent and perspiring haste, which wants to 'get everything done' at once, including every old or new book: – this art does not so easily get anything done, it teaches to read *well*, that is to say, to read slowly, deeply, looking cautiously before and aft, with reservations, with doors left open, with delicate eyes and fingers . . . My patient friends, this book desires for itself only perfect readers and philologists: *learn* to read me well! –

Ruta, near Genoa, in the autumn of 1886

BOOK I

1

Supplemental rationality. – All things that live long are gradually so saturated with reason that their origin in unreason thereby becomes improbable. Does not almost every precise history of an origination impress our feelings as paradoxical and wantonly offensive? Does the good historian not, at bottom, constantly *contradict*?

2

Prejudice of the learned. – The learned judge correctly that people of all ages have believed they *know* what is good and evil, praise- and blameworthy. But it is a prejudice of the learned that *we now know better* than any other age.

3

Everything has its day. – When man gave all things a sex he thought, not that he was playing, but that he had gained a profound insight: – it was only very late that he confessed to himself what an enormous error this was, and perhaps even now he has not confessed it completely. – In the same way man has ascribed to all that exists a connection with morality and laid an *ethical significance* on the world's back. One day this will have as much value, and no more, as the belief in the masculinity or femininity of the sun has today.

4

Against the imagined disharmony of the spheres. – We must again rid the world of much *false* grandeur, because it offends against the justice which all things may lay claim to from us! And to that end it is necessary not to want to see the world as being more disharmonious than it is!

5

Be grateful! – The greatest accomplishment of past mankind is that we no longer have to live in continual fear of wild animals, of barbarians, of gods and of our own dreams.

6

The conjurer and his opposite. – What is astonishing in the realm of science is the opposite of what is astonishing in the art of the conjurer. For the latter wants to persuade us to see a very simple causality where in truth a very complicated causality is at work. Science, on the contrary, compels us to abandon belief in simple causalities precisely where everything seems so easy to comprehend and we are the fools of appearance. The 'simplest' things are *very complicated* – a fact at which one can never cease to marvel!

7

Learning to feel differently about space. – Is it the real things or the imaginary things which have contributed most to human happiness? What is certain is that the *extent of the space* between the highest happiness and the deepest unhappiness has been produced only with the aid of the imaginary things. *This* kind of feeling of space is, consequently, being continually reduced under the influence of science: just as science has taught us, and continues to teach us, to feel that the earth is small and the solar-system itself no more than a point.

8

Transfiguration. – Those that suffer helplessly, those that dream confusedly, those that are entranced by things supernatural – these are the *three divisions* into which Raphael divided mankind. This is no longer how we see the world – and Raphael too would no longer *be able* to see it as he did: he would behold a new transfiguration.

9

Concept of morality of custom. – In comparison with the mode of life of whole millennia of mankind we present-day men live in a very immoral age: the power of custom is astonishingly enfeebled and the moral sense so rarefied and lofty it may be described as having more or less evaporated. That is why the fundamental insights into the origin of morality are so difficult for us latecomers, and even when we have acquired them we find it impossible to enunciate them, because they sound so uncouth or because they seem to slander morality! This is, for example, already the case with the *chief proposition*: morality is nothing other (therefore *no more!*) than obedience to customs, of whatever kind they may be; customs, however, are the *traditional* way of behaving and evaluating. In things in which no tradition commands there is no morality; and the less life is determined by tradition, the smaller the circle of morality. The free human being is immoral because in all things he is *determined* to depend upon himself and not upon a tradition: in all the original conditions of mankind, 'evil' signifies the same as 'individual', 'free', 'capricious', 'unusual', 'unforeseen', 'incalculable'. Judged by the standard of these conditions, if an action is performed *not* because tradition commands it but for other motives (because of its usefulness to the individual, for example), even indeed for precisely the motives which once founded the tradition, it is called immoral and is felt to be so by him who performed it: for it was not performed in obedience to tradition. What is tradition? A higher authority which one obeys, not because it commands what is *useful* to us, but because it *commands*. – What distinguishes this feeling in the presence of tradition from the feeling of fear in general? It is fear in the presence of a higher intellect which here commands, of an incomprehensible, indefinite power, of something more than personal – there is *superstition* in this fear. – Originally all education and care of health, marriage, cure of sickness, agriculture, war, speech and silence, traffic with one another and with the gods belonged within the domain of morality: they demanded one observe prescriptions *without thinking of oneself* as an individual. Originally, therefore, everything was custom, and whoever wanted to elevate himself above it had to become lawgiver and medicine man and a kind of demi-god: that is to say, he had to *make customs* – a dreadful, mortally dangerous thing! Who is the most moral man? *First*, he who obeys the law most frequently: who, like the Brahmin, bears a consciousness of the law with him everywhere and into every minute division of time, so that he is continually inventive in creating opportunities for obeying the law. *Then*, he who obeys it even in the most difficult cases. The most moral man is he who *sacrifices* the most to custom: what, however, are the greatest sacrifices? The way in which this question is answered determines the development of several divers kinds of morality; but the most important distinction remains that which divides the morality of *most frequent obedience* from that of the *most difficult* obedience. Let us not deceive ourselves as to the motivation of that morality which demands difficulty of obedience to custom as the mark of morality! Self-overcoming is demanded, *not* on account of the useful consequences it may have for the individual, but so that the hegemony of custom, tradition, shall be made evident in despite of the private desires and advantages of the individual: the individual is to sacrifice himself – that is the commandment of morality of custom. – Those moralists, on the other hand, who, following in the footsteps of Socrates, offer the *individual* a morality of self-control and temperance as a means to his own *advantage*, as his personal key to happiness, *are the exceptions* – and if it seems otherwise to us that is because we have been brought up in their after-effect: they all take a new path under the highest disapprobation of all advocates of morality of custom – they cut themselves off from the community, as immoral men, and are in the profoundest sense evil. Thus to a virtuous Roman of the old stamp every *Christian* who 'considered first of all his *own* salvation' appeared – evil. – Everywhere that a community, and consequently a morality of custom exists, the idea also predominates that punishment for breaches of custom will fall before all on the community: that supernatural punishment whose forms of expression and limitations are so hard to comprehend and are explored with so much superstitious fear. The community can compel the individual to compensate another individual or the community for the immediate injury his action has brought in its train; it can also take a kind of revenge on the individual for having, as a supposed after-effect of his action, caused the clouds and storms of divine anger to have gathered over the community – but it feels the individual's guilt above all as *its own* guilt and bears the punishment as *its own* punishment – : 'customs have grown lax', each wails in his soul, 'if such actions as this are possible'. Every individual action, every individual mode of thought arouses dread; it is impossible to compute what precisely the rarer, choicer, more original spirits in the whole course of history have had to suffer through being felt as evil and dangerous, indeed through *feeling themselves to be so*. Under the dominion of the morality of custom, originality of every kind has acquired a bad conscience; the sky above the best men is for this reason to this very moment gloomier than it need be.

10

Sense for morality and sense for causality in counteraction. – In the same measure as the sense for causality increases, the extent of the domain of morality decreases: for each time one has understood the necessary effects and has learned how to segregate them from all the accidental effects and incidental consequences (*post hoc*), one has destroyed a countless number of *imaginary causalities* hitherto believed in as the foundations of customs – the real world is much smaller than the imaginary – and each time a piece of anxiety and constraint has vanished from the world, each time too a piece of respect for the authority of custom: morality as a whole has suffered a diminution. He who wants, on the contrary, to augment it must know how to prevent the results from being *subject to control*.

11

Popular morality and popular medicine. – The morality which prevails in a community is constantly being worked at by everybody: most people produce example after example of the alleged *relationship between cause and effect*, between guilt and punishment, confirm it as well founded and strengthen their faith: some observe actions and their consequences afresh and draw conclusions and laws from their observations: a very few take exception here and there and thus diminish faith on these points. – All, however, are at one in the wholly crude, *unscientific* character of their activity; whether it is a matter of producing examples, making observations or taking exception, whether it is a matter of proving, confirming, expressing or refuting a law – both material and form are worthless, as are the material and form of all popular medicine. Popular medicine and popular morality belong together and ought not to be evaluated so differently as they still are: both are the *most dangerous* pseudo-sciences.

12
Consequence as supplement. – Formerly people believed that the outcome of an action was not a consequence but a free supplement – namely God's. Is a greater confusion conceivable? The action and its outcome had to be worked at separately, with quite different means and practices!

13
Towards the re-education of the human race. – Men of application and goodwill assist in this one work: to take the concept of punishment which has overrun the whole world and root it out! There exists no more noxious weed! Not only has it been implanted into the consequences of our actions – and how dreadful and repugnant to reason even this is, to conceive cause and effect as cause and punishment! – but they have gone further and, through this infamous mode of interpretation with the aid of the concept of punishment, robbed of its innocence the whole purely chance character of events. Indeed, they have gone so far in their madness as to demand that we feel our very existence to be a punishment – it is as though the education of the human race had hitherto been directed by the fantasies of jailers and hangmen!

14
Significance of madness in the history of morality. – When in spite of that fearful pressure of 'morality of custom' under which all the communities of mankind have lived, many millennia before the beginnings of our calendar and also on the whole during the course of it up to the present day (we ourselves dwell in the little world of the exceptions and, so to speak, in the evil zone): – when, I say, in spite of this, new and deviate ideas, evaluations, drives again and again broke out, they did so accompanied by a dreadful attendant: almost

everywhere it was madness which prepared the way for the new idea, which broke the spell of a venerated usage and superstition. Do you understand why it had to be madness which did this? Something in voice and bearing as uncanny and incalculable as the demonic moods of the weather and the sea and therefore worthy of a similar awe and observation? Something that bore so visibly the sign of total unfreedom as the convulsions and froth of the epileptic, that seemed to mark the madman as the mask and speaking-trumpet of a divinity? Something that awoke in the bearer of a new idea himself reverence for and dread of himself and no longer pangs of conscience and drove him to become the prophet and martyr of his idea? – while it is constantly suggested to us today that, instead of a grain of salt, a grain of the spice of madness is joined to genius, all earlier people found it much more likely that wherever there is madness there is also a grain of genius and wisdom – something 'divine', as one whispered to oneself. Or rather: as one said aloud forcefully enough. 'It is through madness that the greatest good things have come to Greece', Plato said, in concert with all ancient mankind. Let us go a step further: all superior men who were irresistibly drawn to throw off the yoke of any kind of morality and to frame new laws had, *if they were not actually mad*, no alternative but to make themselves or pretend to be mad – and this indeed applies to innovators in every domain and not only in the domain of priestly and political dogma: – even the innovator of poetical metre had to establish his credentials by madness. (A certain convention that they were mad continued to adhere to poets even into much gentler ages: a convention of which Solon, for example, availed himself when he incited the Athenians to reconquer Salamis.) – 'How can one make oneself mad when one is not mad and does not dare to appear so?' – almost all the significant men of ancient civilisation have pursued this train of thought; a secret teaching of artifices and dietetic hints was propagated on this subject, together with the feeling that such reflections and purposes were innocent, indeed holy. The recipes for becoming a medicine-man among the Indians, a saint among the Christians of the Middle Ages, an angekok among Greenlanders, a pajee among Brazilians are essentially the same: senseless fasting, perpetual sexual abstinence, going into the desert or ascending a mountain or a pillar, or 'sitting in an aged willow tree which looks upon a lake' and thinking of nothing at all except what might bring on an ecstasy and mental disorder. Who would venture to take a look into the wilderness of bitterest and most superfluous agonies of soul in which probably the most fruitful men of all times have languished! To listen to the sighs of these solitary and agitated minds: 'Ah, give me madness, you heavenly powers! Madness, that I may at last believe in myself! Give deliriums and convulsions, sudden lights and darkness, terrify me with frost and fire such as no mortal has ever felt, with deafening din and prowling figures, make me howl and whine and crawl like a beast: so that I may only come to believe in myself! I am consumed by doubt, I have killed the law, the law anguishes me as a corpse does a living man: if I am not *more* than the law I am the vilest of all men. The new spirit which is in me, whence is it if it is not from you? Prove to me that I am yours; madness alone can prove it.' And only too often this fervour achieved its goal all too well: in that age in which Christianity proved most fruitful in saints and desert solitaries, and thought it was proving itself by this fruitfulness, there were in Jerusalem vast madhouses for abortive saints, for those who had surrendered to it their last grain of salt.

15

The oldest means of solace. – First stage: man sees in every feeling of indisposition and misfortune something for which he has to make someone else suffer – in doing so he becomes conscious of the power he still possesses and this consoles him. Second stage: man sees in every feeling of indisposition and misfortune a punishment, that is to say, an atonement for guilt and the means of *getting free* from the evil spell of a real or supposed injustice. When he realises this *advantage* which misfortune brings with it, he no longer believes he has to make someone else suffer for it – he renounces this kind of satisfaction because he now has another.

16

First proposition of civilisation. – Among barbarous peoples there exists a species of customs whose purpose appears to be custom in general: minute and fundamentally superfluous stipulations (as for example those among the Kamshadales forbidding the scraping of snow from the shoes with a knife, the impaling of a coal on a knife, the placing of an iron in the fire – and he who contravenes them meets death!) which, however, keep continually in the consciousness the constant proximity of custom, the perpetual compulsion to practise customs: so as to strengthen the mighty proposition with which civilisation begins: any custom is better than no custom.

17

Nature, good and evil. – At first, men imagined themselves into nature:
they saw everywhere themselves and their kind, especially their evil
and capricious qualities, as it were hidden among the clouds,
storms, beasts of prey, trees and plants: it was then they invented 'evil
nature'. Then there came along an age when they again imagined
themselves out of nature, the age of Rousseau: they were so fed up
with one another they absolutely had to have a corner of the world
into which man and his torments could not enter: they invented
'good nature'.

18

The morality of voluntary suffering. – Of all pleasures, which is the
greatest for the men of that little, constantly imperilled community
which is in a constant state of war and where the sternest morality
prevails? – for souls, that is to say, which are full of strength,
revengefulness, hostility, deceit and suspicion, ready for the most
fearful things and made hard by deprivation and morality? The
pleasure of *cruelty*: just as it is reckoned a *virtue* in a soul under such
conditions to be inventive and insatiable in cruelty. In the act of
cruelty the community refreshes itself and for once throws off the
gloom of constant fear and caution. Cruelty is one of the oldest
festive joys of mankind. Consequently it is imagined that the gods
too are refreshed and in festive mood when they are offered the
spectacle of cruelty – and thus there creeps into the world the idea
that *voluntary suffering*, self-chosen torture, is meaningful and valuable.
Gradually, custom created within the community a practice corresponding to this idea: all excessive well-being henceforth aroused a
degree of mistrust, all hard suffering inspired a degree of confidence;
people told themselves: it may well be that the gods frown upon us
when we are fortunate and smile upon us when we suffer – though
certainly they do not feel pity! For pity is reckoned contemptible and
unworthy of a strong, dreadful soul; – they smile because they are
amused and put into a good humour by our suffering: for to practise
cruelty is to enjoy the highest gratification of the feeling of power.
Thus the concept of the 'most moral man' of the community came to
include the virtue of the most frequent suffering, of privation, of the
hard life, of cruel chastisement – *not*, to repeat it again and again, as a
means of discipline, of self-control, of satisfying the desire for
individual happiness – but as a virtue which will put the community

in good odour with the evil gods and which steams up to them like a perpetual propitiatory sacrifice on the altar. All those spiritual leaders of the peoples who were able to stir something into motion within the inert but fertile mud of their customs have, in addition to madness, also had need of voluntary torture if they were to inspire belief – and first and foremost, as always, their own belief in themselves! The more their spirit ventured on to new paths and was as a consequence tormented by pangs of conscience and spasms of anxiety, the more cruelly did they rage against their own flesh, their own appetites and their own health – as though to offer the divinity a substitute pleasure in case he might perhaps be provoked by this neglect of and opposition to established usages and by the new goals these paths led to. Let us not be too quick to think that we have by now freed ourselves completely from such a logic of feeling! Let the most heroic souls question themselves on this point. Every smallest step in the field of free thought, of a life shaped personally, has always had to be fought for with spiritual and bodily tortures: not only the step forward, no! the step itself, movement, change of any kind has needed its innumerable martyrs through all the long path-seeking and foundation-laying millennia which, to be sure, are not what one has in mind when one uses the expression 'world history' – that ludicrously tiny portion of human existence; and even within this so-called world history, which is at bottom merely much ado about the latest news, there is no more really vital theme than the age-old tragedy of the martyrs *who wanted to stir up the swamp*. Nothing has been purchased more dearly than that little bit of human reason and feeling of freedom that now constitutes our pride. It is this pride, however, which now makes it almost impossible for us to empathise with those tremendous eras of 'morality of custom' which precede 'world history' as the *actual and decisive eras of history which determined the character of mankind*: the eras in which suffering counted as virtue, cruelty counted as virtue, dissembling counted as virtue, revenge counted as virtue, denial of reason counted as virtue, while on the other hand well-being was accounted a danger, desire for knowledge was accounted a danger, peace was accounted a danger, pity was accounted a danger, being pitied was accounted an affront, work was accounted an affront, madness was accounted godliness, and change was accounted immoral and pregnant with disaster! – Do you think all this has altered and that mankind must therefore have changed its character? O observers of mankind, learn better to observe yourselves!

19

Morality makes stupid. – Custom represents the experiences of men of earlier times as to what they supposed useful and harmful – but the *sense for custom* (morality) applies, not to these experiences as such, but to the age, the sanctity, the indiscussability of the custom. And so this feeling is a hindrance to the acquisition of new experiences and the correction of customs: that is to say, morality is a hindrance to the creation of new and better customs: it makes stupid.

20

Freedoers and freethinkers. – Freedoers are at a disadvantage compared with freethinkers because people suffer more obviously from the consequences of deeds than from those of thoughts. If one considers, however, that both the one and the other are in search of gratification, and that in the case of the freethinker the mere thinking through and enunciation of forbidden things provides this gratification, both are on an equal footing with regard to motive: and with regard to consequences the decision will even go against the freethinker, provided one does not judge – as all the world does – by what is most immediately and crassly obvious. One has to take back much of the defamation which people have cast upon all those who broke through the spell of a custom by means of a *deed* – in general, they are called criminals. Whoever has overthrown an existing law of custom has hitherto always first been accounted a *bad man*: but when, as did happen, the law could not afterwards be reinstated and this fact was accepted, the predicate gradually changed; – history treats almost exclusively of these *bad men* who subsequently became *good men*!

21

'Observance of the law'. – If obedience to a moral precept produces a result different from the one promised and expected, and instead of the promised good fortune the moral man unexpectedly encounters ill fortune and misery, the conscientious and fearful will always be able to recourse to saying: 'something was overlooked in the way it was *performed*'. In the worst event, a profoundly sorrowful and crushed mankind will even decree: 'it is impossible to perform the precept properly, we are weak and sinful through and through and in the depths of us incapable of morality, consequently we can lay no claim to success and good fortune. Moral precepts and promises are for better beings than we are.'

22

Works and faith. – Protestant teachers continue to propagate the fundamental error that all that matters is faith, and that out of faith works must necessarily proceed. This is simply not true: but it has so seductive a sound it has confused other intelligences than Luther's (namely those of Socrates and Plato): even though the evidence of every experience of every day speaks against it. The most confident knowledge or faith cannot provide the strength or the ability needed for a deed, it cannot replace the employment of that subtle, many-faceted mechanism which must first be set in motion if anything at all of an idea is to translate itself into action. Works, first and foremost! That is to say, doing, doing, doing! The 'faith' that goes with it will soon put in an appearance – you can be sure of that!

23
What we are most subtle in. – Because for many thousands of years it was thought that *things* (nature, tools, property of all kinds) were also alive and animate, with the power to cause harm and to evade human purposes, the feeling of impotence has been much greater and much more common among men than it would otherwise have been: for one needed to secure oneself against things, just as against men and animals, by force, constraint, flattering, treaties, sacrifices – and here is the origin of most superstitious practices, that is to say, of a considerable, *perhaps preponderant* and yet wasted and useless constituent of all the activity hitherto pursued by man! – But because the feeling of impotence and fear was in a state of almost continuous stimulation so strongly and for so long, the *feeling of power* has evolved to such a degree of *subtlety* that in this respect man is now a match for the most delicate gold-balance. It has become his strongest propensity; the means discovered for creating this feeling almost constitute the history of culture.

24
The proof of a prescription. – In general, the validity or invalidity of a prescription – a prescription for baking bread, for example – is demonstrated by whether or not the result it promises is achieved, always presupposing it is carried out correctly. It is otherwise now with moral prescriptions: for here the results are either invisible or indistinct. These prescriptions rest on hypotheses of the smallest possible scientific value which can be neither demonstrated nor refuted from their results: – but formerly, when the sciences were at their rude beginnings and very little was required for a thing to be regarded as *demonstrated* – formerly, the validity or invalidity of a prescription of morality was determined in the same way as we now

determine that of any other prescription: by indicating whether or not it has succeeded in doing what it promised. If the natives of Russian America have the prescription: you shall not throw an animal bone into the fire or give it to the dogs – its validity is demonstrated with: 'if you do so you will have no luck in hunting'. But one has almost always in some sense 'no luck in hunting'; it is not easy to *refute* the validity of the prescription in this direction, especially when a community and not an individual is regarded as suffering the punishment; some circumstance will always appear which seems to confirm the prescription.

25

Custom and beauty. – Among the things that can be said in favour of custom is this: when someone subjects himself to it completely, from the very heart and from his earliest years on, his organs of attack and defence – both bodily and spiritual – degenerate: that is to say, he grows increasingly beautiful! For it is the exercise of these organs and the disposition that goes with this exercise which keeps one ugly and makes one uglier. That is why the old baboon is uglier than the young one, and why the young female baboon most closely resembles man: is the most beautiful baboon, that is to say. – One could from this draw a conclusion as to the origin of the beauty of women!

26

Animals and morality. – The practices demanded in polite society: careful avoidance of the ridiculous, the offensive, the presumptuous, the suppression of one's virtues as well as of one's strongest inclinations, self-adaptation, self-deprecation, submission to orders of rank – all this is to be found as social morality in a crude form everywhere, even in the depths of the animal world – and only at this depth do we see the purpose of all these amiable precautions: one wishes to elude one's pursuers and be favoured in the pursuit of one's prey. For this reason the animals learn to master themselves and alter their form, so that many, for example, adapt their colouring to the colouring of their surroundings (by virtue of the so-called 'chromatic function'), pretend to be dead or assume the forms and colours of another animal or of sand, leaves, lichen, fungus (what English researchers designate 'mimicry'). Thus the individual hides himself in the general concept 'man', or in society, or adapts himself to princes, classes, parties, opinions of his time and place: and all the subtle ways we have of appearing fortunate, grateful, powerful, enamoured have their easily discoverable parallels in the animal world. Even the sense for truth, which is really the sense for security, man has in common with the animals: one does not want to let oneself be deceived, does not want to mislead oneself, one hearkens mistrustfully to the promptings of one's own passions, one constrains oneself and lies in wait for oneself; the animal understands all this just as man does, with it too self-control springs from the sense for what is real (from prudence). It likewise assesses the effect it produces upon the perceptions of other animals and from this learns to look back upon itself, to take itself 'objectively', it too has its degree of self-knowledge. The animal assesses the movements of its friends and foes, it learns their peculiarities by heart, it prepares itself for them: it renounces war once and for all against individuals of a certain species, and can likewise divine from the way they approach that certain kinds of animals have peaceful and conciliatory intentions. The beginnings of justice, as of prudence, moderation, bravery – in short, of all we designate as the *Socratic virtues*, are *animal*: a consequence of that drive which teaches us to seek food and elude enemies. Now if we consider that even the highest human being has only become more elevated and subtle in the nature of his food and in his conception of what is inimical to him, it is not improper to describe the entire phenomenon of morality as animal.

27

The value of belief in suprahuman passions. – The institution of marriage obstinately maintains the belief that love, though a passion, is yet capable of endurance; indeed, that enduring, lifelong love can be established as the rule. Through tenaciously adhering to a noble belief, despite the fact that it is very often and almost as a general rule refuted and thus constitutes a *pia fraus*, marriage has bestowed upon love a higher nobility. All institutions which accord to a passion *belief in its endurance* and responsibility for its endurance, contrary to the nature of passion, have raised it to a new rank: and thereafter he who is assailed by such a passion no longer believes himself debased or endangered by it, as he formerly did, but enhanced in his own eyes and those of his equals. Think of institutions and customs which have created out of the fiery abandonment of the moment perpetual fidelity, out of the enjoyment of anger perpetual vengeance, out of despair perpetual mourning, out of a single and unpremeditated word perpetual obligation. This transformation has each time introduced a very great deal of hypocrisy and lying into the world:

but each time too, and at this cost, it has introduced a new *suprahuman* concept which elevates mankind.

28

Mood as argument. – 'What is the cause of a cheerful resolution for action?' – mankind has been much exercised by this question. The oldest and still the most common answer is: 'God is the cause; it is his way of telling us he approves of our intention.' When in former times one consulted the oracle over something one proposed to do, what one wanted from it was this feeling of cheerful resolution; and anyone who stood in doubt before several possible courses of action advised himself thus: 'I shall do that which engenders this feeling.' One thus decided, not for the most reasonable course, but for that course the image of which inspired the soul with hope and courage. The good mood was placed on the scales as an argument and outweighed rationality: it did so because it was interpreted super-stitiously as the effect of a god who promises success and who in this manner gives expression to his reason as the highest rationality. Now consider the consequences of such a prejudice when clever and power-hungry men availed themselves – and continue to avail themselves – of it! 'Create a mood!' – one will then require no reasons and conquer all objections!

29

The actors of virtue and sin. – Among the men of antiquity famed for their virtue there were, it appears, a countless number who *play-acted before themselves*: the Greeks especially, as actors incarnate, will have done this quite involuntarily and have approved it. Everyone, moreover, was with his virtue in *competition* with the virtue of another or of all others: how should one not have employed every kind of art to bring one's virtue to public attention, above all before oneself, even if only for the sake of practice! Of what use was a virtue one could not exhibit or which did not know how to exhibit itself! – Christianity put paid to these actors of virtue: in their place it invented the repellent flaunting of sin, it introduced into the world sinfulness *one has lyingly made up* (to this very day it counts as 'good form' among good Christians).

30

Refined cruelty as virtue. – Here is a morality which rests entirely on the *drive to distinction* – do not think too highly of it! For what kind of a drive is that and what thought lies behind it? We want to make the

sight of us *painful* to another and to awaken in him the feeling of envy
and of his own impotence and degradation; by dropping on to his
tongue a drop of *our* honey, and while doing him this supposed
favour looking him keenly and mockingly in the eyes, we want to
make him savour the bitterness of his fate. This person has become
humble and is now perfect in his humility – seek for those whom he
has for long wished to torture with it! you will find them soon
enough! That person is kind to animals and is admired on account of
it – but there are certain people on whom he wants to vent his cruelty
by this means. There stands a great artist: the pleasure he anticipated
in the envy of his defeated rivals allowed his powers no rest until he
had become great – how many bitter moments has his becoming
great not cost the souls of others! The chastity of the nun: with what
punitive eyes it looks into the faces of women who live otherwise!
how much joy in revenge there is in these eyes! – The theme is brief,
the variations that might be played upon it might be endless but
hardly tedious – for it is still a far too paradoxical and almost pain-
inducing novelty that the morality of distinction is in its ultimate
foundation pleasure in refined cruelty. In its ultimate foundation –
in this case that means: in its first generation. For when the habit of
some distinguishing action is *inherited*, the thought that lies behind it
is not inherited with it (thoughts are not hereditary, only feelings):
and provided it is not again reproduced by education, even the
second generation fails to experience any· pleasure in cruelty in
connection with it, but only pleasure in the habit as such. *This*
pleasure, however, is the first stage of the 'good'.

31
Pride in the spirit. – The *pride* of mankind, which resists the theory of
descent from the animals and establishes the great gulf between man
and nature – this pride has its basis in a *prejudice* as to what spirit is:
and this prejudice is relatively *young*. During the great prehistoric age
of mankind, spirit was presumed to exist everywhere and was not
held in honour as a privilege of man. Because, on the contrary, the
spiritual (together with all drives, wickedness, inclinations) had been
rendered common property, and thus common, one was not
ashamed to have descended from animals or trees (the *noble* races
thought themselves honoured by such fables), and saw in the spirit
that which unites us with nature, not that which sunders us from it.
Thus one schooled oneself in *modesty* – and likewise in consequence
of a *prejudice*.

32

The brake. – To suffer for the sake of morality and then to be told that
this kind of suffering is founded on an *error*: this arouses indignation.
For there is a unique consolation in affirming through one's
suffering a 'profounder world of truth' than any other world is, and
one would much *rather* suffer and thereby feel oneself *exalted* above
reality (through consciousness of having thus approached this
'profounder world of truth') than be without suffering but also
without this feeling that one is exalted. It is thus pride, and the
customary manner in which pride is gratified, which stands in the
way of a new *understanding* of morality. What force, therefore, will
have to be employed if this brake is to be removed? More pride? A
new pride?

33

Contempt for causes, for consequences and for reality. – Whenever an evil
chance event – a sudden storm or a crop failure or a plague – strikes a
community, the suspicion is aroused that custom has been offended
in some way or that new practices now have to be devised to
propitiate a new demonic power and caprice. This species of
suspicion and reflection is thus a direct avoidance of any investigation
of the real natural causes of the phenomenon: it takes the demonic
cause for granted. This is one spring of the perversity of the human
intellect which we have inherited: and the other spring arises close
beside it, in that the real natural *consequences* of an action are, equally
on principle, accorded far less attention than the supernatural (the
so-called punishments and mercies administered by the divinity).
Certain ablutions are, for example, prescribed at certain times: one
bathes, not so as to get clean, but because it is prescribed. One learns
to avoid, not the real consequences of uncleanliness, but the
supposed displeasure of the gods at the neglect of an ablution.
Under the pressure of superstitious fear one suspects there must be
very much more to this washing away of uncleanliness, one
interprets a second and third meaning into it, one spoils one's sense
for reality and one's pleasure in it, and in the end accords reality a
value only *insofar as it is capable of being a symbol*. Thus, under the spell
of the morality of custom, man despises first the causes, secondly the
consequences, thirdly reality, and weaves all his higher feelings (of
reverence, of sublimity, of pride, of gratitude, of love) *into an
imaginary world*: the so-called higher world. And the consequences
are perceptible even today: wherever a man's feelings are *exalted*, that

imaginary world is involved in some way. It is a sad fact, but for the moment the man of science has to be suspicious of *all higher feelings*, so greatly are they nourished by delusion and nonsense. It is not that they are thus in themselves, or must always remain thus: but of all the gradual *purifications* awaiting mankind, the purification of the higher feelings will certainly be one of the most gradual.

34
Moral feelings and moral concepts. – It is clear that moral feelings are transmitted in this way: children observe in adults inclinations for and aversions to certain actions and, as born apes, *imitate* these inclinations and aversions; in later life they find themselves full of these acquired and well-exercised affects and consider it only decent to try to account for and justify them. This 'accounting', however, has nothing to do with either the origin or the degree of intensity of the feeling: all one is doing is complying with the rule that, as a rational being, one has to have reasons for one's For and Against, and that they have to be adducible and acceptable reasons. To this extent the history of moral feelings is quite different from the history of moral concepts. The former are powerful *before* the action, the latter especially after the action in face of the need to pronounce upon it.

35
Feelings and their origination in judgments. – 'Trust your feelings!' – But feelings are nothing final or original; behind feelings there stand judgments and evaluations which we inherit in the form of feelings (inclinations, aversions). The inspiration born of a feeling is the grandchild of a judgment – and often of a false judgment! – and in any event not a child of your own! To trust one's feelings – means to give more obedience to one's grandfather and grandmother and their grandparents than to the gods which are in *us*: our reason and our experience.

36
A piece of foolish piety with a concealed purpose. – What! the inventors of the earliest cultures, the most ancient devisers of tools and measuring-rods, of carts and ships and houses, the first observers of the celestial order and the rules of the twice-times-table – are they something incomparably different from and higher than the inventors and observers of our own day? Do these first steps possess a value with which all our voyages and world-circumnavigations in the realm of

discoveries cannot compare? That is the prejudice, that is the argument for the deprecation of the modern spirit. And yet it is palpably obvious that chance was formerly the greatest of all discoverers and observers and the benevolent inspirer of those inventive ancients, and that more spirit, discipline and scientific imagination is employed in the most insignificant invention nowadays than the sum total available in whole eras of the past.

37

False conclusions from utility. – When one has demonstrated that a thing is of the highest utility, one has however thereby taken not one step towards explaining its origin: that is to say, one can never employ utility to make it comprehensible that a thing must necessarily exist. But it is the contrary judgment that has hitherto prevailed – and even into the domain of the most rigorous science. Even in the case of astronomy, has the (supposed) utility in the way the satellites are arranged (to compensate for the diminished light they receive owing to their greater distance from the sun, so that their inhabitants shall not go short of light) not been advanced as the final objective of this arrangement and the explanation of its origin? It reminds us of the reasoning of Columbus: the earth was made for man, therefore if countries exist they must be inhabited. 'Is it probable that the sun should shine on nothing, and that the nocturnal vigils of the stars are squandered upon pathless seas and countries unpeopled?'

38

Drives transformed by moral judgments. – The same drive evolves into the painful feeling of *cowardice* under the impress of the reproach custom has imposed upon this drive: or into the pleasant feeling of *humility* if it happens that a custom such as the Christian has taken it to its heart and called it *good.* That is to say, it is attended by either a good or a bad conscience! In itself it has, *like every drive*, neither this moral character nor any moral character at all, nor even a definite attendant sensation of pleasure or displeasure: it acquires all this, as its second nature, only when it enters into relations with drives already baptised good or evil or is noted as a quality of beings the people has already evaluated and determined in a moral sense. – Thus the older Greeks felt differently about *envy* from the way we do; Hesiod counted it among the effects of the *good,* beneficent Eris, and there was nothing offensive in attributing to the gods something of envy: which is comprehensible under a condition of things the soul of which was contest; contest, however, was evaluated and determined

as good. The Greeks likewise differed from us in their evaluation of
hope: they felt it to be blind and deceitful; Hesiod gave the strongest
expression to this attitude in a fable whose sense is so strange no
more recent commentator has understood it – for it runs counter to
the modern spirit, which has learned from Christianity to believe in
hope as a virtue. With the Greeks, on the other hand, to whom the
gateway to knowledge of the future seemed not to be entirely closed
and in countless cases where we content ourselves with hope
elevated inquiry into the future into a religious duty, hope would,
thanks to all these oracles and soothsayers, no doubt become
somewhat degraded and sink to something evil and dangerous. –
The Jews felt differently about *anger* from the way we do, and called it
holy: thus they saw the gloomy majesty of the man with whom it
showed itself associated at an elevation which a European is
incapable of imagining; they modelled their angry holy Jehovah on
their angry holy prophets. Measured against these, the great men of
wrath among Europeans are as it were creations at second hand.

39
'Pure spirit' a prejudice. – Wherever the teaching of *pure spirituality* has
ruled, it has destroyed nervous energy with its excesses: it has taught
deprecation, neglect or tormenting of the body and men to torment
and deprecate themselves on account of the drives which fill them; it
has produced gloomy, tense and oppressed souls – which believed,
moreover, they knew the cause of their feeling of wretchedness and
were perhaps able to abolish it! 'It must reside in the body! the body
is still *flourishing* too well!' – thus they concluded, while in fact the
body was, by means of the pains it registered, raising protest after
protest against the mockery to which it was constantly being
subjected. A general chronic over-excitability was finally the lot of
these virtuous pure-spirits: the only *pleasure* they could still recognise
was in the form of ecstasy and other precursors of madness – and
their system attained its summit when it came to take ecstasy for the
higher goal of life and the standard by which all earthly things stood
condemned.

40
Speculation on usages. – Countless prescriptions of custom hastily read
off from some unique strange occurence very soon became incomprehensible; the intention behind them could be ascertained with as
little certainty as could the nature of the punishment which would
follow their transgression; doubts existed even as to the performance

of the ceremonial – but inasmuch as there was vast speculation about it, the object of such speculation increased in value and precisely the most absurd aspect of a usage at length passed over into the holiest sanctity. Do not think lightly of the human energy expended over the millennia in this way, and least of all of the effect of this *speculation over usages*! We have here arrived at the tremendous exercise ground of the intellect – it is not only that the religions were woven here: this is also the venerable if dreadful prehistoric world of science, here is where the poet, the thinker, the physician, the lawgiver first grew. Fear of the incomprehensible which in an ambiguous way demanded ceremonies of us gradually passed over into the stimulus of the hard to comprehend, and where one did not know how to explain one learned to create.

41

Towards an evaluation of the vita contemplativa. – Let us, as men of the *vita contemplativa*, not forget what kind of evil and ill-fortune has come upon the man of the *vita activa* through the after-effects of contemplation – in short, what counter-reckoning the *vita activa* has in store for *us* if we boast too proudly before it of our good deeds. *First*: the so-called *religious* natures, whose numbers preponderate among the contemplative and who consequently constitute their commonest species, have at all times had the effect of making life hard for practical men and, where possible, intolerable to them: to darken the heavens, to blot out the sun, to cast suspicion on joy, to deprive hope of its value, to paralyse the active hand – this is what they have known how to do, just as much as they have had their consolations, alms, helping hand and benedictions for wretched feelings and times of misery. *Secondly*: the artists, somewhat rarer than the religious yet still a not uncommon kind of man of the *vita contemplativa*, have as individuals usually been unbearable, capricious, envious, violent and unpeaceable: this effect has to be set against the cheering and exalting effects of their works. *Thirdly*: the philosophers, a species in which religious and artistic powers exist together but in such a fashion that a third thing, dialectics, love of demonstrating, has a place beside them, have been the author of evils in the manner of the religious and the artists and have in addition through their inclination for dialectics brought boredom to many people; but their number has always been very small. *Fourthly*: the thinkers and the workers in science; they have rarely aimed at producing effects but have dug away quietly under their mole-hills. They have thus caused little annoyance or discomfort, and often, as objects of mockery and laughter, have without desiring it even alleviated the life of the men of the *vita activa*. Science has, moreover, become something very useful to everyone: if *on account of this utility* very many predestined for the *vita activa* now, in the sweat of their brow and not without brain-racking and imprecations, beat out for themselves a path to science, this distress is not the fault of the host of thinkers and workers in science; it is 'self-inflicted pain'.

42

Origin of the vita contemplativa. – In rude ages, where pessimistic judgments as to the nature of man and world prevail, the individual in the feeling of possessing all his powers is always intent upon acting in accordance with these judgments and thus translating idea into action through hunting, robbing, attacking, mistreatment and murder, including the paler reflections of these actions such as are alone tolerated within the community. But if his powers decline, if he feels weary or ill or melancholy or satiated and as a consequence for the time being devoid of desires and wishes, he is then a relatively better, that is to say less harmful man, and his pessimistic ideas discharge themselves only in words and thoughts, for example about the value of his comrades or his wife or his life or his gods – his judgments will be *unfavourable* judgments. In this condition he becomes thinker and prophet, or he expands imaginatively on his superstition and devises new usages, or he mocks his enemies – but whatever he may think about, all the products of his thinking are bound to reflect the condition he is in, which is one in which fear and weariness are on the increase and his valuation of action and active enjoyment on the decrease; the content of these products of his thinking must correspond to the content of these poetical, thoughtful, priestly moods; unfavourable judgment is bound to predominate. Later on, all those who continually acted as the single individual had formerly acted while in this condition, and who thus judged unfavourably and whose lives were melancholy and poor in deeds, came to be called poets or thinkers or priests or medicine-men – because they were so inactive one would have liked to have despised such men and ejected them from the community; but there was some danger attached to that – they were versed in superstition and on the scent of divine forces, one never doubted that they commanded unknown sources of power. This is the estimation under which *the oldest race of contemplative natures* lived – despised to just the extent they were not dreaded! In this muffled shape, in this ambiguous guise, with an evil heart and often an anguished head, did contemplation first appear on earth, at once weak and fearsome, secretly despised and publicly loaded with superstitious reference! Here, as always, it is a case of *pudenda origo*!

43

The many forces that now have to come together in the thinker. – To abstract oneself from sensory perception, to exalt oneself to contemplation of abstractions – that was at one time actually felt as *exaltation*: we can no longer quite enter into this feeling. To revel in pallid images of words and things, to sport with such invisible, inaudible, impalpable beings, was, out of contempt for the sensorily tangible, seductive and evil world, felt as a life in another *higher* world. 'These *abstracta* are certainly not seductive, but they can offer us guidance!' – with that one lifted oneself upwards. It is not the content of these sportings of spirituality, it is they themselves which constituted 'the higher life' in the prehistoric ages of science. Hence Plato's admiration for dialectics and his enthusiastic belief that dialectics necessarily pertained to the good, unsensory man. It is not only knowledge which has been discovered gradually and piece by piece, the means of knowing as such, the conditions and operations which precede knowledge in man, have been discovered gradually and piece by piece too. And each time the newly discovered operation or the novel condition seemed to be, not a means to knowledge, but in itself the content, goal and sum total of all that was worth knowing. The thinker needs imagination, self-uplifting, abstraction, desensualization, invention, presentiment, induction, dialectics, deduction, the critical faculty, the assemblage of material, the impersonal mode of thinking, contemplativeness and comprehensiveness, and not least justice and love for all that exists – but all these means to knowledge once counted individually in the history of the *vita contemplativa* as goals, and final goals, and bestowed on their inventors that feeling of happiness which appears in the human soul when it catches sight of a *final* goal.

44

Origin and significance. – Why is it that this thought comes back to me again and again and in ever more varied colours? – that *formerly*, when investigators of knowledge sought out the origin of things they always believed they would discover something of incalculable significance for all later action and judgment, that they always *presupposed*, indeed, that the *salvation* of man must depend on *insight into the origin of things*: but that now, on the contrary, the more we advance towards origins, the more our interest diminishes; indeed, that all the evaluations and 'interestedness' we have implanted into things begin to lose their meaning the further we go back and the closer we approach the things themselves. *The more insight we possess into an origin the less significant does the origin appear*: while *what is nearest to us*, what is around us and in us, gradually begins to display colours and beauties and enigmas and riches of significance of which earlier mankind had not an inkling. Formerly, thinkers prowled around angrily like captive animals, watching the bars of their cages and leaping against them in order to smash them down: and *happy* seemed he who through a gap in them believed he saw something of what was outside, of what was distant and beyond.

45

A tragic ending for knowledge. – Of all the means of producing exaltation, it has been human sacrifice which has at all times most exalted and elevated man. And perhaps every other endeavour could still be thrown down by *one* tremendous idea, so that it would achieve victory over the most victorious – the idea of *self-sacrificing mankind*. But to whom should mankind sacrifice itself? One could already take one's oath that, if ever the constellation of this idea appears above the horizon, the knowledge of truth would remain as the one tremendous goal commensurate with such a sacrifice, because for this goal no sacrifice is too great. In the meantime, the problem of the extent to which mankind can as a whole take steps towards the advancement of knowledge has never yet been posed; not to speak of what drive to knowledge could drive mankind to the point of dying with the light of an anticipatory wisdom in its eyes. Perhaps, if one day an alliance has been established with the inhabitants of other stars for the purpose of knowledge, and knowledge has been communicated from star to star for a few millennia: perhaps enthusiasm for knowledge may then rise to such a high-water mark!

46

Doubt about doubt. – 'What a good pillow doubt is for a well-constructed head!' – this saying of Montaigne's always provoked Pascal, for no one longed for a good pillow as much as he did. Whatever was wrong? –

47

Words lie in our way! – Wherever primitive mankind set up a word, they believed they had made a discovery. How different the truth is! – they had touched on a problem, and by supposing they had *solved* it they had created a hindrance to its solution. – Now with every piece of knowledge one has to stumble over dead, petrified words, and one will sooner break a leg than a word.

48

'Know yourself' is the whole of science. – Only when he has attained a final knowledge of all things will man have come to know himself. For things are only the boundaries of man.

49

The new fundamental feeling: our conclusive transitoriness. – Formerly one sought the feeling of the grandeur of man by pointing to his divine *origin*: this has now become a forbidden way, for at its portal stands the ape, together with other gruesome beasts, grinning knowingly as if to say: no further in this direction! One therefore now tries the opposite direction: the way mankind is *going* shall serve as proof of his grandeur and kinship with God. Alas this, too, is vain! At the end of this way stands the funeral urn of the *last* man and gravedigger (with the inscription *'nihil humani a me alienum puto'*). However high mankind may have evolved – and perhaps at the end it will stand even lower than at the beginning! – it cannot pass over into a higher order, as little as the ant and the earwig can at the end of its 'earthly course' rise up to kinship with God and eternal life. The becoming drags the has-been along behind it: why should an exception to this eternal spectacle be made on behalf of some little star or for any little species upon it! Away with such sentimentalities!

50

Faith in intoxication. – Men who enjoy moments of exaltation and ecstasy and who, on account of the contrast other states present and because of the way they have squandered their nervous energy, are ordinarily in a wretched and miserable condition, regard these moments as their real 'self' and their wretchedness and misery as the *effect of what is 'outside the self'*; and thus they harbour feelings of revengefulness towards their environment, their age, their entire world. Intoxication counts as their real life, as their actual ego: they see in everything else the opponent and obstructor of intoxication, no matter whether its nature be spiritual, moral, religious or artistic.

Mankind owes much that is bad to these wild inebriates: for they are insatiable sowers of the weeds of dissatisfaction with oneself and one's neighbour, of contempt for the age and the world, and especially of world-weariness. Perhaps a whole Hell of *criminals* could not produce an effect so oppressive, poisonous to air and land, uncanny and protracted as does this noble little community of unruly, fantastic, half-crazy people of genius who cannot control themselves and can experience pleasure in themselves only when they have quite lost themselves: while the criminal very often gives proof of exceptional self-control, self-sacrifice and prudence, and keeps these qualities awake in those who fear him. Through him the sky above life may perhaps become perilous and gloomy, but the air stays sharp and invigorating. – In addition to all this, these enthusiasts seek with all their might to implant the faith in intoxication as being that which is actually living in life: a dreadful faith! Just as savages are quickly ruined and then perish through 'fire-water', so mankind as a whole has been slowly and thoroughly ruined through the feelings made drunk by *spiritual* fire-waters and by those who have kept alive the desire for them: perhaps it will go on to perish by them.

51
Such as we still are! – 'Let us be forbearing towards the great one-eyed!' – said John Stuart Mill: as though it were necessary to beg for forbearance where one is accustomed to render them belief and almost worship! I say: let us be forbearing towards the two-eyed, great and small – for, *such as we are*, we shall never attain to anything higher than forbearance!

52
Where are the new physicians of the soul? – It has been the means of comfort which have bestowed upon life that fundamental character of suffering it is now believed to possess; the worst sickness of mankind originated in the way in which they have combated their sicknesses, and what seemed to cure has in the long run produced something worse than that which it was supposed to overcome. The means which worked immediately, anaesthetising and intoxicating, the so-called consolations, were ignorantly supposed to be actual cures; the fact was not even noticed, indeed, that these instantaneous alleviations often had to be paid for with a general and profound worsening of the complaint, that the invalid had to suffer from the

after-effect of intoxication, later from the withdrawal of intoxication, and later still from an oppressive general feeling of restlessness, nervous agitation and ill-health. Past a certain degree of sickness one never recovered – the physicians of the soul, those universally believed in and worshipped, saw to that. – It is said of Schopenhauer, and with justice, that after they had been neglected for so long he again took seriously the sufferings of mankind: where is he who, after they have been neglected for so long, will again take seriously the antidotes to these sufferings and put in the pillory the unheard-of quack-doctoring with which, under the most glorious names, mankind has hitherto been accustomed to treat the sicknesses of its soul?

53
Misuse of the conscientious. – It has been the conscientious and *not* the conscienceless who have had to suffer so dreadfully from the oppression of Lenten preachers and the fears of Hell, especially when they were at the same time people of imagination. Thus life has been made most gloomy precisely for those who had need of cheerfulness and pleasant pictures – not only for their own refreshment and recovery from themselves, but so that mankind might take pleasure in them and absorb from them a ray of their beauty. Oh, how much superfluous cruelty and vivisection have proceeded from those religions which invented sin! And from those people who desired by means of it to gain the highest enjoyment of their power!

54
Thinking about illness! – To calm the imagination of the invalid, so that at least he should not, as hitherto, have to suffer *more* from thinking about his illness than from the illness itself – that, I think, would be something! It would be a great deal! Do you now understand our task?

55
'Ways'. – The supposed 'shorter ways' have always put mankind into great danger; at the glad tidings that such a shorter way has been found, they always desert their way – and *lose their way.*

56
The apostate of the free spirit. – Who could possibly feel an aversion for pious people strong in their faith? To the contrary, do we not regard them with a silent respect and take pleasure in them, with a profound regret that these excellent people do not feel as we do? But whence

comes that sudden deep repugnance without apparent cause which we feel for him who once *had* all freedom of spirit and in the end *became* 'a believer'? If we recall it, it is as if we had beheld some disgusting sight which we want to expunge from our soul as quickly as we can! Would we not turn our back even upon the person we most revered if he became suspicious to us in this respect? And not at all on account of a moral prejudice, but out of a sudden disgust and horror! Why do we feel so strongly about it? Perhaps we shall be given to understand that at bottom we are not altogether sure of ourselves? That we planted thorn-bushes of the most pointed contempt around us in good time, so that at the decisive moment, when old age has made us weak and forgetful, we should not be able to climb out over our own contempt? – Quite honestly, this supposition is erroneous, and he who makes it knows nothing of that which moves and determines the free spirit: how little contemptible does he find his *changes* of opinion in themselves! How greatly, on the contrary, does he honour in the *capacity* to change his opinions a rare and high distinction, especially when it extends into old age! And his ambition (*not* his pusillanimity) reaches up even to the forbidden fruits of *spernere se sperni* and *spernere se ipsum*: certainly he does not feel in the face of these things the fear experienced by the vain and complacent! Besides which, he counts the theory of the *innocence of all opinions* as being as well founded as the theory of the innocence of all actions: how then could he appear before the apostate of spiritual freedom in the role of judge and hangman! The sight of him would, rather, touch him as the sight of someone with a repulsive disease touches a physician: physical disgust at something fungous, mollified, bloated, suppurating, momentarily overpowers reason and the will to help. It is in this way that our goodwill is overcome by the idea of the tremendous *dishonesty* which must have prevailed in the apostate of the free spirit: by the idea of a general degeneration reaching even into the skeleton of his character. –

57

Other fears, other securities. – Christianity had brought into life a quite novel and limitless *perilousness*, and therewith quite novel securities, pleasures, recreations and evaluations of all things. Our century denies this perilousness, and does so with a good conscience: and yet it continues to drag along with it the old habits of Christian security, Christian enjoyment, recreation, evaluation! It even drags them into its noblest arts and philosophies! How worn out and feeble, how insipid and awkward, how arbitrarily fanatical and, above all, how insecure all this must appear, now that that fearful antithesis to it, the omnipresent *fear* of the Christian for his *eternal* salvation, has been lost!

58

Christianity and the affects. – Within Christianity there is audible also a great popular protest against philosophy: the reason of the sages of antiquity had advised men against the affects, Christianity wants to *restore* them. To this end, it denies to virtue as it was conceived by the philosophers – as the victory of reason over affect – all moral value, condemns rationality in general, and challenges the affects to reveal themselves in their extremest grandeur and strength: as *love* of God, *fear* of God, as fanatical *faith* in God, as the blindest *hope* in God.

59

Error as comfort. – You can say what you like: Christianity wanted to free men from the burden of the demands of morality by, as it supposed, showing a *shorter way to perfection*: just as some philosophers thought they could avoid wearisome and tedious dialectics and the collection of rigorously tested facts by pointing out a 'royal road to truth'. It was an error in each case – yet nonetheless a great comfort to the exhausted and despairing in the wilderness.

60

All spirit in the end becomes bodily visible. – Christianity has embraced within itself all the spirit of countless people who joy in submission, all those coarse and subtle enthusiasts for humility and worship, and has thereby emerged from a rustic rudeness – such as is very much in evidence, for example, in the earliest likeness of the apostle Peter – into a very *spirited* religion, with a thousand wrinkles, reservations and subterfuges in its countenance; it has made European humanity sharp-witted, and not only theologically cunning. From this spirit, and in concert with the power and very often the deepest conviction and honesty of devotion, it has *chiselled out* perhaps the most refined figures in human society that have ever yet existed: the figures of the higher and highest Catholic priesthood, especially when they have descended from a noble race and brought with them an inborn grace of gesture, the eye of command, and beautiful hands and feet. Here the human face attains to that total spiritualisation produced by the continual ebb and flow of the two species of happiness (the feeling of power and the feeling of surrender) after a well considered mode of

life has tamed the beast in man; here an activity which consists in
blessing, forgiving sins and representing the divinity keeps awake the
feeling of a suprahuman mission in the soul, *and indeed also in the body*;
here there reigns that noble contempt for the fragility of the body
and of fortune's favour which pertains to born soldiers; one takes
pride in obeying, which is the distinguishing mark of all aristocrats;
in the tremendous impossibility of one's task lies one's excuse and
one's ideal. The surpassing beauty and refinement of the princes of
the church has always proved to the people the *truth* of the church; a
temporary brutalisation of the priesthood (as in the time of Luther)
has always brought with it a belief in the opposite. – And is *this*
human beauty and refinement which is the outcome of a harmony
between figure, spirit and task also to go to the grave when the
religions come to an end? And can nothing higher be attained, or
even imagined?

61

The needful sacrifice. – These serious, excellent, upright, deeply
sensitive people who are still Christians from the very heart: they owe
it to themselves to try for once the experiment of living for some
length of time without Christianity, they owe it to *their faith* in this way
for once to sojourn 'in the wilderness' – if only to win for themselves
the right to a voice on the question whether Christianity is necessary.
For the present they cleave to their native soil and thence revile the
world beyond it: indeed, they are provoked and grow angry if
anyone gives them to understand that what lies beyond their native
soil is the whole wide world! that Christianity is, after all, only a little
corner! No, your evidence will be of no weight until you have lived
for years on end without Christianity, with an honest, fervent zeal to
endure life in the antithesis of Christianity: until you have wandered
far, far away from it. Only if you are driven back, not by homesickness
but by *judgment* on the basis of a rigorous *comparison*, will your
homecoming possess any significance! – The men of the future will
one day deal in this way with all evaluations of the past; one has
voluntarily *to live through* them once again, and likewise their
antithesis – if one is at last to possess the *right* to pass them through
the sieve.

62

On the origin of religions. – How can a person regard his own opinion
about things as a revelation? This is the problem of the origin of

religions: on each occasion there was a person to hand in whom this phenomenon was possible. The precondition is that he already believed in the fact of revelation. Then, one day, he suddenly acquires *his* new idea, and the happiness engendered by a great hypothesis encompassing the universe and all existence enters his consciousness with such force he does not dare to consider himself the creator of such happiness and ascribes the cause of it, and again the cause of the cause of this new idea to his god: as his god's revelation. How should a man be the originator of such great joy! – that is the pessimistic doubt which fills him. And other secret levers are at work within him, too: for example, one *strengthens* an opinion in one's own estimation when one feels it to be a revelation, one therewith abolishes its hypothetical nature, one removes it from all criticism, indeed from all doubt, one makes it holy. One thus debases oneself to the status of an organon, to be sure, but our idea, as an idea of god's, will in the end be victorious – the feeling that with this idea one will finally prove the victor gains ascendancy over the feeling of debasement. Another feeling, too, is playing its game in the background: if one exalts *what one has produced* above oneself, and seems to be disregarding one's own worth, this is nonetheless attended by a rejoicing of paternal love and paternal pride which compensates, and more than compensates, for everything.

63

Hatred of one's neighbour. – Supposing we felt towards another as he feels towards himself – that which Schopenhauer calls sympathy but which would be better designated empathy – then we would have to hate him if, like Pascal, he found himself hateful. And that is probably how Pascal in fact felt towards mankind as a whole; as did the earliest Christians, who, under Nero, were, as Tacitus reports, 'convicted' of *odium generis humani.*

64

The despairing. – Christianity possesses the hunter's instinct for all those who can by one means or another be brought to despair – of which only a portion of mankind is capable. It is constantly on their track, it lies in wait for them. Pascal attempted the experiment of seeing whether, with the aid of the most incisive knowledge, everyone could not be brought to despair: the experiment miscarried, to his twofold despair.

65

Brahminism and Christianity. – There are recipes for the feeling of power, firstly for those who can control themselves and who are thereby accustomed to a feeling of power; then for those in whom precisely this is lacking. Brahminism has catered for men of the former sort, Christianity for men of the latter.

66

Capacity for visions. – Throughout the whole Middle Ages, the actual and decisive sign of the highest humanity was that one was capable of visions – that is to say, of a profound mental disturbance! And the objective of medieval prescriptions for the life of all higher natures (the *religiosi*) was at bottom to make one *capable* of visions! It is thus no wonder that an over-estimation of the half-mad, the fantastic, the fanatical – of so-called men of genius – should have spilled over into our time; 'they have seen things that others do not see' – precisely! and this should make us cautious towards them, not credulous!

67

Price of believers. – He who sets such store on being believed in that he offers Heaven in exchange for this belief, and offers it to everyone, even to a thief on the cross – must have suffered from fearful self-doubt and come to know every kind of crucifixion: otherwise he would not purchase his believers at so high a price.

68

The first Christian. – All the world still believes in the writings of the 'Holy Spirit' or stands in the after-effect of this belief: when one opens the Bible one does so to 'edify' oneself, to discover a signpost of consolation in one's own personal distress, great or small – in short, one reads oneself into and out of it. That it also contains the history of one of the most ambitious and importunate souls, of a mind as superstitious as it was cunning, the history of the apostle Paul – who, apart from a few scholars, knows that? But without this remarkable history, without the storms and confusions of such a mind, of such a soul, there would be no Christianity; we would hardly have heard of a little Jewish sect whose master died on the cross. To be sure: if this history had been understood at the right time, if the writings of Paul had been read, not as the revelations of the 'Holy Spirit', but with a free and honest exercise of one's own spirit and without thinking all the time of our own personal needs – *really read*, that is to say (but for fifteen hundred years there were no such readers) – Christianity would long since have ceased to exist: for these pages of the Jewish Pascal expose the origin of Christianity as thoroughly as the pages of the French Pascal expose its destiny and that by which it will perish. That the ship of Christianity threw overboard a good part of the Jewish ballast, that it went and was able to go among the heathen – that is a consequence of the history of this one man, of a very tormented, very pitiable, very unpleasant man who also found himself unpleasant. He suffered from a fixed idea, or more clearly from a *fixed question* which was always present to him and would never rest: what is the Jewish *law* really concerned with? and, in particular, what is the *fulfilment of this law?* In his youth he had himself wanted to satisfy it, voracious for this highest distinction the Jews were able to conceive – this people which had taken the fantasy of moral sublimity higher than any other people and which alone achieved the creation of a holy God, together with the idea of sin as an offence against this holiness. Paul had become at once the fanatical defender and chaperone of this God and his law, and was constantly combating and on the watch for transgressors and doubters, harsh and malicious towards them and with the extremest inclination for punishment. And then he discovered in himself that he himself – fiery, sensual, melancholy, malevolent in hatred as he was – *could* not fulfil the law, he discovered indeed what seemed to him the strangest thing of all: that his extravagant lust for power was constantly combating and on the watch for transgressors and goad. Is it really 'carnality' which again and again makes him a transgressor? And not rather, as he later suspected, behind it the law itself, which *must* continually prove itself unfulfillable and with irresistible magic lures on to transgression? But at that time he did not yet possess this way out of his difficulty. Many things lay on his conscience – he hints at enmity, murder, sorcery, idolatry, uncleanliness, drunkenness and pleasure in debauch – and however much he tried to relieve this conscience, and even more his lust for domination, through the extremest fanaticism in revering and defending the law, there were moments when he said to himself: 'It is all in vain! The torture of the unfulfilled law cannot be overcome.' Luther may have felt a similar thing when he wanted in his monastery to become the perfect man of the spiritual ideal: and similarly to Luther, who one day began to hate the spiritual ideal and the Pope and the saints and the whole clergy with a hatred the more deadly the less he dared to admit it to himself – a similar thing happened to Paul. The law was the cross to which he felt himself nailed: how he hated it! how he had to drag it along! how he sought about for a means of *destroying* it – and no longer to fulfil it! And at last the liberating idea came to him,

40

together with a vision, as was bound to happen in the case of this epileptic: to him, the zealot of the law who was inwardly tired to death of it, there appeared on a lonely road Christ with the light of God shining in his countenance, and Paul heard the words: 'Why persecutest thou *me?*' What essentially happened then is rather this: his *mind* suddenly became clear: 'it is *unreasonable*', he says to himself, 'to persecute precisely this Christ! For here is the way out, here is perfect revenge, here and nowhere else do I have and hold the *destroyer of the law!*' Sick with the most tormented pride, at a stroke he feels himself recovered, the moral despair is as if blown away, destroyed – that is to say, *fulfilled*, there on the Cross! Hitherto that shameful *death* had counted with him as the principal argument against the 'Messiahdom' of which the followers of the new teaching spoke: but what if it were *necessary* for the *abolition* of the law! – The tremendous consequences of this notion, this solution of the riddle, whirl before his eyes, all at once he is the happiest of men – the destiny of the Jews – no, of all mankind – seems to him to be tied to this notion, to this second of his sudden enlightenment, he possesses the idea of ideas, the key of keys, the light of lights; henceforth history revolves around him! For from now on he is the teacher of the *destruction of the law*! To die to evil – that means also to die to the law; to exist in the flesh – that means also to exist in the law! To become one with Christ – that means also to become with him the destroyer of the law; to have died with him – that means also to have died to the law! Even if it is still possible to sin, it is no longer possible to sin against the law: 'I am outside the law.' 'If I were now to accept the law again and submit to it I should be making Christ an accomplice of sin', for the law existed so that sins might be committed, it continually brought sin forth as a sharp juice brings forth a disease; God could never have resolved on the death of Christ if a fulfilment of the law had been in any way possible without this death; now not only has all guilt been taken away, guilt as such has been destroyed; now the law is dead, now the carnality in which it dwelt is dead – or at least dying constantly away, as though decaying. Yet but a brief time within this decay! – that is the Christian's lot, before, become one with Christ, he arises with Christ, participates with Christ in divine glory and becomes a 'son of God', like Christ. – With that the intoxication of Paul is at its height, and likewise the importunity of his soul – with the idea of becoming one with Christ all shame, all subordination, all bounds are taken from it, and the

41

intractable lust for power reveals itself as an anticipatory revelling in *divine* glories. – This is the *first Christian*, the inventor of Christianness! Before him there were only a few Jewish sectarians.

69

Inimitable. – There exists a tremendous span and tension *between* envy and friendship, between self-contempt and pride: the Greek dwelt in the former, the Christian in the latter.

70

What a crude intellect is good for. – The Christian church is an encyclopaedia of prehistoric cults and conceptions of the most diverse origin, and that is why it is so capable of proselytising: it always could, and it can still go wherever it pleases and it always found, and always finds something similar to itself to which it can adapt itself and gradually impose upon it a Christian meaning. It is not what is Christian in it, but the universally heathen character of its *usages*, which has favoured the spread of this world-religion; its ideas, rooted in both the Jewish and the Hellenic worlds, have from the first known how to raise themselves above national and racial niceties and exclusiveness as though these were merely prejudices. One may admire this *power* of causing the most various elements to coalesce, but one must not forget the contemptible quality that adheres to this power: the astonishing crudeness and self-satisfiedness of the church's intellect during the time it was in process of formation, which permitted it to accept *any food* and to digest opposites like pebbles.

71

Christian revenge on Rome. – Nothing, perhaps, is so wearying as the sight of a perpetual conqueror – for two centuries the world had seen Rome subdue one people after another, the circle was closed, the whole future seemed to be fixed, all things were ordered as though to last for ever – when the Empire *built*, indeed, it built with the notion of *'aere perennius'*; we, who know only the 'melancholy of ruins', can barely understand that quite different *melancholy of eternal construction* from which one had to try to rescue oneself by some means or other – through frivolity, for example, as in the case of Horace. Others sought other antidotes to this weariness bordering on despair, to the deadly awareness that every impulse of head or heart was henceforth without hope, that the great spider was everywhere, that it would implacably consume all blood wherever it might well forth. – This centuries-long speechless hatred for Rome on the part of its wearied spectators, which extended as far as Rome ruled, at last discharged itself in *Christianity*, in as much as Christianity welded together Rome, the 'world' and 'sin' into *one* sensation: it avenged itself on Rome by imagining the sudden destruction of the world to be near at hand; it avenged itself on Rome by re-establishing a future – Rome had known how to turn everything into its *own* pre-history and present – and a future, moreover, in comparison with which Rome no longer appeared the most important thing; it avenged itself on Rome by dreaming of a last *judgment* – and the crucified Jew as symbol of salvation was the profoundest mockery of the splendidly arrayed provincial Roman governors, for they now appeared as symbols of ill-fortune and of 'world' ripe for destruction.

72

The 'after death'. – Christianity discovered the idea of punishment in Hell throughout the whole Roman Empire: all the numerous secret cults had brooded on it with especial satisfaction as on the most promising egg of their power. Epicurus believed he could confer no greater benefit on his fellows than by tearing up the roots of *this* belief: his triumph, which resounds the most beautifully in the mouth of the gloomy and yet enlightened disciple of his teaching, the Roman Lucretius, came too early – Christianity took the belief in these subterranean terrors, which was already dying out, under its especial protection, and it acted prudently in so doing! How, without this bold recourse to complete heathendom, could it have carried off victory over the popularity of the cults of Mithras and Isis! It thereby brought the timorous over to its side – the firmest adherents of a new faith! The Jews, as a people firmly attached to life – like the Greeks and more than the Greeks – had paid little attention to these ideas: definitive death as the punishment for the sinner, and never to rise again as the severest threat – that was sufficient admonition for these strange people, who did not desire to get rid of their bodies but, with their refined Egyptianism, hoped to retain them for all eternity. (A Jewish martyr, whose fate is recorded in the Second Book of the Maccabees, has no thought of renouncing possession of his torn-out intestines: he wants to *have* them at the resurrection – such is the Jewish way!) To the first Christians the idea of eternal torment was very remote: they thought they were *redeemed* 'from death' and from day to day expected a transformation and not that they would die. (What a strange effect the first death must have had on these

43

expectant people! What a mixture of amazement, rejoicing, doubt, shame, fervour – truly a theme for great artists!) Paul knew of nothing better he could say of his Redeemer than that he had *opened* the gates of immortality to everyone – he did not yet believe in the resurrection of the unredeemed; indeed, as would follow from his teaching of the unfulfillability of the law and of death as the consequence of sin, he suspected that hitherto no one (or only very few, and then through mercy and not their own deserts) had become immortal: it was only now that immortality had *begun* to open its doors – and in the end only a very few would be selected: as the arrogance of the elect cannot refrain from adding. – Elsewhere, where the drive to life was not as great as it was among Jews and Jewish Christians and the prospect of immortality did not automatically seem preferable to the prospect of definitive death, that heathen and yet not altogether un-Jewish addition of Hell became a welcome instrument in the hands of proselytisers: there arose the novel teaching that the sinner and unredeemed was immortal, the teaching of eternal damnation, and it was mightier than the idea of *definitive death*, which thereafter faded away. It was only *science* which reconquered it, as it had to do when it at the same time rejected any other idea of death and of any life beyond it. We have grown poorer by *one* interest: the 'after death' no longer concerns us! – an unspeakable benefit, which would be felt as such far and wide if it were not so recent. – And Epicurus triumphs anew!

73

For the 'truth'! – 'For the truth of Christianity there spoke the virtuous behaviour of the Christians, their fortitude in suffering, the firmness of their faith, and above all the way in which Christianity spread and increased in spite of all the difficulties in its path' – this is what you say even today! How pitiable! You must learn that all this argues neither for nor against the truth, that a proof of truth is not the same thing as a proof of truthfulness and that the latter is in no way an argument for the former!

74

Christian mental reservation. – Should the most common mental reservation of the Christian of the first centuries not have been this: 'it is better to *convince* oneself of one's guilt rather than of one's innocence, for one does not quite know how so *mighty* a judge is disposed – but one has to *fear* that he hopes to find before him none but those conscious of their guilt! Given his great power, he will more easily pardon a guilty person than admit that someone is justified in his presence.' – This is how poor people felt in the presence of the Roman provincial governor: 'he is too proud to admit of our innocence' – how should precisely this sensation not have reasserted itself in the Christian representation of the supreme judge!

75

Not European and not noble. – There is something Oriental and something feminine in Christianity: it betrays itself in the idea: 'whom the lord loveth he chastiseth'; for in the Orient women regard chastisements and the strict seclusion of their person from the world as a sign of their husband's love, and complain if this sign is lacking.

76

To think a thing evil means to make it evil. – The passions become evil and malicious if they are regarded as evil and malicious. Thus Christianity has succeeded in transforming Eros and Aphrodite – great powers capable of idealisation – into diabolical kobolds and phantoms by means of the torments it introduces into the consciences of believers whenever they are excited sexually. Is it not dreadful to make necessary and regularly recurring sensations into a source of inner misery, and in this way to want to make inner misery a necessary and regularly recurring phenomenon *in every human being*! In addition to which it remains a misery kept secret and thus more deeply rooted: for not everyone possesses the courage of Shakespeare to confess his Christian gloominess on this point in the way he did in his Sonnets. – Must everything that one has to combat, that one has to keep within bounds or on occasion banish totally from one's mind, always have to be called *evil*! Is it not the way of *common* souls always to think an *enemy* must be *evil*! And ought one to call Eros an enemy? The sexual sensations have this in common with the sensations of sympathy and worship, that one person, by doing what pleases him, gives pleasure to another person – such benevolent arrangements are not to be found so very often in nature! And to calumniate such an arrangement and to ruin it through associating it with a bad conscience! – In the end this *diabolising* of Eros acquired an outcome in comedy: thanks to the dark secretiveness of the church in all things erotic, the 'devil' Eros gradually became more interesting to mankind than all the saints and angels put together: the effect has been that, to this very day, the *love story* is the only thing which *all* circles find equally interesting – and with an exaggeratedness which antiquity would

45

have found incomprehensible and which will one day again elicit laughter. All our thinking and poetising, from the highest to the lowest, is characterised, and more than characterised, by the excessive importance attached to the love story: on this account it may be that posterity will judge the whole inheritance of Christian culture to be marked by something crackbrained and petty.

77

On the torments of the soul. – Everyone now exclaims loudly against torment inflicted by one person on the body of another; indignation is at once ignited against a person capable of doing it; indeed, we tremble at the mere idea of a torment which could be inflicted on a man or an animal, and suffer quite dreadfully when we hear of a definitely attested fact of this kind. But we are still far from feeling so decisively and with such unanimity in regard to torments of the soul and how dreadful it is to inflict them. Christianity has made use of them on an unheard-of scale and continues to preach this species of torture; indeed, it complains quite innocently of falling-off and growing lukewarm when it encounters those who are not in this state of torment – all with the result that even today mankind regards spiritual death-by-fire, spiritual torture and instruments of torture, with the same anxious toleration and indecision as it formerly did the cruelties inflicted on the bodies of men and animals. Hell has, in truth, been more than merely a word: and the newly created and genuine fear of Hell has been attended by a new species of pity corresponding to it, a horrible, ponderously heavy feeling of pity, unknown to former ages, for those 'irrevocably damned to Hell' – a condition, for example, which the stone guest gives Don Juan to understand he is in, and which had no doubt often before during the Christian centuries wrung tears even from stones. Plutarch gives a gloomy picture of the state of a superstitious man in the pagan world: this picture pales when contrasted with the Christian of the Middle Ages who *supposes* he is no longer going to escape 'eternal torment'. Dreadful portents appear to him: perhaps a stork holding a snake in its beak but *hesitating* to swallow it. Or nature suddenly blanches or fiery colours flutter across the ground. Or he is approached by the figures of dead relatives, their faces bearing the traces of fearful sufferings. Or when he is asleep the dark walls of his room grow bright and there appear on them in a yellow exhalation the images of torture-instruments and a confusion of snakes and devils. Indeed, what a dreadful place Christianity had already made of the earth when it everywhere erected the crucifix and thereby designated the earth as the place 'where the just man is *tortured* to death'! And when the powerful oratory of great Lenten preachers for once fetched into the light of publicity all the hidden suffering of the individual, the torments of the 'closet'; when a Whitfield, for instance, preached 'like a dying man to the dying', now violently weeping, now stamping loudly, and passionately and unashamedly, in the most abrupt and cutting tones, directed the whole weight of his attack upon some one individual present and in a fearful manner excluded him from the community – then the earth really did seem to want to transform itself into the 'vale of misery'! Whole masses then come together appeared to fall victim to a madness; many were paralysed with fear; others lay unconscious and motionless; some were seized with violent trembling or rent the air for hours with piercing cries. Everywhere a loud breathing, as of people half-choked gasping for air. 'And truly', says one eye-witness of such a sermon, 'almost all the sounds to be heard were those of people *dying in bitter torment.*' – Let us never forget that it was Christianity which made of the *death-bed* a bed of torture, and that with the scenes that have since then been enacted upon it, with the terrifying tones which here seemed to be realised for the first time, the senses and the blood of countless witnesses have been poisoned for the rest of their life and for that of their posterity! Imagine a harmless human being who cannot get over once having heard such words as these: 'Oh eternity! Oh that I had no soul! Oh that I had never been born! I am damned, damned, lost for ever. A week ago you could have helped me. But now it is all over. Now I belong to the Devil. I go with him to Hell. Break, break, poor hearts of stone! Will you not break? What more can be done for hearts of stone? I am damned that you may be saved! There he is! Yes, there he is! Come, kind Devil! Come!' –

78

Justice which punishes. – Misfortune and guilt – Christianity has placed these two things on a balance: so that, when misfortune consequent on guilt is great, even now the greatness of the guilt itself is still involuntarily measured by it. But this is not *antique*, and that is why the Greek tragedy, which speaks so much yet in so different a sense of misfortune and guilt, is a great liberator of the spirit in a way in which the ancients themselves could not feel it. They were still so innocent as not to have established an 'adequate relationship' between guilt and misfortune. The guilt of their tragic heroes is, indeed, the little stone over which they stumble and perhaps break an arm or put out an eye: antique sensibility commented: 'Yes, he should have gone his way a little more cautiously and with less haughtiness!' But it was reserved for Christianity to say: 'Here is a great misfortune and behind it there *must* lie hidden a great, *equally great* guilt, even though it may not be clearly visible! If you, unfortunate man, do not feel this you are *obdurate* – you will have to suffer worse things!' – Moreover, in antiquity there still existed actual misfortune, pure innocent misfortune; only in Christendom did everything become punishment, well-deserved punishment: it also makes the sufferer's imagination suffer, so that with every misfortune he feels himself morally reprehensible and cast out. Poor mankind! – The Greeks have a word for indignation at another's unhappiness: this affect was inadmissible among Christian peoples and failed to develop, so that they also lack a name for this *more manly* brother of pity.

79

A suggestion. – If, as Pascal and Christianity maintain, our ego is always *hateful*, how could we ever allow and accept that another should love it – whether god or man! It would be contrary to all decency to let oneself be loved while being all the time well aware that one *deserves* only hatred – not to speak of other defensive sensations. – 'But this precisely is the realm of clemency.' – Is your love of your neighbour an act of clemency, then? Your pity an act of clemency? Well, if you are capable of this, go a step further: love yourselves as an act of clemency – then you will no longer have any need of your god, and the whole drama of Fall and Redemption will be played out to the end in you yourselves!

80

The compassionate Christian. – The reverse side of Christian compassion for the suffering of one's neighbour is a profound suspicion of all the joy of one's neighbour, of his joy in all that he wants to do and can.

81

The saint's humanity. – A saint had fallen among believers and could no longer endure their unremitting hatred of sin. At last he said: 'God created all things excepting sin alone: is it any wonder if he is ill-disposed towards it? – But man created sin – and is he to cast out this only child of his merely because it displeases God, the grandfather of sin! Is that humane? Honour to him to whom honour is due! – but

heart and duty ought to speak firstly for the child – and only secondly
for the honour of the grandfather!'

82
Spiritual assault. – 'This you have to decide within yourself, for your
life is at stake': with this cry Luther springs at us and thinks we feel the
knife at our throat. But we fend him off with the words of one higher
and more considerate than he: 'We are free to refrain from forming
an opinion about this thing or that, and thus to spare our soul
distress. For things themselves are by their nature incapable of *forcing*
us to make judgments.'

83
Poor mankind! – One drop of blood too much or too little in the brain
can make our life unspeakably wretched and hard, so that we have to
suffer more from this drop of blood than Prometheus suffered from
his vulture. But the worst is when one does not even *know* that this
drop of blood is the cause. But 'the Devil'! Or 'sin'! –

84
The philology of Christianity. – How little Christianity educates the sense
of honesty and justice can be gauged fairly well from the character of
its scholars' writings: they present their conjectures as boldly as if
they were dogmas and are rarely in any honest perplexity over the
interpretation of a passage in the Bible. Again and again they say 'I
am right, for it is written – ' and then follows an interpretation of such
impudent arbitrariness that a philologist who hears it is caught
between rage and laughter and asks himself: is it possible? Is this
honourable? Is it even decent? – How much dishonesty in this
matter is still practised in Protestant pulpits, how grossly the
preacher exploits the advantage that no one is going to interrupt him
here, how the Bible is pummelled and punched and the *art of reading
badly* is in all due form imparted to the people: only he who never
goes to church or never goes anywhere else will underestimate that.
But after all, what can one expect from the effects of a religion which
in the centuries of its foundation perpetrated that unheard-of
philological farce concerning the Old Testament: I mean the
attempt to pull the Old Testament from under the feet of the Jews
with the assertion it contained nothing but Christian teaching and
belonged to the Christians as the *true* people of Israel, the Jews being
only usurpers. And then there followed a fury of interpretation and

construction that cannot possibly be associated with a good conscience: however much Jewish scholars protested, the Old Testament
was supposed to speak of Christ and only of Christ, and especially of
his Cross; wherever a piece of wood, a rod, a ladder, a twig, a tree, a
willow, a staff is mentioned, it is supposed to be a prophetic allusion
to the wood of the Cross; even the erection of the one-horned beast
and the brazen serpent, even Moses spreading his arms in prayer,
even the spits on which the Passover lamb was roasted – all allusions
to the Cross and as it were preludes to it! Has anyone who asserted
this ever *believed* it? Consider that the church did not shrink from
enriching the text of the Septuagint (e.g. in Psalm 96, verse 10) so as
afterwards to employ the smuggled-in passage in the sense of
Christian prophecy. For they were conducting a *war* and paid more
heed to their opponents than to the need to stay honest.

85
Subtle deficiency. – Do not mock the mythology of the Greeks because
it so little resembles your profound metaphysics! You ought to
admire a people who at precisely this point called its sharp
understanding to a halt and for a long time had sufficient tact to
avoid the perils of scholasticism and sophistical superstition!

86
Christian interpreters of the body. – Whatever proceeds from the
stomach, the intestines, the beating of the heart, the nerves, the bile,
the semen – all those distempers, debilitations, excitations, the
whole chance operation of the machine of which we still know so
little! – had to be seen by a Christian such as Pascal as a moral and
religious phenomenon, and he had to ask whether God or Devil,
good or evil, salvation or damnation was to be discovered in them!
Oh what an unhappy interpreter! How he had to twist and torment
his system! How he had to twist and torment himself so as to be in the
right!

87
The moral miracle. – In the sphere of morality, Christianity knows only
the miracle: the sudden change in all value-judgments, the sudden
abandonment of all customary modes of behaviour, the sudden
irresistible inclination for new persons and objects. It conceives this
phenomenon to be the work of God and calls it a rebirth, it accords it
a unique, incomparable value: everything else which calls itself
morality but has no reference to this miracle thus becomes a matter

of indifference to the Christian – indeed, inasmuch as it involves a feeling of pride and well-being, it may even become an object of fear to him. In the New Testament, the canon of virtue, of the fulfilled law, is set up: but in such a way that it is the canon of *impossible virtue*: those still *striving* after morality are in the face of such a canon to learn to feel themselves ever *more distant* from their goal, they are to *despair* of virtue, and in the end *throw themselves on the bosom* of the merciful – only if it ended in this way could the Christian's moral effort be regarded as possessing any value, with the presupposition therefore that it always remains an unsuccessful, miserable, melancholy *effort*; only thus could it *serve* to bring about that ecstatic moment when he experiences the 'breakthrough of grace' and the moral miracle: – but this wrestling for morality is not *necessary*, for that miracle not seldom overtakes the sinner when he is as it were leprous with sin: indeed, the leap from the deepest and most all-pervading sinfulness into its opposite even seems to be somewhat easier and, as a more striking *demonstration* of the miracle, also somewhat *more desirable*. – For the rest, *what* such a sudden, irrational and irresistible *reversal*, such an exchange of the profoundest wretchedness for the profoundest well-being, signifies physiologically (whether it is perhaps a masked epilepsy?) – that must be determined by the psychiatrists, who have indeed plenty of occasion to observe similar 'miracles' (in the form of homicidal mania, for example, or suicide mania). The relatively *'more pleasant consequences'* in the case of the Christian make no essential difference.

88

Luther the great benefactor. – Luther's most significant achievement was the mistrust he aroused for the saints and the whole Christian *vita contemplativa*: only since then has the way again become open to an unchristian *vita contemplativa* in Europe and a limit set to contempt for worldly activity and the laity. Luther, who remained an honest miner's son after they had shut him up in a monastery and here, for lack of other depths and 'mineshafts', descended into himself and bored out terrible dark galleries – Luther finally realised that a saintly life of contemplation was impossible to him and that his inborn 'activeness' of soul and body would under these conditions destroy him. For all too long he sought the way to holiness with self-castigations – finally he came to a decision and said to himself: 'there *is* no real *vita contemplativa*! We have allowed ourselves to be deceived! The saints have not been worth any more than all the rest of us.' –

That, to be sure, was a rustic boorish way of making one's point – but for Germans of that time the right and only way: how it edified them now to read in their Lutheran catechism: 'except for the Ten Commandments there is *no* work that could be *pleasing* to God – the *celebrated* spiritual works of the saints are self-fabrications'.

89
Doubt as sin. – Christianity has done its utmost to close the circle and declared even doubt to be sin. One is supposed to be cast into belief without reason, by a miracle, and from then on to swim in it as in the brightest and least ambiguous of elements: even a glance towards land, even the thought that one perhaps exists for something else as well as swimming, even the slightest impulse of our amphibious nature – is sin! And notice that all this means that the foundation of belief and all reflection on its origin is likewise excluded as sinful. What is wanted are blindness and intoxication and an eternal song over the waves in which reason has drowned!

90
Egoism against egoism. – How many there are who still conclude: 'life could not be endured if there were no God!' (or, as it is put among the idealists: 'life could not be endured if its foundation lacked an ethical significance!') – therefore there *must* be a God (or existence *must* have an ethical significance)! The truth, however, is merely that he who is accustomed to these notions does not desire a life without them: that these notions may therefore be necessary to him and for his preservation – but what presumption it is to decree that whatever is necessary for my preservation must actually *exist*! As if my preservation were something necessary! How if others felt in the opposite way! if those two articles of faith were precisely the conditions under which they did not wish to live and under which they no longer found life worth living! – And that is how things are now!

91
God's honesty. – A god who is all-knowing and all-powerful and who does not even make sure that his creatures understand his intention – could that be a god of goodness? Who allows countless doubts and dubieties to persist, for thousands of years, as though the salvation of mankind were unaffected by them, and who on the other hand holds out the prospect of frightful consequences if any mistake is made as to the nature of the truth? Would he not be a cruel god if he

possessed the truth and could behold mankind miserably tormenting itself over the truth? – But perhaps he is a god of goodness notwithstanding – and merely *could* not express himself more clearly! Did he perhaps lack the intelligence to do so? Or the eloquence? So much the worse! For then he was perhaps also in error as to that which he calls his 'truth', and is himself not so very far from being the 'poor deluded devil'! Must he not then endure almost the torments of Hell to have to see his creatures suffer so, and go on suffering even more through all eternity, for the sake of knowledge of him, and *not* be able to help and counsel them, except in the manner of a deaf-and-dumb man making all kinds of ambiguous signs when the most fearful danger is about to fall on his child or his dog? – A believer who reaches this oppressive conclusion ought truly to be forgiven if he feels more pity for this suffering god than he does for his 'neighbours' – for they are no longer his neighbours if that most solitary and most primeval being is also the most suffering being of all and the one most in need of comfort. – All religions exhibit traces of the fact that they owe their origin to an early, immature intellectuality in man – they all take astonishingly *lightly* the duty to tell the truth: they as yet know nothing of a *duty of God* to be truthful towards mankind and clear in the manner of his communications. – On the 'hidden god', and on the reasons for keeping himself thus hidden and never emerging more than half-way into the light of speech, no one has been more eloquent than Pascal – a sign that he was never able to calm his mind on this matter: but his voice rings as confidently as if he had at one time sat behind the curtain with this hidden god. He sensed a piece of immorality in the *'deus absconditus'* and was very fearful and ashamed of admitting it to himself: and thus, like one who is afraid, he talked as loudly as he could.

92
At the deathbed of Christianity. – Really active people are now inwardly without Christianity, and the more moderate and reflective people of the intellectual middle class now possess only an adapted, that is to say marvellously *simplified* Christianity. A god who in his love arranges everything in a manner that will in the end be best for us; a god who gives to us and takes from us our virtue and our happiness, so that as a whole all is meet and fit and there is no reason for us to take life sadly, let alone to exclaim against it; in short, resignation and modest demands elevated to godhead – that is the best and most vital thing that still remains of Christianity. But one should notice that

Christianity has thus crossed over into a gentle *moralism*: it is not so much 'God, freedom and immortality' that have remained, as benevolence and decency of disposition, and the belief that in the whole universe too benevolence and decency of disposition will prevail: it is the *euthanasia* of Christianity.

93

What is truth? – Who would not acquiesce in the *conclusion* the faithful like to draw: 'Science cannot be true, for it denies God. Consequently it does not come from God; consequently it is not true – for God is the truth.' It is not the conclusion but the premise which contains the error: how if God were *not* the truth and it were precisely this which is proved? if he were the vanity, the lust for power, the impatience, the terror, the enraptured and fearful delusion of men?

94

Cure for the depressed. – Paul himself was of the opinion that a sacrifice was needed if God's profound displeasure at the commission of sins was to be removed: and since then Christians have never ceased to discharge their dissatisfaction with themselves on to a *sacrifice* – whether this sacrifice be the 'world' or 'history' or 'reason' or the joy or peace of other people – something *good* has to die for *their* sin (even if only in effigy)!

95

Historical refutation as the definitive refutation. – In former times, one sought to prove that there is no God – today one indicates how the belief that there is a God could *arise* and how this belief acquired its weight and importance: a counter-proof that there is no God thereby becomes superfluous. – When in former times one had refuted the 'proofs of the existence of God' put forward, there always remained the doubt whether better proofs might not be adduced than those just refuted: in those days atheists did not know how to make a clean sweep.

96

'In hoc signo vinces'. – However much progress Europe may have made in other respects, in religious matters it has not yet attained to the free-minded naivety of the ancient Brahmins: a sign that there was more thinking, and that more pleasure in thinking was customarily inherited, four thousand years ago in India than is the case with us today. For those Brahmins believed, firstly that the priests were more powerful than the gods, and secondly that the power of the priests

resided in the observances: which is why their poets never wearied of celebrating the observances (prayers, ceremonies, sacrifices, hymns, verses) as the real givers of all good things. However much poetising and superstition may have crept in here between the lines, these propositions are *true*! A step further, and one threw the gods aside – which is what Europe will also have to do one day! Another step further, and one no longer had need of the priests and mediators either, and the teacher of the *religion of self-redemption*, the Buddha, appeared: – how distant Europe still is from this level of culture! When, finally, all the observances and customs upon which the power of the gods and of the priests and redeemers depends will have been abolished, when, that is to say, morality in the old sense will have died, then there will come – well, what will come then? But let us not speculate idly: let us first of all see to it that Europe overtakes what was done several thousands of years ago in India, among the nation of thinkers, in accordance with the commandments of reason! There are today among the various nations of Europe perhaps ten to twenty million people who no longer 'believe in God' – is it too much to ask that they should *give a sign* to one another? Once they have thus come to *know* one another, they will also have made themselves known to others – they will at once constitute a *power* in Europe and, happily, a power *between* the nations! Between the classes! Between rich and poor! Between rulers and subjects! Between the most unpeaceable and the most peaceable, peace-bringing people!

BOOK II

97

To become moral is not in itself moral. – Subjection to morality can be slavish or vain or self-interested or resigned or gloomily enthusiastic or an act of despair, like subjection to a prince: in itself it is nothing moral.

98

Mutation of morality. – There is a continual moiling and toiling going on in morality – the effect of *successful crimes* (among which, for example, are included all innovations in moral thinking).

99

Wherein we are all irrational. – We still draw the conclusions of judgments we consider false, of teachings in which we no longer believe – our feelings make us do it.

100

Awakening from a dream. – Wise and noble men once believed in the music of the spheres: wise and noble men still believe in the 'moral significance of existence'. But one day this music of the spheres too will no longer be audible to them! They will awaken and perceive that their ears had been dreaming.

101

Suspicious. – To admit a belief merely because it is a custom – but that means to be dishonest, cowardly, lazy! – And so could dishonesty, cowardice and laziness be the preconditions of morality?

102

The oldest moral judgments. – What really are our reactions to the behaviour of someone in our presence? – First of all, we see what there is in it *for us* – we regard it only from this point of view. We take *this* effect as the *intention* behind the behaviour – and finally we ascribe the harbouring of such intentions as a *permanent* quality of the person whose behaviour we are observing and thenceforth call him, for instance, 'a harmful person'. Threefold error! Threefold primeval blunder! Perhaps inherited from the animals and their power of judgment! Is the *origin of all morality* not to be sought in the detestable petty conclusions: 'what harms *me* is something *evil* (harmful in itself); what is useful *to me* is something *good* (beneficent and advantageous in itself); what harms me *once or several times* is the inimical as such and in itself; what is useful to me *once or several times* is the friendly as such and in itself'. *O pudenda origo!* Does that not mean; to imagine that the paltry, occasional, often chance *relationship* of

59

another with ourself is his *essence* and most essential being, and to assert that with the whole world and with himself he is capable only of those relationships we have experienced with him once or several times? And does there not repose behind this veritable folly the most immodest of all secret thoughts: that, because good and evil are measured according to our reactions, we ourselves must constitute the principle of the good? –

103

There are two kinds of deniers of morality. – 'To deny morality' – this can mean, *first*: to deny that the moral motives which men *claim* have inspired their actions really have done so – it is thus the assertion that morality consists of words and is among the coarser or more subtle deceptions (especially self-deceptions) which men practise, and is perhaps so especially in precisely the case of those most famed for virtue. *Then* it can mean: to deny that moral judgments are based on truths. Here it is admitted that they really are motives of action, but that in this way it is *errors* which, as the basis of all moral judgment, impel men to their moral actions. This is *my* point of view: though I should be the last to deny that *in very many cases* there is some ground for suspicion that the other point of view – that is to say, the point of view of La Rochefoucauld and others who think like him – may also be justified and in any event of great general application. – Thus I deny morality as I deny alchemy, that is, I deny their premises: but I do *not* deny that there have been alchemists who believed in these premises and acted in accordance with them. – I also deny immorality: *not* that countless people *feel* themselves to be immoral, but there is any *true* reason so to feel. It goes without saying that I do not deny – unless I am a fool – that many actions called immoral ought to be avoided and resisted, or that many called moral ought to be done and encouraged – but I think the one should be encouraged and the other avoided *for other reasons than hitherto*. We have to *learn to think differently* – in order at last, perhaps very late on, to attain even more: *to feel differently.*

104

Our evaluations. – All actions may be traced back to evaluations, all evaluations are either *original* or *adopted* – the latter being by far the most common. Why do we adopt them? From fear – that is to say, we consider it more advisable to pretend they are our own – and accustom ourself to this pretence, so that at length it becomes our own nature. Original evaluation: that is to say, to assess a thing according to the extent to which it pleases or displeases us alone and no one else – something excessively rare! – But must our evaluation of another, in which there lies the motive for our generally availing ourselves of *his* evaluation, at least not proceed from *us*, be our *own* determination? Yes, but we arrive at it as *children*, and rarely learn to change our view; most of us are our whole lives long the fools of the way we acquired in childhood of judging our neighbours (their minds, rank, morality, whether they are exemplary or reprehensible) and of finding it necessary to pay homage to their evaluations.

105

Pseudo-egoism. – Whatever they may think and say about their 'egoism', the great majority nonetheless do nothing for their ego their whole life long: what they do is done for the phantom of their ego which has formed itself in the heads of those around them and has been communicated to them; – as a consequence they all of them dwell in a fog of impersonal, semi-personal opinions, and arbitrary, as it were poetical evaluations, the one for ever in the head of someone else, and the head of this someone else again in the heads of others: a strange world of phantasms – which at the same time knows how to put on so sober an appearance! This fog of habits and opinions lives and grows almost independently of the people it envelops; it is in this fog that there lies the tremendous effect of general judgments about 'man' – all these people, unknown to themselves, believe in the bloodless abstraction 'man', that is to say, in a fiction; and every alteration effected to this abstraction by the judgments of individual powerful figures (such as princes and philosophers) produces an extraordinary and grossly disproportionate effect on the great majority – all because no individual among this majority is capable of setting up a real ego, accessible to him and fathomed by him, in opposition to the general pale fiction and thereby annihilating it.

106

Against the definitions of the goal of morality. – Everywhere today the goal of morality is defined in approximately the following way: it is the preservation and advancement of mankind; but this definition is an expression of the desire for a formula, and nothing more. Preservation *of what?* is the question one immediately has to ask. Advancement *to what?* Is the essential thing – the answer to this *of what?* and *to what?* – not precisely what is left out of the formula? So what, then, can it contribute to any teaching of what our duty is that is not already, if

tacitly and thoughtlessly, regarded in advance as fixed? Can one
deduce from it with certainty whether what is to be kept in view is the
longest possible existence of mankind? Or the greatest possible
deanimalisation of mankind? How different the means, that is to say
the practical morality, would have to be in these two cases! Suppose
one wanted to bestow on mankind the highest degree of rationality
possible to it: this would certainly not guarantee it the longest period
of duration possible to it! Or suppose one conceived the attainment
of mankind's 'highest happiness' as being the *to what* and *of what* of
morality: would one mean the highest degree of happiness that
individual men could gradually attain to? Or a – necessarily
incalculable – average-happiness which could finally be attained to
by all? And why should the way to that have to be morality? Has
morality not, broadly speaking, opened up such an abundance of
sources of displeasure that one could say, rather, that with every
refinement of morals mankind has hitherto become *more discontented*
with himself, his neighbour and the lot of his existence? Did the
hitherto most moral man not entertain the belief that the only
justified condition of mankind in the face of morality was the
profoundest misery?

107

Our right to our folly. – How is one to act? To what end is one to act? – In
the case of the individual's most immediate and crudest wants these
questions are easy enough to answer, but the more subtle, comprehensive and weighty the realms of action are into which one rises, the
more uncertain, consequently more arbitrary, will the answer be.
But it is precisely here that arbitrariness of decision is to be excluded!
– thus commands the authority of morality: an obscure fear and awe
are at once to direct mankind in the case of precisely those actions
the aims and means of which are least *immediately* obvious! This
authority of morality paralyses thinking in the case of things about
which it might be dangerous to think *falsely* – : this is how it is
accustomed to justify itself before its accusers. Falsely: here that
means 'dangerously' – but dangerously for whom? Usually it is not
really the danger to the performer of the action which the wielders of
authoritative morality have in view, but the danger to *themselves*, the
possibility that their power and influence may be diminished if the
right to act arbitrarily and foolishly according to the light, bright or
dim, of one's own reason is accorded to everybody: they themselves,

of course, unhesitatingly exercise the right to arbitrariness and folly
– they issue *commands* even where the questions 'how am I to act? to
what end am I to act?' are hardly possible or at least extremely
difficult to answer. – And if the *reason* of mankind is of such
extraordinarily slow growth that it has often been denied that it has
grown at all during the whole course of mankind's existence, what is
more to blame than this solemn presence, indeed omnipresence, of
moral commands which absolutely prohibit the utterance of *individual*
questions as to How? and To what end? Have we not been brought
up to *feel pathetically* and to flee into the dark precisely when reason
ought to be taking as clear and cold a view as possible! That is to say,
in the case of all our higher and weightier affairs.

108

A few theses. – *Insofar* as the individual is seeking happiness, one ought
not to tender him any prescriptions as to the path to happiness: for
individual happiness springs from one's own unknown laws, and
prescriptions from without can only obstruct and hinder it. – The
prescriptions called 'moral' are in truth directed against individuals
and are in no way aimed at promoting their happiness. They have
just as little to do with the 'happiness and welfare of mankind' – a
phrase to which is it in any case impossible to attach any distinct
concepts, let alone employ them as guiding stars on the dark ocean
of moral aspirations. – It is not true, as prejudice would have it, that
morality is more favourable to the evolution of reason than
immorality is. – It is not true that the *unconscious goal* in the evolution
of every conscious being (animal, man, mankind, etc) is its 'highest
happiness': the case, on the contrary, is that every stage of evolution
possesses a special and incomparable happiness neither higher nor
lower but simply its own. Evolution does not have happiness in view,
but evolution and nothing else. – Only if mankind possessed a
universally recognised *goal* would it be possible to propose 'thus and
thus is the *right* course of action': for the present there exists no such
goal. It is thus irrational and trivial to impose the demands of
morality upon mankind. – To *recommend* a goal to mankind is
something quite different: the goal is then thought of as something
which *lies in our own discretion*; supposing the recommendation
appealed to mankind, it could in pursuit of it also *impose* upon itself a
moral law, likewise at its own discretion. But up to now the moral law
has been supposed to stand *above* our own likes and dislikes: one did

not want actually to *impose* this law upon oneself, one wanted to *take* it from somewhere or *discover* it somewhere or *have it commanded to one* from somewhere.

109

Self-mastery and moderation and their ultimate motive. – I find no more than six essentially different methods of combating the vehemence of a drive. First, one can avoid opportunities for gratification of the drive, and through long and ever longer periods of non-gratification weaken it and make it wither away. Then, one can impose upon oneself strict regularity in its gratification: by thus imposing a rule upon the drive itself and enclosing its ebb and flood within firm time-boundaries, one has then gained intervals during which one is no longer troubled by it – and from there one can perhaps go over to the first method. Thirdly, one can deliberately give oneself over to the wild and unrestrained gratification of a drive in order to generate disgust with it and with disgust to acquire a power over the drive: always supposing one does not do like the rider who rode his horse to death and broke his own neck in the process – which, unfortunately, is the rule when this method is attempted. Fourthly, there is the intellectual artifice of associating its gratification in general so firmly with some very painful thought that, after a little practice, the thought of its gratification is itself at once felt as very painful (as, for example, when the Christian accustoms himself to associating the proximity and mockery of the Devil with sexual enjoyment or everlasting punishment in Hell with a murder for revenge, or even when he thinks merely of the contempt which those he most respects would feel for him if he, for example, stole money; or, as many have done a hundred times, a person sets against a violent desire to commit suicide a vision of the grief and self-reproach of his friends and relations and therewith keeps himself suspended in life: – henceforth these ideas within him succeed one another as cause and effect). The same method is also being employed when a man's pride, as for example in the case of Lord Byron or Napoleon, rises up and feels the domination of his whole bearing and the ordering of his reason by a single affect as an affront: from where there then arises the habit and desire to tyrannise over the drive and make it as it were gnash its teeth. ('I refuse to be the slave of any appetite', Byron wrote in his diary.) Fifthly, one brings about a dislocation of one's quanta of strength by imposing on oneself a particularly difficult and strenuous labour, or by deliberately subjecting oneself to a new stimulus and pleasure and thus directing one's thoughts and plays of physical forces into other channels. It comes to the same thing if one for the time being favours another drive, gives it ample opportunity for gratification and thus makes it squander that energy otherwise available to the drive which through its vehemence has grown burdensome. Some few will no doubt also understand how to keep in check the individual drive that wanted to play the master by giving all the other drives he knows of a temporary encouragement and festival and letting them eat up all the food the tyrant wants to have for himself alone. Finally, sixth: he who can endure it and finds it reasonable to weaken and depress his *entire* bodily and physical organisation will naturally thereby also attain the goal of weakening an individual violent drive: as he does, for example, who, like the ascetic, starves his sensuality and thereby also starves and ruins his vigour and not seldom his reason as well. – Thus: avoiding opportunities, implanting regularity into the drive, engendering satiety and disgust with it and associating it with a painful idea (such as that of disgrace, evil consequences or offended pride), then dislocation of forces and finally a general weakening and exhaustion – these are the six methods: *that* one *desires* to combat the vehemence of a drive at all, however, does not stand within our own power; nor does the choice of any particular method; nor does the success or failure of this method. What is clearly the case is that in this entire procedure our intellect is only the blind instrument of *another drive* which is a *rival* of the drive whose vehemence is tormenting us: whether it be the drive to restfulness, or the fear of disgrace and other evil consequences, or love. While 'we' believe we are complaining about the vehemence of a drive, at bottom it is one drive *which is complaining about another*; that is to say: for us to become aware that we are suffering from the *vehemence* of a drive presupposes the existence of another equally vehement or even more vehement drive, and that a *struggle* is in prospect in which our intellect is going to have to take sides.

110
That which sets itself up in opposition. – One can observe the following process in oneself, and I wish it might often be observed and confirmed. There arises in us the scent of a kind of *pleasure* we have not known before, and as a consequence there arises a new *desire*. The question now is: *what* is it that *sets itself up in opposition* to this desire. If it is things and considerations of the common sort, or

65

people for whom we feel little respect – then the goal of the new desire dresses itself in the sensation 'noble, good, praiseworthy, worthy of sacrifice', the entire moral disposition we have inherited thenceforth takes it into itself, adds it to the goals it already possesses which it feels to be moral – and now we believe we are striving, not after a pleasure, but after something moral: which belief greatly enhances the confidence with which we strive.

111

To the admirers of objectivity. – He who as a child was aware of the existence of manifold and strong feelings, but of little subtle judgment and pleasure in intellectual justice, in the relatives and acquaintances among whom he grew up, and who thus used up the best of his energy and time in the imitation of feelings: he will as an adult remark in himself that every new thing, every new person, at once arouses in him liking or dislike or envy or contempt; under the pressure of this experience, towards which he feels himself powerless, he admires *neutrality of sentiment*, or 'objectivity', as a matter of genius or of the rarest morality, and refuses to believe that this too is only *the child of habit and discipline*.

112

On the natural history of rights and duties. – Our duties – are the rights of others over us. How have they acquired such rights? By taking us to be capable of contracting and of requiting, by positing us as similar and equal to them, and as a consequence entrusting us with something, educating, reproving, supporting us. We fulfil our duty – that is to say: we justify the idea of our power on the basis of which all these things were bestowed upon us, we give back in the measure in which we have been given to. It is thus our pride which bids us do our duty – when we do something for others in return for something they have done for us, what we are doing is restoring our self-regard – for in doing something for us, these others have impinged upon our sphere of power, and would have continued to have a hand in it if we did not with the performance of our 'duty' practise a requital, that is to say impinge upon their power. The rights of others can relate only to that which lies within our power; it would be unreasonable if they wanted of us something we did not possess. Expressed more precisely: only to that which they believe lies within our power, provided it is the same thing we believe lies within our power. The same error could easily be made on either side: the feeling of duty depends upon our having the same *belief* in regard to the extent of our power as others have: that is to say, that we *are able* to promise certain things and bind ourselves to perform them ('freedom of will'). – My rights – are that part of my power which others have not merely conceded me, but which they wish me to preserve. How do these others arrive at that? First: through their prudence and fear and caution: whether in that they expect something similar from us in return (protection of their own rights); or in that they consider that a struggle with us would be perilous or to no purpose; or in that they see in any diminution of our force a disadvantage to themselves, since we would then be unsuited to forming an alliance with them in opposition to a hostile third power. *Then*: by donation and cession. In this case, others have enough and more than enough power to be able to dispose of some of it and to guarantee to him they have given it to the portion of it they have given: in doing so they presuppose a feeble sense of power in him who lets himself be thus donated to. That is how rights originate: recognised and guaranteed degrees of power. If power-relationships undergo any material alteration, rights disappear and new ones are created – as is demonstrated in the continual disappearance and reformation of rights between nations. If our power is materially diminished, the feeling of those who have hitherto guaranteed our rights changes: they consider whether they can restore us to the full possession we formerly enjoyed – if they feel unable to do so, they henceforth deny our 'rights'. Likewise, if our power is materially increased, the feeling of those who have hitherto recognised it but whose recognition is no longer needed changes: they no doubt attempt to suppress it to its former level, they will try to intervene and in doing so will allude to their 'duty' – but this is only a useless playing with words. Where rights *prevail*, a certain condition and degree of power is being maintained, a diminution and increment warded off. The rights of others constitute a concession on the part of our sense of power to the sense of power of those others. If our power appears to be deeply shaken and broken, our rights cease to exist: conversely, if we have grown very much more powerful, the rights of others, as we have previously conceded them, cease to exist for us. – The 'man who wants to be fair' is in constant need of the subtle tact of a balance: he must be able to assess degrees of power and rights, which, given the transitory nature of human things, will never stay in equilibrium for very long but will usually be rising or sinking: – being fair is consequently difficult and demands much practice and good will, and very much very good *sense*. –

113

The striving for distinction. – The striving for distinction keeps a constant
eye on the next man and wants to know what his feelings are: but the
empathy which this drive requires for its gratification is far from
being harmless or sympathetic or kind. We want, rather, to perceive
or divine how the next man outwardly or inwardly *suffers* from us,
how he loses control over himself and surrenders to the impressions
our hand or even merely the sight of us makes upon him; and even
when he who strives after distinction makes and wants to make a
joyful, elevating or cheering impression, he nonetheless enjoys this
success not inasmuch as he has given joy to the next man or elevated
or cheered him, but inasmuch as he has *impressed* himself on the soul
of the other, changed its shape and ruled over it at his own sweet will.
The striving for distinction is the striving for domination over the
next man, though it be a very indirect domination and only felt or
even dreamed. There is a long scale of degrees of this secretly desired
domination, and a complete catalogue of them would be almost the
same thing as a history of culture, from the earliest, still grotesque
barbarism up to the grotesqueries of over-refinement and morbid
idealism. The striving for distinction brings with it *for the next man* –
to name only a few steps on the ladder: torment, then blows, then
terror, then fearful astonishment, then wonderment, then envy,
then admiration, then elevation, then joy, then cheerfulness, then
laughter, then derision, then mockery, then ridicule, then giving
blows, then imposing torment: – here at the end of the ladder stands
the *ascetic* and martyr, who feels the highest enjoyment by himself
enduring, as a consequence of his drive for distinction, precisely that
which, on the first step of the ladder, his counterpart the *barbarian*
imposes on others on whom and before whom he wants to
distinguish himself. The triumph of the ascetic over himself, his
glance turned inwards which beholds man split asunder into a
sufferer and a spectator, and henceforth gazes out into the outer
world only in order to gather as it were wood for his own pyre, this
final tragedy of the drive for distinction in which there is only one
character burning and consuming himself – this is a worthy
conclusion and one appropriate to the commencement: in both
cases an unspeakable happiness at the *sight of torment!* Indeed,
happiness, conceived of as the liveliest feeling of power, has perhaps
been nowhere greater on earth than in the souls of superstitious
ascetics. The Brahmins give expression to this in the story of King
Visvamitra, who derived such strength from *practising penance* for a

thousand years that he undertook to construct a new *Heaven*. I
believe that in this whole species of inner experience we are now
incompetent novices groping after the solution of riddles: they knew
more about these infamous refinements of self-enjoyment 4,000
years ago. The creation of the world: perhaps it was then thought of
by some Indian dreamer as an ascetic operation on the part of a god!
Perhaps the god wanted to banish himself into active and moving
nature as into an instrument of torture, in order thereby to feel his
bliss and power doubled! And supposing it was a god of love: what
enjoyment for such a god to create *suffering* men, to suffer divinely
and superhumanly from the ceaseless torment of the sight of them,
and thus to tyrannise over himself! And even supposing it was not
only a god of love, but also a god of holiness and sinlessness: what
deliriums of the divine ascetic can be imagined when he creates sin
and sinners and eternal damnation and a vast abode of eternal
affliction and eternal groaning and sighing! – It is not altogether
impossible that the souls of Dante, Paul, Calvin and their like may
also once have penetrated the gruesome secrets of such voluptuousness
of power – and in face of such souls one can ask: is the circle of
striving for distinction really at an end with the ascetic? Could this
circle not be run through again from the beginning, holding fast to
the basic disposition of the ascetic and at the same time that of the
pitying god? That is to say, doing hurt to others in order thereby to
hurt *oneself*, in order then to triumph over oneself and one's pity and
to revel in an extremity of power! – Excuse these extravagant
reflections on all that may have been possible on earth through the
psychical extravagance of the lust for power!

114
On the knowledge acquired through suffering. – The condition of sick
people who suffer dreadful and protracted torment from their
suffering and whose minds nonetheless remain undisturbed is not
without value for the acquisition of knowledge – quite apart from the
intellectual benefit which accompanies any profound solitude, any
unexpected and permitted liberation from duties. He who suffers
intensely looks *out* at things with a terrible coldness: all those little
lying charms with which things are usually surrounded when the eye
of the healthy regards them do not exist for him; indeed, he himself
lies there before himself stripped of all colour and plumage. If until
then he has been living in some perilous world of fantasy, this
supreme sobering-up through pain is the means of extricating him

from it: and perhaps the only means. (It is possible that this is what happened to the founder of Christianity on the cross: for the bitterest of all exclamations 'my God, why hast thou forsaken me!' contains, in its ultimate significance, evidence of a general disappointment and enlightenment over the delusion of his life; at the moment of supreme agony he acquired an insight into himself of the kind told by the poet of the poor dying Don Quixote.) The tremendous tension imparted to the intellect by its desire to oppose and counter pain makes him see everything he now beholds in a new light: and the unspeakable stimulus which any new light imparts to things is often sufficiently powerful to defy all temptation to self-destruction and to make continuing to live seem to the sufferer extremely desirable. He thinks with contempt of the warm, comfortable misty world in which the healthy man thoughtlessly wanders; he thinks with contempt of the noblest and most beloved of the illusions in which he himself formerly indulged; he takes pleasure in conjuring up this contempt as though out of the deepest depths of Hell and thus subjecting his soul to the bitterest pain: for it is through this counterweight that he holds his own against the physical pain – he feels that this counterweight is precisely what is now needed! With dreadful clearsightedness as to the nature of his being, he cries to himself: 'for once be your own accuser and executioner, for once take your suffering as the punishment inflicted by yourself upon yourself! Enjoy your superiority as judge; more, enjoy your wilful pleasure, your tyrannical arbitrariness! Raise yourself above your life as above your suffering, look down into the deep and the unfathomable depths!' Our pride towers up as never before: it discovers an incomparable stimulus in opposing such a tyrant as pain is, and in answer to all the insinuations it makes to us that we should bear witness against life in becoming precisely the *advocate* of *life* in the face of this tyrant. In this condition one defends oneself desperately against all pessimism, that it may not appear to be a *consequence* of our condition and humiliate us in defeat. The stimulus to justness of judgment has likewise never been greater than it is now, for now it represents a triumph over ourself, over a condition which, of all conditions, would make unjustness of judgment excusable – but we do not want to be excused, it is precisely now that we want to show that we can be 'without need of excuse'. We experience downright convulsions of arrogance. – And then there comes the first glimmering of relief, of convalescence – and almost the first effect is that we fend off the dominance of this arrogance: we

call ourselves vain and foolish to have felt it – as though we had
experienced something out of the ordinary! We humiliate our
almighty pride, which has enabled us to endure our pain, without
gratitude, and vehemently desire an antidote to it: we want to
become estranged from ourself and depersonalised, after pain has
for too long and too forcibly made us *personal*. 'Away, away with this
pride!' we cry, 'it was only one more sickness and convulsion!' We
gaze again at man and nature – now with a more desiring eye: we
recall with a sorrowful smile that we now know something new and
different about them, that a veil has fallen – but we find it so *refreshing*
again to see *life in a subdued light* and to emerge out of the terrible
sobering brightness in which as sufferers we formerly saw things and
saw through things. We are not annoyed when the charms of health
resume their game – we look on as if transformed, gentle and still
wearied. In this condition one cannot hear music without weeping. –

115
The so-called 'ego'. – Language and the prejudices upon which
language is based are a manifold hindrance to us when we want to
explain inner processes and drives: because of the fact, for example,
that words really exist only for *superlative* degrees of these processes
and drives; and where words are lacking, we are accustomed to
abandon exact observation because exact thinking there becomes
painful; indeed, in earlier times one involuntarily concluded that
where the realm of words ceased the realm of existence ceased also.
Anger, hatred, love, pity, desire, knowledge, joy, pain – all are names
for *extreme* states: the milder, middle degrees, not to speak of the
lower degrees which are continually in play, elude us, and yet it is
they which weave the web of our character and our destiny. These
extreme outbursts – and even the most moderate *conscious* pleasure
or displeasure, while eating food or hearing a note, is perhaps,
rightly understood, an extreme outburst – very often rend the web
apart, and then they constitute violent exceptions, no doubt usually
consequent on built-up congestions: – and, as such, how easy it is for
them to mislead the observer! No less easy than it is for them to
mislead the person in whom they occur. *We are none of us* that which
we appear to be in accordance with the states for which alone we have
consciousness and words, and consequently praise and blame; those
cruder outbursts of which alone we are aware make us *misunderstand*
ourselves, we draw a conclusion on the basis of data in which the
exceptions outweigh the rule, we misread ourselves in this apparently

most intelligible of handwriting on the nature of our self. *Our opinion of ourself*, however, which we have arrived at by this erroneous path, the so-called 'ego', is thenceforth a fellow worker in the construction of our character and our destiny. –

116

The unknown world of the 'subject'. – That which, from the earliest times to the present moment, men have found so hard to understand is their ignorance of themselves! Not only in regard to good and evil, but in regard to what is much more essential! The primeval delusion still lives on that one knows, and knows quite precisely in every case, *how human action is brought about.* Not only 'God, who sees into the heart', not only the doer who premeditates his deed – no, everyone else too is in no doubt that he understands what is essentially involved in the process of action in every other person. 'I know what I want, what I have done, I am free and responsible for it, I hold others responsible, I can call by its name every moral possibility and every inner motion which precedes action; you may act as you will – in this matter I understand myself and understand you all!' – that is how everyone formerly thought, that is how almost everyone still thinks. Socrates and Plato, in this regard great doubters and admirable innovators, were nonetheless innocently credulous in regard to that most fateful of prejudices, that profoundest of errors, that 'right knowledge *must be followed* by right action' – in this principle they were still the heirs of the universal madness and presumption that there exists knowledge as to the essential nature of an action. 'For it would be *terrible* if insight into the nature of right action were not followed by right action' – this is the only kind of proof these great men deemed necessary for demonstrating the truth of this idea, the opposite seemed to them crazy and unthinkable – and yet this opposite is precisely the naked reality demonstrated daily and hourly from time immemorial! Is the 'terrible' truth not that no amount of knowledge about an act *ever* suffices to ensure its performance, that the space between knowledge and action has never yet been bridged even in one single instance? Actions are *never* what they appear to us to be! We have expended so much labour on learning that external things are not as they appear to us to be – very well! the case is the same with the inner world! Moral actions are in reality 'something other than that' – more we cannot say: and all actions are essentially unknown. The opposite was and is the universal belief: we have the oldest realism against us; up to now mankind has thought: 'an action is what it appears to us to be'. (In re-reading these words a very express passage of Schopenhauer occurs to me which I shall here adduce as evidence that he too remained an adherent of this moral realism, and did so without the slightest compunction: 'Each one of us is truly a competent and perfectly moral judge, with an exact knowledge of good and evil, holy in loving good and abhorring evil – each of us is all this insofar as it is not our actions but those of others which are under investigation and we have merely to approve or disapprove, while the burden of performance rests on others' shoulders. Consequently, everyone can, as a confessor, wholly and completely deputise for God.')

117

In prison. – My eyes, however strong or weak they may be, can see only a certain distance, and it is within the space encompassed by this distance that I live and move, the line of this horizon constitutes my immediate fate, in great things and small, from which I cannot escape. Around every being there is described a similar concentric circle, which has a mid-point and is peculiar to him. Our ears enclose us within a comparable circle, and so does our sense of touch. Now, it is by these horizons, within which each of us encloses his senses as if behind prison walls, that we *measure* the world, we say that this is near and that far, this is big and that small, this is hard and that soft: this measuring we call sensation – and it is all of it an error! According to the average quantity of experiences and excitations possible to us at any particular point of time one measures one's life as being short or long, poor or rich, full or empty: and according to the average human life one measures that of all other creatures – all of it an error! If our eyes were a hundredfold sharper, man would appear to us tremendously tall; it is possible, indeed, to imagine organs by virtue of which he would be felt as immeasurable. On the other hand, organs could be so constituted that whole solar systems were viewed contracted and packed together like a single cell: and to beings of an opposite constitution a cell of the human body could present itself, in motion, construction and harmony, as a solar system. The habits of our senses have woven us into lies and deception of sensation: these again are the basis of all our judgments and 'knowledge' – there is absolutely no escape, no backway or bypath into the *real world*! We sit within our net, we spiders, and whatever we may catch in it, we can catch nothing at all except that which allows itself to be caught in precisely *our* net.

118

What is our neighbour! – What do we understand to be the boundaries
of our neighbour: I mean that with which he as it were engraves and
impresses himself into and upon us? We understand nothing of him
except the *change in us* of which he is the cause – our knowledge of
him is like hollow space *which has been shaped*. We attribute to him the
sensations his actions evoke in us, and thus bestow upon him a false,
inverted positivity. According to our knowledge of ourself we make
of him a satellite of our own system: and when he shines for us or
grows dark and we are the ultimate cause in both cases – we
nonetheless believe the opposite! World of phantoms in which we
live! Inverted, upsidedown, empty world, yet dreamed of as *full* and
upright!

119

Experience and invention. – However far a man may go in self-
knowledge, nothing however can be more incomplete than his
image of the totality of *drives* which constitute his being. He can
scarcely name even the cruder ones: their number and strength,
their ebb and flood, their play and counterplay among one another,
and above all the laws of their *nutriment* remain wholly unknown to
him. This nutriment is therefore a work of chance: our daily
experiences throw some prey in the way of now this, now that drive,
and the drive seizes it eagerly; but the coming and going of these
events as a whole stands in no rational relationship to the nutritional
requirements of the totality of the drives: so that the outcome will
always be twofold – the starvation and stunting of some and the
overfeeding of others. Every moment of our lives sees some of the
polyp-arms of our being grow and others of them wither, all
according to the nutriment which the moment does or does not bear
with it. Our experiences are, as already said, all in this sense means of
nourishment, but the nourishment is scattered indiscriminately
without distinguishing between the hungry and those already
possessing a superfluity. And as a consequence of this chance
nourishment of the parts, the whole, fully grown polyp will be
something just as accidental as its growth has been. To express it
more clearly: suppose a drive finds itself at the point at which it
desires gratification – or exercise of its strength, or discharge of its
strength, or the saturation of an emptiness – these are all metaphors –:
it then regards every event of the day with a view to seeing how it can
employ it for the attainment of its goal; whether a man is moving, or

resting or angry or reading or speaking or fighting or rejoicing, the drive will in its thirst as it were taste every condition into which the man may enter, and as a rule will discover nothing for itself there and will have to wait and go on thirsting: in a little while it will grow faint, and after a couple of days or months of non-gratification it will wither away like a plant without rain. Perhaps this cruelty perpetrated by chance would be more vividly evident if all the drives were as much in earnest as is *hunger*, which is not content with *dream food*; but most of the drives, espccially the so-called moral ones, *do precisely this* – if my supposition is allowed that the meaning and value of our *dreams* is precisely to *compensate* to some extent for the chance absence of 'nourishment' during the day. Why was the dream of yesterday full of tenderness and tears, that of the day before yesterday humorous and exuberant, an earlier dream adventurous and involved in a continuous gloomy searching? Why do I in this dream enjoy indescribable beauties of music, why do I in another soar and fly with the joy of an eagle up to distant mountain peaks? These inventions, which give scope and discharge to our drives to tenderness or humorousness or adventurousness or to our desire for music and mountains – and everyone will have his own more striking examples to hand – are interpretations of nervous stimuli we receive while we are asleep, *very free*, very arbitrary interpretations of the motions of the blood and intestines, of the pressure of the arm and the bedclothes, of the sounds made by church bells, weather-cocks, night-revellers and other things of the kind. That this text, which is in general much the same on one night as on another, is commented on in such varying ways, that the inventive reasoning faculty *imagines* today a *cause* for the nervous stimuli so very different from the cause it imagined yesterday, though the stimuli are the same: the explanation of this is that today's prompter of the reasoning faculty was different from yesterday's – a different *drive* wanted to gratify itself, to be active, to exercise itself, to refresh itself, to discharge itself – today this drive was at high flood, yesterday it was a different drive that was in that condition. – Waking life does not have this *freedom* of interpretation possessed by the life of dreams, it is less inventive and unbridled – but do I have to add that when we are awake our drives likewise do nothing but interpret nervous stimuli and, according to their requirements, posit their 'causes'? that there is no *essential* difference between waking and dreaming? that when we compare very different stages of culture we even find that freedom of waking interpretation in the one is in no way inferior to

75

the freedom exercised in the other while dreaming? that our moral judgments and evaluations too are only images and fantasies based on a physiological process unknown to us, a kind of acquired language for designating certain nervous stimuli? that all our so-called consciousness is a more or less fantastic commentary on an unknown, perhaps unknowable, but felt text? – Take some trifling experience. Suppose we were in the market place one day and we noticed someone laughing at us as we went by: this event will signify this or that to us according to whether this or that drive happens at that moment to be at its height in us – and it will be a quite different event according to the kind of person we are. One person will absorb it like a drop of rain, another will shake it from him like an insect, another will try to pick a quarrel, another will examine his clothing to see if there is anything about it that might give rise to laughter, another will be led to reflect on the nature of laughter as such, another will be glad to have involuntarily augmented the amount of cheerfulness and sunshine in the world – and in each case a drive has gratified itself, whether it be the drive to annoyance or to combativeness or to reflection or to benevolence. This drive seized the event as its prey: why precisely this one? Because, thirsty and hungry, it was lying in wait. – One day recently at eleven o'clock in the morning a man suddenly collapsed right in front of me as if struck by lightning, and all the women in the vicinity screamed aloud; I myself raised him to his feet and attended to him until he had recovered his speech – during this time not a muscle of my face moved and I felt nothing, neither fear nor sympathy, but I did what needed doing and went coolly on my way. Suppose someone had told me the day before that tomorrow at eleven o'clock in the morning a man would fall down beside me in this fashion – I would have suffered every kind of anticipatory torment, would have spent a sleepless night, and at the decisive moment instead of helping the man would perhaps have done what he did. For in the meantime all possible drives would have *had time* to imagine the experience and to comment on it. – What then are our experiences? Much *more* that which we put into them than that which they already contain! Or must we go so far as to say: in themselves they contain nothing? To experience is to invent? –

120

To reassure the sceptic. – 'I have no idea how I am *acting*! I have no idea how I *ought to act*!' – you are right, but be sure of this: *you will be acted upon*! at every moment! Mankind has in all ages confused the active and the passive: it is their everlasting grammatical blunder.

121

'Cause and effect'. – In this mirror – and our intellect is a mirror – something is taking place that exhibits regularity, a certain thing always succeeds another certain thing – this we *call*, when we perceive it and want to call it something, cause and effect – we fools! As though we had here understood something or other, or could understand it! For we have seen nothing but *pictures* of 'causes and effects'! And it is precisely this *pictorialness* that makes impossible an insight into a more essential connection than that of mere succession.

122

Purposes in nature. – The impartial investigator who pursues the history of the eye and the forms it has assumed among the lowest creatures, who demonstrates the whole step-by-step evolution of the eye, must arrive at the great conclusion that vision was *not* the intention behind the creation of the eye, but that vision appeared, rather, after *chance* had put the apparatus together. A single instance of this kind – and 'purposes' fall away like scales from the eyes!

123

Rationality. – How did rationality arrive in the world? Irrationally, as might be expected: by a chance accident. If we want to know what that chance accident was we shall have to guess it, as one guesses the answer to a riddle.

124

What is willing! – We laugh at him who steps out of his room at the moment when the sun steps out of its room, and then says: '*I will* that the sun shall rise'; and at him who cannot stop a wheel, and says: '*I will* that it shall roll'; and at him who is thrown down in wrestling, and says: 'here I lie, but *I will* lie here!' But, all laughter aside, are we ourselves ever acting any differently whenever we employ the expression: '*I will*'?

125

On the 'realm of freedom'. – We can think many, many more things than we can do or experience – that is to say, our thinking is superficial and content with the surface; indeed, it does not notice that it is the surface. If our intellect had *evolved* strictly in step with our strength and the extent to which we exercise our strength, the dominant principle of our thinking would be that we can understand only that which we can *do* – *if* understanding is possible at all. A man is thirsty and cannot get water, but the pictures his thought produces bring water ceaselessly before his eyes, as though nothing were easier to procure – the superficial and easily satisfied character of the intellect cannot grasp the actual need and distress, and yet it feels superior; it is proud of being able to do more, to run faster, to be at its goal almost in a twinkling – and thus it is that the realm of thought appears to be, in comparison with the realm of action, willing and experience, a *realm of freedom*: while in reality it is, as aforesaid, only a realm of surfaces and self-satisfaction.

126

Forgetting. – It has not yet been proved that there is any such thing as forgetting; all we know is that the act of recollection does not lie within our power. We have provisionally set into this gap in our power that word 'forgetting', as if it were one more addition to our faculties. But what, after all, does lie within our power! – if that word stands in a gap in our power, ought the other words not to stand in a gap in our *knowledge of our power*?

127

For a purpose. – Of all actions, those performed for a purpose have been least understood, no doubt because they have always been counted the most understandable and are to our consciousness the most commonplace. The great problems are to be encountered in the street.

128

Dream and responsibility. – You are willing to assume responsibility for everything! Except, that is, for your dreams! What miserable weakness, what lack of consistent courage! Nothing is *more* your own than your dreams! Nothing *more* your own work! Content, form, duration, performer, spectator – in these comedies you are all of this yourself! And it is precisely here that you rebuff and are ashamed of yourselves, and even Oedipus, the wise Oedipus, derived consolation from the thought that we cannot help what we dream! From this I conclude that the great majority of mankind must be conscious of having abominable dreams. If it were otherwise, how greatly this nocturnal poetising would have been exploited for the enhancement of human arrogance! – Do I have to add that the wise Oedipus was right, that we really are not responsible for our dreams – but just as little for our waking life, and that the doctrine of freedom of will has human pride and feeling of power for its father and mother? Perhaps I say this too often: but at least that does not make it an error.

129
Alleged conflict of motives. – One speaks of a 'conflict of motives', but designates with this phrase a conflict which is *not* one of motives. That is to say: before an act there step into our reflective consciousness one after another the *consequences* of various acts all of which we believe we can perform, and we compare these consequences. We believe we have resolved upon an act when we have decided that its consequences will be more favourable than those of any other; before reaching this conclusion we often honestly torment ourselves on account of the great difficulty of divining what the consequences will be, of seeing all their implications, and of being certain we have included them all without omission: so that the result obtained still has to be divided by chance. Indeed, to come to the worst difficulty: all these consequences, so hard to determine individually, now have to be weighed against one another on the *same* scales; but usually it happens that, on account of the differences in the *quality* of all these possible consequences, we lack the scales and the weights for this casuistry of advantage. Supposing, however, we got through that too, and chance had placed on our scales consequences that admit of being weighed against one another: we would then in fact possess in our *picture of the consequences* of a certain action a *motive* for performing this action – yes! *one* motive! But at the moment when we finally do act, our action is often enough determined by a different species of motives than the species here under discussion, those involved in our 'picture of the consequences'. What here comes into play is the way we habitually expend our energy; or some slight instigation from a person whom we fear or honour or love; or our indolence, which prefers to do what lies closest to hand; or an excitation of our imagination brought about at the decisive moment by some immediate, very trivial event; quite incalculable physical influences come into play; caprice and waywardness come into play; some emotion or other happens quite by chance to leap forth: in short, there come into play motives in part unknown to us, in part known very ill, which we can *never* take account of *beforehand*. *Probably* a struggle takes place between these as well, a battling to and fro, a rising and falling of the scales – and this would be the actual 'conflict

of motives': – something quite invisible to us of which we would be quite unconscious. I have calculated the consequences and the outcomes and in doing so have set *one* very essential motive in the battle-line – but I have not set up this battle-line itself, nor can I even see it: the struggle itself is hidden from me, and likewise the victory as victory; for, though I certainly learn what I finally *do*, I do not learn which motive has therewith actually proved victorious. *But we are accustomed* to *exclude* all these unconscious processes from the accounting and to reflect on the preparation for an act only to the extent that it is conscious: and we thus confuse conflict of motives with comparison of the possible consequences of different actions – a confusion itself very rich in consequences and one highly fateful for the evolution of morality!

130

Purposes? Will? – We have accustomed ourselves to believe in the existence of two realms, the realm of *purposes* and *will* and the realm of *chance*; in the latter everything happens senselessly, things come to pass without anyone's being able to say why or wherefore. – We stand in fear of this mighty realm of the great cosmic stupidity, for in most cases we experience it only when it falls like a slate from the roof on to that other world of purposes and intentions and strikes some treasured purpose of ours dead. This belief in the two realms is a primeval romance and fable: we clever dwarfs, with our will and purposes, are oppressed by those stupid, arch-stupid giants, chance accidents, overwhelmed and often trampled to death by them – but in spite of all that we would not like to be without the harrowing poetry of their proximity, for these monsters often arrive when our life, involved as it is in the spider's web of purposes, has become too tedious or too filled with anxiety, and provide us with a sublime diversion by for once *breaking* the web – not that these irrational creatures would do so intentionally! Or even notice they had done so! But their coarse bony hands tear through our net as if it were air. – The Greeks called this realm of the incalculable and of sublime eternal narrow-mindedness Moira, and set it around their gods as the horizon beyond which they could neither see nor exert influence: it is an instance of that secret defiance of the gods encountered among many peoples – one worships them, certainly, but one keeps in one's hand a final trump to be used against them; as when the Indians and Persians think of them as being dependent on the *sacrifice* of mortals, so that in the last resort mortals can let the gods go hungry or even starve them to death; or when the harsh, melancholy Scandinavian creates the notion of a coming 'twilight of the gods' and thus enjoys a silent revenge in retaliation for the continual fear his evil gods produce in him. Christianity, whose basic feeling is neither Indian nor Persian nor Greek nor Scandinavian, acted differently: it bade us to worship the *spirit of power* in the dust and even to kiss the dust itself – the sense of this being that that almighty 'realm of stupidity' was not as stupid as it looked, that it was *we*, rather, who were stupid in failing to see that behind it there stood our dear God who, though his ways were dark, strange and crooked, would in the end 'bring all to glory'. This new fable of a loving god who had hitherto been mistaken for a race of giants or for Moira and who himself span out purposes and nets more refined even than those produced by our own understanding – so that they *had* to seem incomprehensible, indeed unreasonable to it – this fable represented so bold an inversion and so daring a paradox that the ancient world, grown over-refined, could not resist it, no matter how mad and *contradictory* the thing might sound; for, between ourselves, there was a contradiction in it: if our understanding cannot divine the understanding and the purposes of God, whence did it divine this quality of its understanding? and this quality of God's understanding? – In more recent times men have in fact come seriously to doubt whether the slate that falls from the roof was really thrown down by 'divine love' – and have again begun to go back to the old romance of giants and dwarfs. Let us therefore *learn*, because it is high time we did so: in our supposed favoured realm of purposes and reason the giants are likewise the rulers! And our purposes and our reason are not dwarfs but giants! And our nets are just as often and just as roughly broken *by us ourselves* as they are by slates from the roof! And all is not purpose that is called purpose, and even less is all will that is called will! And if you want to conclude from this: 'so there is only one realm, that of chance accidents and stupidity?' – one will have to add: yes, perhaps there is only one realm, perhaps there exists neither will nor purposes, and we have only imagined them. Those iron hands of necessity which shake the dice-box of chance play their game for an infinite length of time: so that there *have* to be throws which exactly resemble purposiveness and rationality of every degree. *Perhaps* our acts of will and our purposes are nothing but just such throws – and we are only too limited and too vain to comprehend our extreme limitedness: which consists in the fact that we ourselves shake the dice-box with iron hands, that we ourselves in our most intentional actions do no more than play the game of necessity. Perhaps! – To get out of this *perhaps* one would have to have been already a guest in the underworld and beyond all surfaces, sat at Persephone's table and played dice with the goddess herself.

131

Fashions in morality. – How the overall moral judgments have shifted! The great men of antique morality, Epictetus for instance, knew nothing of the now normal glorification of thinking of others, of living for others; in the light of our moral fashion they would have to be called downright immoral, for they strove with all their might *for* their *ego* and *against* feeling with others (that is to say, with the sufferings and moral frailties of others). Perhaps they would reply to us: 'If you are so boring or ugly an object to yourself, by all means think of others more than of yourself! It is right you should!'

132

The echo of Christianity in morality. – '*On n'est bon que par la pitié: il faut donc qu'il y ait quelque pitié dans tous nos sentiments*' – thus says morality today! And why is that? – That men today feel the sympathetic, disinterested, generally useful social actions to be the *moral* actions – this is perhaps the most general effect and conversion which Christianity has produced in Europe: although it was not its intention nor contained in its teaching. But it was the residuum of Christian states of mind left when the very much antithetical, strictly egoistic fundamental belief in the 'one thing needful', in the absolute importance of eternal *personal* salvation, together with the dogmas upon which it rested, gradually retreated and the subsidiary belief in 'love', in 'love of one's neighbour', in concert with the tremendous practical effect of ecclesiastical charity, was thereby pushed into the foreground. The more one liberated oneself from the dogmas, the more one sought as it were a *justification* of this liberation in a cult of philanthropy: not to fall short of the Christian ideal in this, but where possible to outdo it, was a secret spur with all French freethinkers from Voltaire up to Auguste Comte: and the latter did in fact, with his moral formula *vivre pour autrui*, outchristian Christianity. In Germany it was Schopenhauer, in England John Stuart Mill who gave the widest currency to the teaching of the sympathetic affects and of pity or the advantage of others as the principle of behaviour: but they themselves were no more than an echo – those teachings have shot up with a mighty impetus everywhere and in the crudest and subtlest forms together from about the time of the French Revolution onwards, every socialist system has placed itself as if involuntarily on the common ground of these teachings. There is today perhaps no more firmly credited prejudice than this: that one *knows* what really constitutes the moral. Today it seems *to do everyone good* when they hear that society is on the way to *adapting* the individual to general requirements, and that *the happiness and at the same time the sacrifice of the individual* lies in feeling himself to be a useful member and instrument of the whole: except that one is at present very uncertain as to where this whole is to be sought, whether in an existing state or one still to be created, or in the nation, or in a brotherhood of peoples, or in new little economic communalities. At present there is much reflection, doubt, controversy over this subject, and much excitement and passion; but there is also a wonderful and fair-sounding unanimity in the demand that the ego has to deny itself until, in the form of adaptation to the whole, it again acquires its firmly set circle of rights and duties – until it has become something quite novel and different. What is wanted – whether this is admitted or not – is nothing less than a fundamental remoulding, indeed weakening and abolition of the *individual*: one never tires of enumerating and indicting all that is evil and inimical, prodigal, costly, extravagant in the form individual existence has assumed hitherto, one hopes to manage more cheaply, more safely, more equitably, more uniformly if there exist only *large bodies and their members*. Everything that in any way corresponds to this body- and membership-building drive and its ancillary drives is felt to be *good*, this is the *moral undercurrent* of our age; individual empathy and social feeling here play into one another's hands. (Kant still stands outside this movement: he expressly teaches that we must be insensible towards the suffering of others if our beneficence is to possess moral value – which Schopenhauer, in a wrath easy to comprehend, calls *Kantian insipidity*.)

133

'No longer to think of oneself'. – Let us reflect seriously upon this question: why do we leap after someone who has fallen into the water in front of us, even though we feel no kind of affection for him? Out of pity: at that moment we are thinking only of the other person – thus says thoughtlessness. Why do we feel pain and discomfort in common with someone spitting blood, though we may even be ill-disposed towards him? Out of pity: at that moment we are not thinking of ourself – thus says the same thoughtlessness. The truth is:

in the feeling of pity – I mean in that which is usually and misleadingly called pity – we are, to be sure, not consciously thinking of ourself but are doing so *very strongly unconsciously*; as when, if our foot slips – an act of which we are not immediately conscious – we perform the most purposive counter-motions and in doing so plainly employ our whole reasoning faculty. An accident which happens to another offends us: it would make us aware of our impotence, and perhaps of our cowardice, if we did not go to assist him. Or it brings with it in itself a diminution of our honour in the eyes of others or in our own eyes. Or an accident and suffering incurred by another constitutes a signpost to some danger to us; and it can have a painful effect upon us simply as a token of human vulnerability and fragility in general. We repel this kind of pain and offence and requite it through an act of pity; it may contain a subtle self-defence or even a piece of revenge. That at bottom we are thinking very strongly of ourselves can be divined from the decision we arrive at in every case in which we *can* avoid the sight of the person suffering, perishing or complaining: we decide *not* to do so if we can present ourselves as the more powerful and as a helper, if we are certain of applause, if we want to feel how fortunate we are in contrast, or hope that the sight will relieve our boredom. It is misleading to call the *Leid* (suffering) we may experience at such a sight, and which can be of very varying kinds, *Mit-Leid* (pity), for it is under all circumstances a suffering which he who is suffering in our presence is *free* of: it is our own, as the suffering he feels is his own. But it is *only this suffering of our own* which we get rid of when we perform deeds of pity. But we never do anything of this kind out of *one* motive; as surely as we want to free ourselves of suffering by this act, just as surely do we give way to an *impulse to pleasure* with the same act – pleasure arises at the sight of a contrast to the condition we ourselves are in; at the notion that we can help if only we want to; at the thought of the praise and recognition we shall receive if we do help; at the activity of helping itself, insofar as the act is successful and as something achieved step by step in itself gives delight to the performer; especially, however, at the feeling that our action sets a limit to an injustice which arouses our indignation (the discharge of one's indignation is itself refreshing). All of this, and other, much more subtle things in addition, constitute 'pity': how coarsely does language assault with its one word so polyphonous a being! – That pity, on the other hand, is the *same kind of thing* as the suffering at the sight of which it arises, or that it possesses an especially subtle, penetrating understanding of suffering, are propositions contradicted by *experience*, and he who glorifies pity precisely on account of these two qualities *lacks* adequate experience in this very realm of the moral. This is what I have to conclude when I see all the incredible things Schopenhauer had to say of pity: he who wanted in this way to force us to believe in his great innovation that pity – which he had observed so imperfectly and described so badly – is the source of each and every moral action, past and future – and precisely on account of the faculties he had *invented* for it. – What in the end distinguishes men without pity from those with it? Above all – to offer only a rough outline here too – they lack the susceptible imagination for fear, the subtle capacity to scent danger; nor is their vanity so quickly offended if something happens that they could have prevented (the cautiousness of their pride tells them not to involve themselves needlessly in the things of others, indeed they love to think that each should help himself and play his own cards). They are, in addition, mostly more accustomed to enduring pain than are men of pity; and since they themselves have suffered, it does not seem to them so unfair that others should suffer. Finally, they find that being soft-hearted is painful to them, just as maintaining a stoic indifference is painful to men of pity; they load that condition with deprecations and believe it to threaten their manliness and the coldness of their valour – they conceal their tears from others and wipe them away, angry with themselves. They are a *different* kind of egoists from the men of pity; – but to call them in an exceptional sense *evil*, and men of pity *good*, is nothing but a moral fashion which is having its day: just as the opposite fashion had its day, and a long day too!

134

To what extent one has to guard against pity. – Pity (*Mitleiden*), insofar as it really causes suffering (*Leiden*) – and this is here our only point of view – is a weakness, like every losing of oneself through a *harmful* affect. It *increases* the amount of suffering in the world: if suffering is here and there indirectly reduced or removed as a consequence of pity, this occasional and on the whole insignificant consequence must not be employed to justify its essential nature, which is, as I have said, harmful. Supposing it was dominant even for a single day, mankind would immediately perish of it. In itself, it has as little a good character as any other drives: only where it is demanded and commended – and this happens where one fails to grasp that it is harmful but discovers a *source of pleasure* in it – does a good conscience adhere to it, only then does one gladly succumb to it and not hesitate to demonstrate it. Under other conditions, where the fact of its harmfulness is grasped, it counts as weakness: or, as with the Greeks, as a morbid recurring affect the perilousness of which can be removed by periodical deliberate discharge. – He who for a period of time made the experiment of intentionally pursuing occasions for pity in his everyday life and set before his soul all the misery available to him in his surroundings would inevitably grow sick and melancholic. He, however, whose desire it is to serve mankind as a physician *in any sense whatever* will have to be very much on his guard against that sensation – it will paralyse him at every decisive moment and apply a ligature to his knowledge and his subtle helpful hand.

135

Being pitied. – To savages the idea of being pitied evokes a moral shudder: it divests one of all virtue. To offer pity is as good as to offer contempt: one does not want to see a contemptible creature suffer, there is no enjoyment in that. To see an enemy suffer, on the other hand, whom one recognises as one's equal in pride and who does not relinquish his pride under torture, and in general any creature who refuses to cry out for pity – cry out, that is, for the most shameful and profoundest humiliation – this is an enjoyment of enjoyments, and beholding it the soul of the savage is elevated to *admiration*: in the end he kills such a valiant creature, if he has him in his power, and thus accords this *indomitable enemy* his last *honour*: if he had wept and wailed and the expression of cold defiance had vanished from his face, if he had shown himself contemptible – well, he would have been let live, like a dog – he would no longer have excited the pride of the spectator of his suffering, and admiration would have given place to pity.

136

Happiness in pity. – If, like the Indians, one posits as the *goal* of all intellectual activity the knowledge of human *misery* and remains faithful to such a terrible objective throughout many generations of the spirit: then in the eyes of such men of *inherited* pessimism *pity* at last acquires a new value as a *life-preservative* power – it makes existence endurable, even though existence may seem worthy of being thrown off in disgust and horror. Pity becomes the antidote to self-destruction, as a sensation which includes pleasure and proffers the taste of superiority in small doses: it skims off our dross, makes the heart full, banishes fear and torpor, incites us to words, complaint, and action – measured against the misery of the knowledge which comes from all sides, hounds the individual into a dark narrow corner and takes away his breath, it is a *relative happiness*. Happiness, however, whatever kind it may be, brings air, light and freedom of movement.

137

Why double your 'ego'! – To view our own experiences with the eyes with which we are accustomed to view them when they are the experiences of others – this is very comforting and a medicine to be recommended. On the other hand, to view and imbibe the experiences of others *as if they were ours* – as is the demand of a philosophy of pity – this would destroy us, and in a very short time: but just try the experiment of doing it, and fantasise no longer! Moreover, the former maxim is certainly *more in accord* with reason and the will to rationality, for we adjudge the value and meaning of an event more objectively when it happens to another than we do when it happens to us: the value, for example, of a death, or a money-loss, or a slander. Pity as a principle of action, with the demand: suffer from another's ill-fortune *as* he himself suffers, would, on the other hand, entail that the ego-stand-point, with its exaggeration and excess, would also become the stand-point of the person feeling pity: so that we would have to suffer from our own ego and at the same time from the ego of the other, and would thus voluntarily encumber ourselves with a double load of irrationality instead of making the burden of our own as light as possible.

138

Growing tenderer. – If we love, honour, admire someone, and then afterwards discover that he is *suffering* – a discovery that always fills us with the greatest astonishment, for we cannot think otherwise than that the happiness that flows across to us from him must proceed from a superabundant well of happiness *of his own* – our feeling of love, reverence and admiration changes in an *essential respect*: it grows *tenderer*; that is to say, the gulf between us and him seems to be bridged, an approximation to identity seems to occur. Only now do we conceive it possible that we might *give back* to him, while he previously dwelt in our imagination as being elevated above our gratitude. This capacity to give back produces in us great joy and exultation. We try to divine what it is will ease his pain, and we give it to him; if he wants words of consolation, comforting looks,

attentions, acts of service, presents – we give them; but above all, if he
wants us to *suffer* at his suffering we give ourselves out to be *suffering*;
in all this, however, we have the *enjoyment of active gratitude* – which, in
short, *is benevolent revenge*. If he wants and takes nothing whatever
from us, we go away chilled and saddened, almost offended: it is as
though our gratitude had been repulsed – and on this point of
honour even the most benevolent man is ticklish. – From all this it
follows that, even in the most favourable case, there is something
degrading in suffering and something elevating and productive of
superiority in pitying – which separates these two sensations from
one another to all eternity.

139

Said to be higher! – You say that the morality of pity is a higher morality
than that of stoicism? Prove it! but note that 'higher' and 'lower' in
morality is not to be measured by a moral yardstick: for there is no
absolute morality. So take your yardstick from elsewhere and –
watch out!

140

Praise and blame. – If a war proves unsuccessful one asks who was to
'blame' for the war; if it ends in victory one praises its instigator. Guilt
is always sought wherever there is failure; for failure brings with it a
depression of spirits against which the sole remedy is instinctively
applied: a new excitation of the *feeling of power* – and this is to be
discovered in the *condemnation* of the 'guilty'. This guilty person is not
to be thought of as a scapegoat for the guilt of others: he is a sacrifice
to the weak, humiliated and depressed, who want to demonstrate on
something that they still have some strength left. To condemn
oneself can also be a means of restoring the feeling of strength after a
defeat. – On the other hand, the glorification of the *instigator* is often
the equally blind result of another drive which wants its sacrifice –
and this time the sacrifice smells sweet and inviting to the sacrificial
beast itself – : for when the feeling of power in a people or a society is
surfeited by a great and glittering success and a *weariness with victory*
sets in, one relinquishes some of one's pride; the feeling of *devotion*
rises up and seeks an object. – Whether we are *praised* or *blamed*, what
we usually constitute is opportunities, and arbitrarily seized opportunities, for our neighbours to discharge the drive to praise or blame
which has become distended in them: in both cases we do them a
favour for which we deserve no credit and they display no gratitude.

141

More beautiful but less valuable. – Picturesque morality: this is the morality of steeply ascending emotions, of abrupt transitions, of pathetic, importunate, fearsome, solemn sounds and gestures. It is the *semi-savage* stage of morality: one must not let its aesthetic charm lure one into according it a higher rank.

142

Empathy. – To understand another person, that is, *to imitate his feelings in ourselves*, we do indeed often go back to the *reason* for his feeling thus or thus and ask for example: *why* is he troubled? – so as then for the same reason to become troubled ourselves; but it is much more usual to omit to do this and instead to produce the feeling in ourselves after the *effects* it exerts and displays on the other person by imitating with our own body the expression of his eyes, his voice, his walk, his bearing (or even their reflection in word, picture, music). Then a similar feeling arises in us in consequence of an ancient association between movement and sensation, which has been trained to move backwards or forwards in either direction. We have brought our skill in understanding the feelings of others to a high state of perfection and in the presence of another person we are always almost involuntarily practising this skill: one should observe especially the play on the faces of women and how they quiver and glitter in continual imitation and reflection of what is felt to be going on around them. But it is music which reveals to us most clearly what masters we are in the rapid and subtle divination of feelings and in empathising: for, though music is an imitation of an imitation of feelings, it nonetheless and in spite of this degree of distance and indefiniteness often enough makes us participants in these feelings, so that, like perfect fools, we grow sad without there being the slightest occasion for sorrow merely because we hear sounds and rhythms which somehow remind us of the tone-of-voice and movements of mourners, or even of no more than their customary usages. It is told of a Danish king that he was wrought up to such a degree of warlike fury by the music of his minstrel that he leaped from his seat and killed five people of his assembled court: there was no war, no enemy, rather the reverse, but the drive which *from the feeling infers the cause* was sufficiently strong to overpower observation and reason. But that is almost always the effect of music (supposing it capable of producing an effect at all –), and one does not require such paradoxical cases to see this: the state of feeling into which

music transports us almost always contradicts the real situation we
are apparently in and the reasoning powers which recognise this real
situation and its causes. – If we ask how we became so fluent in the
imitation of the feelings of others the answer admits of no doubt:
man, as the most timid of all creatures on account of his subtle and
fragile nature, has in his *timidity* the instructor in that empathy, that
quick understanding of the feelings of another (and of animals).
Through long millennia he saw in everything strange and lively a
danger: at the sight of it he at once imitated the expression of the
features and the bearing and drew his conclusion as to the kind of
evil intention behind these features and this bearing. Man has even
applied this interpretation of all movements and lineaments *as
deriving from intention* to inanimate nature – in the delusion that there
is nothing inanimate: I believe that all we call *feeling for nature* at the
sight of sky, meadow, rocks, forest, storms, stars, sea, landscape,
spring, has its origin here – without the primeval habit, born of fear,
of seeing behind all this a second, hidden meaning, we would not
now take pleasure in nature, just as we would take no pleasure in
man and animal without this same instructor in understanding, fear.
For pleasure and pleased astonishment, finally the sense of the
ridiculous, are the later-born children of empathy and the much
younger siblings of fear. – The capacity for understanding – which,
as we have seen, rests on the capacity for *rapid dissimulation* – declines
in proud, arrogant men and peoples, because they have less fear: on
the other hand, every kind of understanding and self-dissembling is
at home among timid peoples; here is also the rightful home of the
imitative arts and of the higher intelligence. – If, from the standpoint
of such a theory of empathy as I have here suggested, I think of the
theory, just at this time much loved and sanctified, of a mystical
process by virtue of which *pity* makes two beings into one and in this
way makes possible the immediate understanding of the one by the
other: when I recall that so clear a head as Schopenhauer's took
pleasure in such frivolous and worthless rubbish and passed this
pleasure on to other clear and not-so-clear heads: then there is no
end to my amazement and compassion! How great must be our joy
in incomprehensible nonsense! How close to the madman does the
sane man stand when he pays heed to his *secret* intellectual desires! –
(*For what* did Schopenhauer really feel so grateful and so deeply
indebted to Kant? The answer was once revealed quite unambigu-
ously: someone had spoken of how Kant's categorical imperative
could be deprived of its *qualitas occulta* and be made comprehensible.

Thereupon Schopenhauer burst out: 'The categorical imperative comprehensible! What a fundamentally perverse idea! What Egyptian darkness! Heaven forbid that it should ever become comprehensible! For that there is something incomprehensible, that *this misery of the understanding* and its concepts is limited, conditional, finite, deceptive: the certainty of this is Kant's greatest gift to us.' – Let us ask ourselves whether anyone who feels happy in believing in the *incomprehensibility* of moral things can be sincerely interested in acquiring a knowledge of them! One who still honestly believes in inspirations from on high, in magic and spiritual apparitions, and in the metaphysical ugliness of the toad!)

143

Alas, if this drive should rage! – Supposing the drive to attachment and care for others (the 'sympathetic affection') were twice as strong as it is, life on earth would be *insupportable*. Only consider what follies people commit, hourly and daily, out of attachment and care *for themselves*, and how intolerably awful they look as a result: how would it be if we became *for others* the object of the follies and importunities with which they had previously tormented only themselves! Would one not flee blindly away as soon as our 'neighbour' drew near? And bestow upon the sympathetic affection the kind of evil names we now bestow upon egoism?

144

Closing one's ears to lamentation. – If we let ourselves be made gloomy by the lamentation and suffering of other mortals and cover our own sky with clouds, who is it who will have to bear the consequences of this gloom? These other mortals, of course, and in addition to the burdens they bear already! We can offer them neither *aid* nor *comfort* if we want to be the echo of their lamentation, or even if we are merely always giving ear to it – unless, that is, we had acquired the art of the Olympians and henceforth *edified* ourselves by the misfortunes of mankind instead of being made unhappy by them. But that is somewhat too Olympian for us: even though we have, with our enjoyment of tragedy, already taken a step in the direction of this ideal divine cannibalism.

145

'Unegoistic!' – This one is hollow and wants to be full, that one is overfull and wants to be emptied – both go in search of an individual who will serve their purpose. And this process, understood in its

highest sense, is in both cases called by the same word: love – what? is love supposed to be something unegoistic?

146

Out beyond our neighbour too. – What? Is the nature of the truly moral to lie in our keeping in view the most immediate and most direct consequences to others of our actions and deciding in accordance with these consequences? But this, though it may be a morality, is a narrow and petty bourgeois one: a higher and freer viewpoint, it seems to me, is to *look beyond* these immediate consequences to others and under certain circumstances to pursue more distant goals *even at the cost of the suffering of others* – for example, to pursue knowledge even though one realises that our free-spiritedness will at first and as an immediate consequence plunge others into doubt, grief and even worse things. May we not at least treat our neighbour as we treat ourselves? And if with regard to ourselves we take no such narrow and petty bourgeois thought for the immediate consequences and the suffering they may cause, why do we *have* to take such thought in regard to our neighbour? Supposing we acted in the sense of self-sacrifice, what would forbid us to sacrifice our neighbour as well? – just as the state and as princes have done hitherto, when they sacrificed one citizen to another 'for the sake of the general interest', as they put it. We too, however, have general, and perhaps more general interests: why may a few individuals of the present generation not be sacrificed to coming generations? their grief, their distress, their despair, their blunders and fears not be deemed necessary, because a new ploughshare is to break up the ground and make it fruitful for all? – Finally: we at the same time communicate to our neighbour the point of view from which he can *feel himself to be a sacrifice,* we persuade him to the task for which we employ him. Are we then without pity? But if we also want to *transcend our own pity* and thus achieve victory over ourselves, is this not a higher and freer viewpoint and posture than that in which one feels secure when one has discovered whether an action *benefits or harms* our neighbour? We, on the other hand, would, through sacrifice – in which we *and our neighbour* are both included – strengthen and raise higher the general feeling of human *power,* even though we might not attain to more. But even this would be a positive enhancement of *happiness.* – Finally, if even this – – but now not a word more! A glance is enough; you have understood me.

147

Cause of 'altruism'. – Men have on the whole spoken of love with such emphasis and so idolised it *because they have had little of it* and have never been allowed to eat their fill of this food: thus it became for them 'food of the gods'. Let a poet depict a utopia in which there obtains *universal love,* he will certainly have to describe a painful and ludicrous state of affairs the like of which the earth has never yet seen – everyone worshipped, encumbered and desired, not by *one* lover, as happens now, but by thousands, indeed by everyone else, as the result of an uncontrollable drive which would then be as greatly execrated and cursed as selfishness had been in former times; and the poets in that state of things – provided they were left alone long enough to write – would dream of nothing but the happy, loveless past, of divine selfishness, of how it was once possible to be alone, undisturbed, unloved, hated, despised on earth, and whatever else may characterise the utter baseness of the dear animal world in which *we* live.

148

Distant prospect. – If only those actions are moral which are performed for the sake of another and only for his sake, as one definition has it, then there are no moral actions! If only those actions are moral which are performed out of freedom of will, as another definition says, then there are likewise no moral actions! – What is it then which is so *named* and which in any event exists and wants explaining? It is the effects of certain intellectual mistakes. – And supposing one freed oneself from these errors, what would become of 'moral actions'? – By virtue of these errors we have hitherto accorded certain actions a higher value than they possess: we have segregated them from the 'egoistic' and 'unfree' actions. If we now realign them with the latter, as we shall have to do, we shall certainly *reduce* their value (the value we feel they possess), and indeed shall do so to an unfair degree, because the 'egoistic' and 'unfree' actions were hitherto evaluated too low on account of their supposed profound and intrinsic difference. – Will they from then on be performed less often because they are now valued less highly? – Inevitably! At least for a good length of time, as long as the balance of value-feelings continues to be affected by the reaction of former errors! But our counter-reckoning is that we shall restore to men their goodwill towards the actions decried as egoistic and restore to these actions their *value – we shall deprive them of their bad conscience!* And since they have hitherto been by far the most frequent actions, and will continue to be so for all future time, we thus remove from the entire aspect of action and life its *evil appearance*! This is a very significant result! When man no longer regards himself as evil he ceases to be so!

BOOK III

149

The need for little deviant acts. – Sometimes to act *against* one's better judgment when it comes to questions of *custom*; to give way in practice while keeping one's reservations to oneself; to do as everyone does and thus to show them consideration as it were in compensation for our deviant opinions: – many tolerably free-minded people regard this, not merely as unobjectionable, but as 'honest', 'humane', 'tolerant', 'not being pedantic', and whatever else those pretty words may be with which the intellectual conscience is lulled to sleep: and thus this person takes his child for Christian baptism though he is an atheist; and that person serves in the army as all the world does, however much he may execrate hatred between nations; and a third marries his wife in church because her relatives are pious and is not ashamed to repeat vows before a priest. 'It doesn't *really matter* if people like us also do what everyone does and always has done' – this is the thoughtless *prejudice*! The *thoughtless* error! For nothing *matters more* than that an already mighty, anciently established and irrationally recognised custom should be once more confirmed by a person recognised as rational: it thereby acquires in the eyes of all who come to hear of it the sanction of rationality itself! All respect to your opinions! But *little deviant acts* are worth more!

150

Chance in marriage. – If I were a god, and a benevolent god, the *marriages* of mankind would make me more impatient than anything else. The individual can go far, far in his seventy years, indeed in his thirty years if that is all he has – it is amazing, even to gods! But when one then sees how he takes the legacy and inheritance of this struggle and victory, the laurel-wreath of his humanity, and hangs it up at the first decent place where a little woman can get at it and pluck it to pieces: when one sees how well he knows how to gain but how ill to preserve, that he gives no thought to the fact, indeed, that through procreation he could prepare the way for an even more victorious life: then, as aforesaid, one grows impatient and says to oneself: 'nothing can come of mankind in the long run, its individuals are squandered, chance in marriage makes a grand rational progress of mankind impossible – let us cease to be eager spectators and fools of this spectacle without a goal!' – It was in this mood that the gods of Epicurus once withdrew into their divine happiness and silence: they were tired of mankind and its love affairs.

151

Here we must invent new ideals. – We ought not to be permitted to come
to a decision affecting our life while we are in the condition of being
in love, nor to determine once and for all the character of the
company we keep on the basis of a violent whim: the oaths of lovers
ought to be publicly declared invalid and marriage denied them: –
the reason being that one ought to take marriage enormously more
seriously! so that in precisely those cases in which marriages have
hitherto taken place they would henceforth usually not take place!
Are most marriages not of a kind that one would prefer not to be
witnessed by a third party? But this third party is almost always
present – the child – and he is more than a witness, he is a scapegoat!

152

Form of oath. – 'If I am now lying I am no longer a decent human being
and anyone may tell me so to my face.' – I recommend this form of
oath in place of the judicial oath with its customary invocation of
God: it is *stronger*. Even the pious person has no reason to oppose it:
for as soon as the sanction of the oath hitherto in use begins to be
applied *vainly*, the pious person must give ear to his catechism, which
prescribes 'thou shalt not take the name of the Lord thy God *in vain*!'

153

A malcontent. – This is one of those old-style fighting men: he has no
love of civilisation, because he thinks the object of civilisation is to
make all the good things of life – honours, plunder, beautiful women
– accessible also to cowards.

154

Consolation of the imperilled. – The Greeks, in a way of life in which great
perils and upheavals were always present, sought in knowledge and
reflection a kind of security and ultimate *refugium*. We, in an
incomparably more secure condition, have transferred this perilousness into knowledge and reflection, and we recover from it, and calm
ourselves down, *with our way of life*.

155

A scepticism become extinct. – Bold and daring undertakings are rarer in
the modern age than they were in ancient times or in the Middle
Ages – probably because the modern age no longer believes in
omens, oracles, soothsayers or the stars. That is to say: we have
become incapable of *believing in a future* determined for *us*, as did the

ancients: who – in this quite different from us – were far less sceptical in regard to what was *coming* than they were in regard to what *is*.

156

Evil through high spirits. – 'If only we don't feel too happy!' – that was the anxiety the Greeks of the best period felt secretly in their hearts. *That* was why they preached to themselves moderation. And we!

157

Cult of 'natural sounds'. – What does it indicate that our culture is not merely tolerant of expressions of pain, of tears, complaints, reproaches, gestures of rage or of humiliation, but approves of them and counts them among the nobler inescapables? – while the spirit of the philosophy of antiquity looked upon them with contempt and absolutely declined to regard them as necessary. Recall, for instance, how Plato – not one of the most inhuman philosophers, that is to say – speaks of the Philoctetes of the tragic stage. Is our modern culture perhaps lacking in 'philosophy'? Would those philosophers of antiquity perhaps regard us one and all as belonging to the 'rabble'?

158

Climate of the flatterer. – One must no longer seek the fawning flatterer in the proximity of princes – they have all acquired a taste for soldiering and the flatterer is repugnant to it. But this flower still blooms in the proximity of bankers and artists.

159

Resurrectors of the dead. – Vain people value a piece of the past more highly from the moment they find they can reproduce it in themselves (especially when this is difficult to do); indeed, where possible they desire to resurrect it again from the dead. And since there are always innumerable vain people, the danger that lies in the study of history as soon as it gets the upper hand of an entire age is indeed not small: too much energy is thrown away on all possible resurrections from the dead. Perhaps the whole movement of romanticism can best be understood from this point of view.

160

Vain, greedy and with very little wisdom. – Your desires are greater than your reason, and your vanity is even greater than your desires – for such people as you are a *great deal* of Christian practice plus a little Schopenhauerian theory would be a very good thing.

161

Beauty appropriate to the age. – If our sculptors, painters and composers want to hit off the spirit of the age they must depict beauty as bloated, gigantic and nervous: just as the Greeks, under the spell of their morality of moderation, saw and depicted beauty as the Apollo Belvedere. We ought really to call him *ugly*! But our stupid 'classicists' have robbed us of all honesty!

162

Contemporary irony. – At the present moment it is the way of Europeans to treat all great interests with irony, because one is so busy in their service one has no time to take them seriously.

163

Contra Rousseau. – If it is true that our civilisation has something pitiable about it, you have the choice of concluding with Rousseau that 'this pitiable civilisation is to blame for our *bad* morality', or against Rousseau that 'our *good* morality is to blame for this pitiableness of our civilisation. Our weak, unmanly, social concepts of good and evil and their tremendous ascendancy over body and soul have finally weakened all bodies and souls and snapped the self-reliant, independent, unprejudiced men, the pillars of a *strong* civilisation: where one still encounters *bad* morality one beholds the last ruins of these pillars.' Thus paradox stands against paradox! The truth cannot possibly be on both sides: and is it on either of them? Test them and see.

164

Perhaps premature. – At the present time it seems that, under all kinds of false, misleading names and mostly amid great uncertainty, those who do not regard themselves as being bound by existing laws and customs are making the first attempts to organise themselves and therewith to create for themselves a *right*: while hitherto they had lived, corrupt and corrupting, denounced as criminals, free-thinkers, immoral persons, and villains, and under the ban of outlawry and bad conscience. One ought to find this on the whole *fair and right*, even though it may make the coming century a dangerous one and put everybody under the necessity of carrying a gun: by this fact alone it constitutes a counter-force which is a constant reminder that there is no such thing as a morality with an exclusive monopoly of the moral, and that every morality that affirms itself alone destroys too much valuable strength and is bought too dear. Men who deviate from the usual path and are so often the inventive and productive men shall no longer be sacrificed; it shall not even be considered disgraceful to deviate from morality, either in deed or thought; numerous novel experiments shall be made in ways of life and modes of society; a tremendous burden of bad conscience shall be expelled from the world – these most universal goals ought to be recognised and furthered by all men who are honest and seek the truth!

165
When morality is not boring. – The chief moral commandments which a people is willing to be taught and have preached at it again and again are related to its chief failings, and thus it is never bored by them. The Greeks, who all too frequently failed to evidence moderation, cold courage, fairmindedness or rationality in general, were glad to give ear to the four Socratic virtues – for they had such need of them and *yet* so little talent for them!

166
At the crossroads. – Disgusting! You want to be part of a system in which one must either be a wheel and nothing else, or get run over by the other wheels! In which it goes without saying that everyone *is* what he has been *made* by decree from above! In which the hunt for 'connections' is among the natural duties! In which no one feels insulted if a man is drawn to his attention with the words 'he could be of use to you some day'! In which one is not ashamed to visit somebody in order to obtain his recommendation! In which one has not the faintest idea how with this easy conformity to such customs one has designated oneself a common piece of nature's pottery which others may use and smash without feeling very much compunction about it; as if one said: 'there will never be a shortage of things like me: take me! Don't stand on ceremony!'

167
Unconditional homage. – When I think of the most read German philosopher, of the most heard German composer and of the most respected German statesman, I have to admit to myself that the Germans, that nation of *unconditional* feelings, are much imposed upon nowadays, and by their own great men. Each of these three cases represents a glorious spectacle: each is a stream in its own, self-fashioned bed, and so mightily agitated it can often seem as though it wanted to flow uphill. And yet, however much respect one may have

for them, who would not on the whole prefer to be of a *different* opinion from Schopenhauer! – And who could be of one opinion with Richard Wagner, on the whole or in detail? however true it may be that, as somebody once said, wherever he takes offence or gives offence a problem lies *buried* – suffice it to say that he himself does not bring it to light. – And finally, how many would want to be wholeheartedly of one opinion with Bismarck, even if he showed any sign of being of one opinion with himself! To be sure: *no principles but strong drives* – a volatile mind in the service of strong drives and for that reason without principles – ought not to be anything strikingly uncommon in a statesman, but on the contrary something right and natural; only hitherto this has *not* been German! just as little as has a loud to-do about music or discord and annoyance about a composer, just as little as has the novel and extraordinary posture chosen by Schopenhauer: not *above* things or on his knees before things – both could have been called German – but *against* things! Incredible! And unpleasant! To range oneself alongside things and yet to do so as their enemy, in the last resort as the enemy of oneself! – what is the unconditional admirer to do with such a model! And what is he to do at all with three such models, who cannot even keep the peace among themselves! Schopenhauer is an enemy of Wagner's music, and Wagner an enemy of Bismarck's politics, and Bismarck an enemy of everything Wagnerian and Schopenhauerian! What is to be done! Where shall we satisfy our thirst for wholesale homage! Might one not select from the composer's music several hundred bars of good music which appeal to the heart because they possess heart: might one not go aside with this little theft and forget all the rest! And do the same in regard to the philosopher and the statesman – select, lay to one's heart, and in particular *forget the rest*! Yes, if only forgetting were not so difficult! There was once a very proud man who would accept nothing, good or bad, but what came from himself: but when he needed *forgetfulness* he found he could not give it to himself and had to summon the spirits three times; they came, they listened to his demand, and at length they said: 'this alone stands not within our power!' Can the Germans not profit from the experience of *Manfred*? Why summon the spirits at all! There is no point in doing so; one may want to forget, but one cannot. And what an enormous amount 'the rest' is that one would have to forget if one wanted to go on being a wholesale admirer of these three great men of our age! It would thus be more advisable to take the opportunity here offered of attempting something novel: namely, to grow more *honest towards oneself* and to make of a nation of credulous emulation and blind and bitter animosity a nation of conditional consent and benevolent opposition; firstly, however, to learn that unconditional homage to people is something ludicrous, that to learn differently in this matter is not discreditable even for Germans, and that there is a profound maxim worth laying to heart: *'Ce qui importe, ce ne sont point les personnes: mais les choses'*. This maxim is, like him who spoke it, great, honest, simple and taciturn – like Carnot, the soldier and republican. – But may one now speak to Germans of a Frenchman in this way, and of a Frenchman who is a republican? Perhaps not; perhaps, indeed, one may not even recall what Niebuhr ventured in his time to tell the Germans: that no one had given him so strong an impression of *true greatness* as Carnot.

168

A model. – What is it I love in Thucydides, why do I honour him more highly than Plato? He takes the most comprehensive and impartial delight in all that is typical in men and events and believes that to each type there pertains a quantum of *good sense*: *this* he seeks to discover. He displays greater practical justice than Plato; he does not revile or belittle those he does not like or who have harmed him in life. On the contrary: through seeing nothing but types he introduces something great into all the things and persons he treats of; for what interest would posterity, to whom he dedicates his work, have in that which was *not* typical! Thus in him, the portrayer of man, that *culture of the most impartial knowledge of the world* finds its last glorious flower: that culture which had in Sophocles its poet, in Pericles its statesman, in Hippocrates its physician, in Democritus its natural philosopher; which deserves to be baptised with the name of its teachers, the *Sophists*, and which from this moment of baptism unfortunately begins suddenly to become pale and ungraspable to us – for now we suspect that it must have been a very immoral culture, since a Plato and all the Socratic schools fought against it! Truth is here so tangled and twisted one does not like the idea of trying to sort it out: let the ancient error (*error veritate simplicior*) continue to run its ancient course! –

169

The Hellenic very foreign to us. – Oriental or modern, Asiatic or European: in contrast to the Hellenic, all these have in common the employment of massiveness and pleasure in great quantity as the language of the sublime; while in Paestum, Pompeii and Athens, and

103

with the whole of Greek architecture, one stands astonished at the *smallness of the masses* by means of which the Greeks know how to express and *love* to express the sublime. – Likewise: how simple the people of Greece appeared *in their own conception of themselves*! How greatly we surpass them in our knowledge of man! But how labyrinthine do our souls appear to us in comparison with theirs! If we desired and dared an architecture corresponding to the nature of *our* soul (we are too cowardly for it!) – our model would have to be the labyrinth! The fact is betrayed by our music, the art which is really our own and in which we really find expression! (For in music men let themselves go, in the belief that when they are *concealed* in music no one is capable of seeing them.)

170

Different perspectives of feeling. – What does our chatter about the Greeks amount to! What do we understand of their art, the soul of which is – passion for naked *male* beauty! It was only from that viewpoint that they were sensible of female beauty. Thus their perspective on female beauty was quite different from ours. And similarly with their love of women: they reverenced differently, they despised differently.

171

The nourishment of modern man. – Modern man understands how to digest many things, indeed almost everything – it is his kind of ambition: but he would be of a higher order if he did *not* understand it; *homo pamphagus* is not the finest of species. We live between a past which had a more perverse and stubborn taste than we and a future which will perhaps have a more discriminating one – we live too much in the middle.

172

Tragedy and music. – Men whose disposition is fundamentally warlike, as for example the Greeks of the age of Aeschylus, are *hard to move*, and when pity does for once overbear their severity it seizes them like a frenzy and as though a 'demonic force' – they then feel themselves under constraint and are excited by a shudder of religious awe. Afterwards they have their doubts about this condition; but for as long as they are in it they enjoy the delight of the miraculous and of being outside themselves, mixed with the bitterest wormwood of suffering: it is a draught appropriate to warriors, something rare, dangerous and bitter-sweet that does not easily fall to one's lot. – It is to souls which experience pity like this that tragedy appeals, to hard

and warlike souls which are difficult to conquer, whether with fear or
with pity, but which find it useful to grow soft from time to time: but
of what use is tragedy to those who are as open to the 'sympathetic
affections' as sails to the winds! When the Athenians had grown
softer and more sensitive, in the age of Plato – ah, but how far they
still were from the emotionality of our urban dwellers! – the
philosophers were already complaining of the harmfulness of
tragedy. An age full of danger such as is even now commencing, in
which bravery and manliness become more valuable, will perhaps
again gradually make souls so hard they will have need of tragic
poets: in the meantime, these would be a little *superfluous* – to put it as
mildly as possible. – For music, too, there may perhaps again come a
better time (it will certainly be a *more evil* one!) when artists have to
make it appeal to men strong in themselves, severe, dominated by
the dark seriousness of their own passion: but of what use is music to
the little souls of this vanishing age, souls too easily moved,
undeveloped, half-selves, inquisitive, lusting after everything!

173

Those who commend work. – In the glorification of 'work', in the
unwearied talk of the 'blessing of work', I see the same covert idea as
in the praise of useful impersonal actions: that of fear of everything
individual. Fundamentally, one now feels at the sight of work – one
always means by work that hard industriousness from early till late –
that such work is the best policeman, that it keeps everyone in
bounds and can mightily hinder the development of reason,
covetousness, desire for independence. For it uses up an extraordinary
amount of nervous energy, which is thus denied to reflection,
brooding, dreaming, worrying, loving, hating; it sets a small goal
always in sight and guarantees easy and regular satisfactions. Thus a
society in which there is continual hard work will have more security:
and security is now worshipped as the supreme divinity. – And now!
Horror! Precisely the 'worker' has become *dangerous*! The place is
swarming with 'dangerous individuals'! And behind them the
danger of dangers – *the* individual!

174

Moral fashion of a commercial society. – Behind the basic principle of the
current moral fashion: 'moral actions are actions performed out of
sympathy for others', I see the social effect of timidity hiding behind
an intellectual mask: it desires, first and foremost, that *all the dangers*
which life once held should be removed from it, and that *everyone*

should assist in this with all his might: hence only those actions which tend towards the common security and society's sense of security are to be accorded the predicate 'good'. – How little pleasure men must nowadays take in themselves when such a tyranny of timidity prescribes to them their supreme moral law, when they so uncontradictingly allow themselves to be ordered to look away from themselves but to have lynx-eyes for all the distress and suffering that exists elsewhere! Are we not, with this tremendous objective of obliterating all the sharp edges of life, well on the way to turning mankind into *sand*? Sand! Small, soft, round, unending sand! Is that your ideal, you heralds of the sympathetic affections? – In the meantime, the question itself remains unanswered whether one is of *more use* to another by immediately leaping to his side and *helping* him – which help can in any case be only superficial where it does not become a tyrannical seizing and transforming – or by *creating* something out of oneself that the other can behold with pleasure: a beautiful, restful, self-enclosed garden perhaps, with high walls against storms and the dust of the roadway but also a hospitable gate.

175

Fundamental idea of a commercial culture. – Today one can see coming into existence the culture of a society of which *commerce* is as much the soul as personal contest was with the ancient Greeks and as war, victory and justice were for the Romans. The man engaged in commerce understands how to appraise everything without having made it, and to appraise it *according to the needs of the consumer*, not according to his own needs; 'who and how many will consume this?' is his question of questions. This type of appraisal he then applies instinctively and all the time: he applies it to everything, and thus also to the productions of the arts and sciences, of thinkers, scholars, artists, statesmen, peoples and parties, of the entire age: in regard to everything that is made he inquires after supply and demand *in order to determine the value of a thing in his own eyes.* This becomes the character of an entire culture, thought through in the minutest and subtlest detail and imprinted in every will and every faculty: it is this of which you men of the coming century will be proud: if the prophets of the commercial class are right to give it into your possession! But I have little faith in these prophets. *Credat Judaeus Apella* – in the words of Horace.

176

Criticism of our fathers. – Why does one nowadays endure the truth

about even the most recent past? Because there is always a
generation which feels itself to be in opposition to this past and in
criticising it enjoys the first fruits of the feeling of power. Formerly
the new generation wanted, on the contrary, to *found* itself on the
older, and it began to *feel* secure in itself when it did not merely adopt
the views of its fathers but where possible took them more *strictly*.
Criticism of the fathers was then considered wicked: nowadays our
younger idealists *begin* with it.

177
Learning solitude. – O you poor devils in the great cities of world
politics, you gifted young men tormented by ambition who consider
it your duty to pass some comment on everything that happens – and
there is always something happening! Who when they raise the dust
in this way think they are the chariot of history! Who, because they
are always on the alert, always on the lookout for the moment when
they can put their word in, lose all genuine productivity! However
much they may desire to do great work, the profound speechlessness
of pregnancy never comes to them! The event of the day drives them
before it like chaff, while they think they are driving the event – poor
devils! – If one wants to represent a hero on the stage one must not
think of making one of the chorus, indeed one must not even know
how to make one of the chorus.

178
Worn out daily. – These young men lack neither character nor talent
nor industry: but they have never been allowed time to choose a
course for themselves; on the contrary, they have been accustomed
from childhood onwards to being given a course by someone else.
When they were mature enough to be 'sent off into the desert',
something else was done – they were employed, they were purloined
from themselves, they were trained to being *worn out daily* and taught
to regard this as a matter of duty – and now they cannot do without it
and would not have it otherwise. Only these poor beasts of burden
must not be denied their 'holidays' – as they call this idleness-ideal of
an overworked century in which one is for once allowed to laze
about, and be idiotic and childish to one's heart's content.

179
As little state as possible. – Political and economic affairs are not worthy
of being the enforced concern of society's most gifted spirits: such a
wasteful use of the spirit is at bottom worse than having none at all.

They are and remain domains for lesser heads, and others than lesser heads ought not to be in the service of these workshops: better for the machinery to fall to pieces again! But as things now stand, with everybody believing he is obliged to *know* what is taking place here every day and neglecting his own work in order to be continually participating in it, the whole arrangement has become a great and ludicrous piece of insanity. The price being paid for 'universal security' is much too high: and the maddest thing is that what is being effected is the very opposite of universal security, a fact our lovely century is undertaking to demonstrate: as if demonstration were needed! To make society safe against thieves and fireproof and endlessly amenable to every kind of trade and traffic, and to transform the state into a kind of providence in both the good and the bad sense – these are lower, mediocre and in no way indispensable goals which ought not to be pursued by means of the highest instruments *which in any way exist* – instruments which ought to be *saved up* for the highest and rarest objectives! Our age may talk about economy but it is in fact a squanderer: it squanders the most precious thing there is, the spirit.

180

Wars. – The great wars of the present age are the effects of the study of history.

181

Ruling. – Some rule out of a desire to rule; others so as not to be ruled: – to the latter ruling is only the less of two evils.

182

Rough consistency. – It is considered a mark of great distinction when people say 'he is a character!' – which means no more than that he exhibits a rough consistency, a consistency apparent even to the dullest eye! But when a subtler and profounder spirit reigns and is consistent in its more elevated manner, the spectators deny the existence of character. That is why statesmen with cunning usually act out their comedy beneath a cloak of rough consistency.

183

The old and the young. – 'There is something immoral about parliaments' – many continue to think – 'for there one is also allowed to hold views *contrary* to those of the government!' – 'One must always hold the view of a thing commanded by our sovereign lord' – this is the Eleventh Commandment in many an honest old head, especially in northern Germany. One laughs at it as at an out-of-date fashion: but formerly it was morality! Perhaps there will one day be laughter at that which nowadays counts as moral among the younger generation brought up under parliamentary institutions: namely, to set the policy of the party above one's own wisdom and to answer every question of public wellbeing in the way that will produce a favourable wind for the party's sails. 'One must hold the view of a thing demanded by the situation of the party' – this would be the canon of conduct. In the service of this morality men are now prepared for every kind of sacrifice, self-overcoming and martyrdom.

184
The state as a product of the anarchists. – In the lands where man is restrained and subdued there are still plenty of backsliding and unsubdued men: at the present moment they collect in the socialist camps more than anywhere else. If it should happen that they should one day lay down *laws*, then you can be sure they will put themselves in iron chains and practise a fearful discipline: *they know themselves*! And they will endure these laws in the consciousness of having imposed them on themselves – the feeling of power, and of *this* power, is too new and delightful for them not to suffer anything for its sake.

185
Beggars. – Beggars ought to be abolished: for one is vexed at giving to them and vexed at not giving to them.

186
Business people. – Your business – is your greatest prejudice: it ties you to your locality, to the company you keep, to the inclinations you feel. Diligent in business – but indolent in spirit, content with your inadequacy, and with the cloak of duty hung over this contentment: that is how you live, that is how you want your children to live!

187
From a possible future. – Is a state of affairs unthinkable in which the malefactor calls himself to account and publicly dictates his own punishment, in the proud feeling that he is thus honouring the law which he himself has made, that by punishing himself he is exercising his power, the power of the lawgiver; he may have committed an offence, but by voluntarily accepting punishment he raises himself above his offence, he does not only obliterate his offence through freeheartedness, greatness and imperturbability, he

performs a public service as well. – Such would be the criminal of a possible future, who, to be sure, also presupposes a future lawgiving – one founded on the idea 'I submit only to the law which I myself have given, in great things and in small.' There are so many experiments still to make! There are so many futures still to dawn!

188

Food and intoxication. – The peoples are so greatly deceived because they are always *seeking* a deceiver: that is to say, a wine to stimulate their senses. If only they can have *that*, they are quite content with bad bread. Intoxication means more to them than nourishment – this is the bait they will always take! What to them are men chosen from among themselves – though they be the most expert practitioners – compared with glittering conquerors or the grand old princely houses! The man of the people at least has to hold out to them the prospect of conquests and grandeur: perhaps they will then come to believe in him. They always obey, and do more than obey, provided they can at the same time become intoxicated! One cannot even offer them peace and plenty unless it includes the laurel-wreath and its mad-making power. But this mob taste, which *prefers intoxication to food*, by no means originated in the depths of the mob: it was rather transported and transplanted thither, and is only growing up there most persistently and luxuriantly, while it takes its origin in the highest intellects and has flourished in them for millennia. The people is the last *virgin soil* in which this glittering weed can still thrive. – What? And is it to them that politics are to be entrusted? So that they can make of them their daily intoxication?

189

On grand politics. – However much utility and vanity, those of individuals as of peoples, may play a part in *grand politics*: the strongest tide which carries them forward is the *need for the feeling of power*, which from time to time streams up out of inexhaustible wells not only in the souls of princes and the powerful but not least in the lower orders of the people. There comes again and again the hour when the masses are *ready* to stake their life, their goods, their conscience, their virtue so as to acquire that higher enjoyment and as a victorious, capriciously tyrannical nation to rule over other nations (or to think it rules). Then the impulses to squander, sacrifice, hope, trust, to be over-daring and to fantasise spring up in such abundance that the ambitious or prudently calculating prince can let loose a war and cloak his crimes in the good conscience of his people. The great conquerors have always mouthed the pathetic language of virtue: they have had around them masses in a condition of elevation who wanted to hear only the most elevated language. Strange madness of moral judgments! When man possesses the feeling of power he feels and calls himself *good*: and it is precisely then that the others upon whom he has to *discharge* his power feel and call him *evil*! – In the fable of the ages of mankind, Hesiod has depicted the same age, that of the Homeric heroes, twice and made *two ages out of one*: from the point of view of those who had to suffer the terrible iron oppression of these adventurous *Gewaltmenschen*, or had heard of it from their forefathers, it appeared *evil*; but the posterity of this knightly generation revered it as the *good* old happy times. In these circumstances, the poet had no other recourse than to do as he did – for he no doubt had around him auditors of both races!

190

German culture as it used to be. – When the Germans began to be interesting to the other nations of Europe – it happened not all that long ago – it was on account of a culture which they now no longer possess, which they have, indeed, with a blind zeal shaken off as though it had been an illness: and yet they have had nothing better to put in its place than the political and nationalist lunacy. To be sure, they have thereby succeeded in becoming much more interesting to the other nations than they formerly were on account of their culture: and so let them be contented! In the meantime, it cannot be denied that this German culture deluded the Europeans, that it was unworthy of the interest, emulation and imitation it inspired. Let us today take a look at Schiller, Wilhelm von Humboldt, Schleiermacher, Hegel, Schelling, read their correspondence and familiarise ourselves with their large circle of adherents: what do they have in common, what is it in them that seems to us, as we are today, now so insupportable, now so pitiable and moving? First, their thirst for appearing morally *excited* at all cost; then, their desire for brilliant, boneless generalities, together with the intention of seeing everything (characters, passions, ages, customs) in as beautiful a light as possible – 'beautiful', unfortunately, in the sense of a vague and bad taste which nonetheless boasted of a Greek ancestry. It is a soft, good-natured, silver-glistering idealism which wants above all to affect noble gestures and a noble voice, a thing as presumptuous as it is harmless, infused with a heartfelt repugnance for 'cold' or 'dry' reality, for the anatomy, for wholehearted passion, for every kind of philosophical temperance and scepticism, but especially for natural science except when it is amenable to being employed as religious symbolism. Goethe observed these goings-on in his own way: standing aside, gently remonstrating, keeping silent, ever more determined to follow his own, better path. Somewhat later on, Schopenhauer also observed them – to him much of the real world and the devilry of the world had again become visible, and what he had to say of it was as rough and uncouth as it was enthusiastic: for this devilry had its *beauty*! – And what was it that misled foreigners that they did not observe German culture in the way in which Goethe and Schopenhauer did, or simply disregard it? It was the dull lustre, the enigmatic Milky-Way shimmer, that lit up this culture: when they saw it, foreigners said: 'that is very, very distant from us, there our seeing, hearing, understanding, enjoyment, evaluation cease; nonetheless they could be stars! Could it be that the Germans have quietly discovered some corner of the heavens and settled down there? We must try to get closer to the Germans.' And they did get closer: but hardly had they done so when these same Germans began to exert themselves to get rid of this Milky-Way shimmer; they knew too well that they had not been in the heavens – but in a cloud!

191

Better people! – They tell me that contemporary art is directed at the greedy, insatiable, undisciplined, disgusted, harassed men of the present day and exhibits to them a picture of blissful exultation and unworldliness to set beside that of their own dissoluteness: so that they can for once forget themselves and breathe again, perhaps indeed bring back with them out of this forgetting an incitement to flight and reformation. Poor artists who have such a public! Whose hidden intentions have to be half priestly, half psychiatric! How much more fortunate was Corneille – 'our great Corneille', as Madame de Sévigné exclaims in the accents of a woman in the presence of a complete *man* – how much more exalted was *his* audience, whom he could improve with pictures of knightly virtue, stern duty, magnanimous self-sacrifice, the heroic restraining of himself! How differently did he and they love existence: not out of a blind, dissolute 'will' which is cursed because it cannot be killed, but as a place where greatness and humanity are *possible* together and where even the strictest constraint of form, subjection to princely and clerical arbitrariness, can suppress neither the pride, nor the chivalry, nor the charm, nor the spirit of every individual, but is felt rather as an antithetical spur and stimulus to an inborn self-reliance and nobility, to an inherited power of will and passion!

192

The desire for perfect opponents. – One cannot deny that the French have been the *most Christian* nation on earth: not because the faith of the masses has been greater in France than elsewhere, but because the most difficult Christian ideals have there been transformed into men and not remained merely ideas, beginnings, falterings. There stands Pascal, in unity of fervour, spirit and honesty the first of all Christians – and consider what had to be united here! There stands Fénelon, the perfect and dazzling expression of *ecclesiastical culture* in all its strength: a golden mean which, as a historian, one might be inclined to declare something impossible, whereas it was only something unspeakably difficult and improbable. There stand Madame de Guyon and her companions, the French Quietists: and all that the fire and eloquence of the apostle Paul endeavoured to discover in the sublime, loving, silent and enraptured semi-divine state of the Christian has here become truth and, thanks to a genuine, feminine, fine and noble old French naivety in word and gesture, has at the same time put off that Jewish importunity which Paul evidenced towards his God. There stands the founder of the Trappist monasteries, who took the ascetic ideal of Christianity with ultimate seriousness and did so, not as an exception among Frenchmen, but quite typically as a Frenchman: for his gloomy creation has to the present moment been at home and remained potent only among Frenchmen; it followed them to Alsace and into Algiers. Let us not forget the Huguenots: the union of worldliness and industriousness, of more refined customs and Christian severity, has hitherto never been more beautifully represented. And in Port-Royal the great world of Christian scholarship saw its last efflorescence: and in France men understand efflorescence better than elsewhere. In no way superficial, a great Frenchman nonetheless always preserves his surface, a natural skin to cover his content and depths – while the depths of a great German are usually kept enclosed in an intricate capsule, as an elixir which seeks to protect itself against the light and against frivolous hands by the hardness and strangeness of its casing. – And now say why this nation possessing these perfect types of Christianness was bound also to produce perfect counter-types of unchristian free-spiritedness! The French free-spirit struggled within himself against great human beings, and not merely against dogmas and sublime abortions, as did the free-spirits of other nations.

193

Esprit and morality. – The German, who knows the secret of how to make spirit, knowledge and heart boring and has accustomed himself to feeling that boredom is moral, fears of French *esprit* that it may put out the eyes of morality – and yet his fear has in it the fascinated dread of the little bird before the rattlesnake. Of the celebrated Germans, none perhaps possessed more *esprit* than Hegel – but he also possessed so great a German fear of it that this fear was responsible for creating the bad style peculiar to him. For the essence of his style is that a kernel is wrapped round and wrapped round again until it can hardly peep through, bashfully and with inquisitive eyes as 'young women peep through their veils', to quote the ancient misogynist Aeschylus – but this kernel is a witty, often indiscreet inspiration on the most intellectual subjects, a daring and subtle phrase-coinage such as is appropriate to the *society of thinkers* as a condiment to science – but swathed in its wrapping it presents itself as the abstrusest of sciences and altogether a piece of the highest moral boredom! Here the Germans had a form of *esprit permitted* them, and they enjoyed it with such unbridled delight that Schopenhauer's excellent, very excellent understanding was brought up short at it – his whole life long he thundered against the spectacle the Germans presented to him, but he was never able to explain it to himself.

194

Vanity of the teachers of morality. – The slightness of the success which the teachers of morality have had on the whole is to be explained by the fact that they wanted too much at one time; that is to say, that they were too ambitious: they were all too anxious to offer prescriptions *for everybody*. This, however, means to be much too indefinite and to preach at the animals in a bid to turn them into humans! One should seek out limited circles and seek and promote morality for them: preach at wolves, for example, in a bid to turn them into dogs. Great success, however, is reserved above all to him who wants to educate, not everybody or even limited circles, but a single individual, and in doing so looks neither to the right nor the left. The previous century is superior to ours in precisely this, that it contained so many individually educated people, together with just as many individual educators who had here discovered the *task* of their life – and with their task also their *dignity*, in their own eyes and in those of all others of 'good society'.

195

So-called classical education. – To discover that our life is *consecrated* to knowledge; that we would throw it off, no! that we should have thrown it off, if this consecration did not defend it against us; to repeat to ourselves, often and with profound emotion, the lines:

Schicksal, ich *folge* dir! Und wollt ich nicht,
ich *müsst'* es doch und unter Seufzer tun!

– Destiny, I follow thee! And if I would not I should have to nonetheless, though sighing as I did so! – And then to look back on our life and also to discover something that can no longer be made good: the squandering of our youth when our educators failed to employ those eager, hot and thirsty years to lead us towards *knowledge* of things but used them for a so-called 'classical education'! The squandering of our youth when we had a meagre knowledge of the Greeks and Romans and their languages drummed into us in a way as clumsy as it was painful and one contrary to the supreme principle of all education, that one should offer food only to him *who hungers for it*! When we had mathematics and physics forced upon us *instead* of our being led into despair at our ignorance and having our little daily life, our activities, and all that went on at home, in the work-place, in the sky, in the countryside from morn to night, reduced to thousands of problems, to annoying, mortifying, irritating problems – so as to show us that we *needed* a knowledge of mathematics and mechanics, and then to teach us our first *delight* in science through showing us the absolute consistency of this knowledge! If only we had been taught to *revere* these sciences, if only our souls had *even once* been made to tremble at the way in which the great men of the past had struggled and been defeated and had struggled anew, at the martyrdom which constitutes the history of *rigorous* science! What we felt instead was the breath of a certain disdain for the actual sciences in favour of history, of 'formal education' and of 'the classics'! And we let ourselves be deceived so easily! Formal education! Could we not have pointed to the finest teachers at our grammar schools, laughed at them and asked: 'are they the products of formal education? And if not, how can they teach it?' And the classics! Did

115

we learn anything of that which these same ancients taught their
young people? Did we learn to speak or write as they did? Did we
practise unceasingly the fencing-art of conversation, dialectics? Did
we learn to move as beautifully and proudly as they did, to wrestle, to
throw, to box as they did? Did we learn anything of the asceticism
practised by all Greek philosophers? Were we trained in a single one
of the antique virtues and in the manner in which the ancients
practised it? Was all reflection on morality not utterly lacking in our
education – not to speak of the only possible critique of morality, a
brave and rigorous attempt to *live* in this or that morality? Was there
ever aroused in us any feeling that the ancients regarded more highly
than the moderns? Were we ever shown the divisions of the day and
of life, and goals beyond life, in the spirit of antiquity? Did we learn
even the ancient languages in the way we learn those of living nations
– namely, so as to speak them with ease and fluency? Not one real
piece of ability, of new capacity, out of years of effort! Only a
knowledge of what men were once capable of knowing! And what
knowledge! Nothing grows clearer to me year by year than that the
nature of the Greeks and of antiquity, however simple and universally
familiar it may seem to lie before us, is very hard to understand,
indeed is hardly accessible at all, and that the facility with which the
ancients are usually spoken of is either a piece of frivolity or an
inherited arrogance born of thoughtlessness. We are deceived by a
similarity of words and concepts: but behind them there always lies
concealed a sensation which *has to be* foreign, incomprehensible or
painful to modern sensibility. And these are supposed to be
domains in which little boys are allowed to run around! Well, we did
it when we were boys, and we brought back with us an almost
unconquerable repugnance for antiquity, the repugnance aroused
by an apparently too great intimacy! For the proud conceit of our
classics teachers goes so far in imagining they are as it were *in
possession of the ancients* that they transfer this arrogance to their
pupils, together with the suspicion that such a possession, while it
certainly does not make us happy, is good enough for poor, foolish,
honest old book-dragons: 'let these dragons brood over their hoard!
for it will be worthy of them!' – it is with this silent thought that our
classical education is concluded. – This can no longer be made good
– so far as we are concerned! But let us not think only of ourselves!

196
The most personal questions of truth. – 'What am I really *doing*? And why

am *I* doing it?' – that is the question of truth which is not taught in our present system of education and is consequently not asked; we have no time for it. On the other hand, to talk of buffooneries with children and not of the truth, to talk of compliments to women who are later to become mothers and not of the truth, to talk of their future and their pleasures to young people and not of the truth – we always have time and inclination for that! – But what, after all, are seventy years! – they run on and are soon over; it matters so little whether the wave knows how and whither it flows! indeed, it could be a piece of prudence *not to know* it. – 'Admitted: but not even *to ask* after it is not a sign of possessing much pride; our education does not make people proud'. – So much the better. – 'Really?'

197
German hostility to the Enlightenment. – Let us consider the intellectual contribution to general culture made by the Germans of the first half of this century, and let us take first the German philosophers: they retreated to the first and oldest stage of speculation, for, like the thinkers of dreamy ages, they were content with concepts instead of explanations – they brought to life again a pre-scientific species of philosophy. Secondly, the German historians and romantics: their general endeavour was to bring into honour older, primitive sensibilities and especially Christianity, the folk-soul, folk-lore, folk-speech, the medieval world, oriental asceticism, the world of India. Thirdly, the natural scientists: they fought against the spirit of Newton and Voltaire and, like Goethe and Schopenhauer, sought to restore the idea of a divine or diabolical nature suffused with ethical and symbolic significance. The whole great tendency of the Germans was against the Enlightenment and against the revolution in society which was crudely misunderstood as its consequence: piety towards everything that exists sought to translate itself into piety towards everything that ever had existed, to the end that heart and spirit might once more become *full* and no room be left for future and novel goals. The cult of feeling was erected in place of the cult of reason, and the German composers, as artists of the invisible, emotional, fabulous, unsatisfied, built at the new temple more successfully than any of the artists of words or of ideas. Even if we take into account the enormous quantity of individual achievement, and the fact that since that time many things have been judged more fairly than they were before, it must nonetheless be said that there was *no small danger* involved when, under the appearance of attaining

a full and final knowledge of the past, the movement as a whole set knowledge in general below feeling and – in the words Kant employed to designate his own task – 'again paved the way for faith by showing knowledge its limitations'. Let us breathe freely again: the hour of this danger has passed! And strange: it is precisely the spirits the Germans so eloquently conjured up which have in the long run most thwarted the intentions of their conjurers – after appearing for a time as ancillaries of the spirit of obscurantism and reaction, the study of history, understanding of origins and evolutions, empathy for the past, newly aroused passion for feeling and knowledge one day assumed a new nature and now fly on the broadest wings above and beyond their former conjurers as new and stronger genii of *that very Enlightenment* against which they were first conjured up. This Enlightenment we must now carry further forward: let us not worry about the 'great revolution' and the 'great reaction' against it which have taken place – they are no more than the sporting of waves in comparison with the truly great flood which bears *us* along!

198

Those who determine their nation's rank. – To have many great inner experiences and to look down on and beyond them with the eye of the spirit – this is what constitutes the men of culture who determine the *rank* of their nation. In France and Italy it is the nobility who have done this; in Germany, where hitherto the nobility have on the whole been among the poor in spirit (perhaps they will not be so for much longer), it is the priests, teachers and their descendants who have done it.

199

We are nobler. – Loyalty, magnanimity, care for one's reputation: these three united in a single disposition – we call *noble*, and in this quality we excel the Greeks. Let us not abandon it, as we might be tempted to do as a result of feeling that the ancient objects of these virtues have lost in estimation (and rightly), but see to it that this precious inherited drive is applied to new objects. – To grasp how, from the viewpoint of our own aristocracy, which is still chivalrous and feudal in nature, the disposition of even the noblest Greeks has to seem of a lower sort and, indeed, hardly decent, one should recall the words with which Odysseus comforted himself in ignominious situations: 'Endure it, my dear heart! you have already endured the lowest things!' And, as a practical application of this mythical model, one

should add the story of the Athenian officer who, threatened with a
stick by another officer in the presence of the entire general staff,
shook this disgrace from himself with the words: 'Hit me! But also
hear me!' (This was Themistocles, that dextrous Odysseus of the
classical age, who was certainly the man to send down to his 'dear
heart' those lines of consolation at so shameful a moment.) The
Greeks were far from making as light of life and death on account of
an insult as we do under the impress of inherited chivalrous
adventurousness and desire for self-sacrifice; or from seeking out
opportunities for risking both in a game of honour, as we do in
duels; or from valuing a good name (honour) more highly than the
acquisition of a bad name if the latter is compatible with fame and
the feeling of power; or from remaining loyal to their class prejudices
and articles of faith if these could hinder them from becoming
tyrants. For this is the ignoble secret of every good Greek aristocrat:
out of the profoundest jealousy he considers each of his peers to
stand on an equal footing with him, but is prepared at any moment
to leap like a tiger upon his prey, which is rule over them all: what are
lies, murder, treachery, selling his native city, to him then! This
species of man found justice extraordinarily difficult and regarded it
as something nearly incredible; 'the just man' sounded to the Greeks
like 'the saint' does among Christians. But when Socrates went so far
as to say: 'the virtuous man is the happiest man' they did not believe
their ears and fancied they had heard something insane. For when he
pictures the happiest man, every man of noble origin included in the
picture the perfect ruthlessness and devilry of the tyrant who
sacrifices everyone and everything to his arrogance and pleasure.
Among people who secretly revelled in fantasies of this kind of
happiness, respect for the state could, to be sure, not be implanted
deeply enough – but I think that people whose lust for power no
longer rages as blindly as that of those noble Greeks also no longer
require the idolisation of the concept of the state with which that lust
was formerly kept in check.

200
Enduring poverty. – The great advantage of having noble origins is that
it enables one more easily to endure poverty.

201
Future of the aristocracy. – The demeanour adopted by the nobility is an
expression of the fact that the consciousness of power is constantly
playing its charming game in their limbs. A person of aristocratic

habits, man or woman, does not like to fall into a chair as if utterly exhausted; where everybody else makes himself comfortable, when travelling on the railway for example, he avoids leaning against his back; he seems not to get tired if he stands for hours on his feet at court; he orders his house, not with a view to comfort, but in a spacious and dignified manner, as though it were the home of grander (and taller) beings; he responds to a provocation with restraint and a clear head, not as though horrified, crushed, mortified, breathless, in the manner of the plebeian. Just as he knows how to present the appearance of being at all times in possession of high physical strength, so, through maintaining a constant cheerfulness and civility even in painful situations, he also wants to preserve the impression that his soul and spirit are equal to every danger and every surprise. In regard to the passions, an aristocratic culture can resemble either a rider who takes delight in making a passionate proud animal move to the Spanish step – picture the age of Louis XIV – or a rider who feels his horse shoot along under him like a force of nature, horse and rider both on the verge of losing their heads but in enjoyment of the delight of keeping one's head at precisely this point: in both cases the aristocratic *culture* breathes power, and if its customs very often demand merely the semblance of the feeling of power, the impression this game produces on the non-aristocratic, and the spectacle of this impression, nonetheless constantly enhance the actual feeling of superiority. – The incontestable advantage possessed by the culture of the nobility on the basis of this feeling of superiority is now beginning to reveal itself on an even higher level: thanks to the work of our free-spirits, it is now no longer reprehensible for those born and raised in the aristocracy to enter the orders of knowledge and there to obtain more intellectual ordinations, learn higher knightly duties, than any heretofore, and to raise their eyes to the ideal of *victorious wisdom* which no previous age has been free to erect for itself with so good a conscience as the age now about to arrive. And finally: with what is the aristocracy henceforth to occupy itself, now it is becoming daily more apparent that it will be *indecent* to engage in politics? –

202

For the promotion of health. – One has hardly begun to reflect on the physiology of the criminal, and yet one already stands before the irrefutable insight that there exists no essential difference between criminals and the insane: presupposing one *believes* that the *usual*

BOOK III   202

mode of moral thinking is the mode of thinking of *spiritual health*. But no belief is still so firmly believed as this is, and so one should not hesitate to accept the consequence and treat the criminal as a mental patient: not, to be sure, with an arrogant show of being merciful, but with the prudence and goodwill of a physician. He needs a change of air, a change of company, a temporary absence, perhaps he needs to be alone and have a new occupation – very well! Perhaps he himself may find it to his advantage to live for a time in custody, so as to secure protection against himself and against a burdensome *tyrannical drive* – very well! One should place before him quite clearly the possibility and the means of becoming cured (the extinction, transformation, sublimation of this drive), also, if things are that bad, the improbability of a cure; one should offer the opportunity of suicide to the incurable criminal who has become an abomination to himself. Keeping this extremest means of relief in reserve, one should neglect nothing in the effort to restore to the criminal his courage and freedom of heart; one should wipe pangs of conscience from his soul as a matter of cleanliness, and indicate to him how he can make good the harm he has done perhaps to only a single person, and more than make it good, through benefits he could bestow on others and perhaps on the whole community. In all this one should show him the greatest consideration! And especially in allowing him anonymity, or a new name and frequent changes of residence, so that his reputation and his future life shall be as little endangered as possible. At present, to be sure, he who has been injured, irrespective of how this injury is to be made good, will still desire his *revenge* and will turn for it to the courts – and for the time being the courts continue to maintain our detestable criminal codes, with their shopkeeper's scales and the *desire to counterbalance guilt with punishment*: but can we not get beyond this? What a relief it would be for the general feeling of life if, together with the belief in guilt, one also got rid of the old instinct for revenge, and even regarded it as a piece of prudence for the promotion of happiness to join Christianity in blessing one's enemies and *to do good* to those who have offended us! Let us do away with the concept *sin* – and let us quickly send after it the concept *punishment*! May these banished monsters henceforth live somewhere other than among men, if they want to go on living at all and do not perish of disgust with themselves! – In the meantime, consider that the loss which society and the individual sustain through the criminal is of exactly the same kind as the loss they sustain through the invalid: the invalid propagates care and ill-

121

humour, produces nothing, consumes what others produce, requires
attendants, physicians, distractions, and lives off the time and efforts
of the healthy. Nonetheless, we should nowadays describe as
inhuman anyone who for this reason desired to take *revenge* on the
invalid. In earlier days, to be sure, that was what one did; in rude
cultures, and even now among certain savage peoples, the invalid is
in fact treated as a criminal, that is to say as a danger to the
community and the abode of some demonic being who has entered
into his body as the consequence of a guilt he has incurred – here the
rule is: every sick person is a guilty person! And we – are we not yet
ready for the opposite view? can we not yet say: every 'guilty person'
is a sick person? – No, the hour for that has not yet arrived. As yet we
lack above all the physicians for whom that which has hitherto been
called practical morality will have to have been transformed into an
aspect of their science and art of healing; we lack in general that
hungry interest in these things which will one day perhaps arrive in a
way not dissimilar to that *Sturm und Drang* of the religious ecstasies of
earlier times; the churches are not yet in the possession of the
promoters of health; neither our lower nor higher schools yet teach
care of the body or dietary theory; as yet we have no quiet groups of
people pledged to renounce the use of the courts and codes of
punishment; no thinker has yet had the courage to evaluate a society
or an individual according to how many parasites it can endure, nor
has there yet been a founder of a state who has wielded the
ploughshare in the spirit of that generous and mild-hearted dictum:
'if thou wouldst cultivate the land, cultivate it with the plough: then
the bird and the wolf who follow behind the plough shall rejoice in
thee – *all creatures shall rejoice in thee*'.

203
Against bad diet. – To the devil with the meals people make nowadays –
in hotels just as much as where the wealthy classes of society live!
Even when eminent scholars forgather they load their table in the
same way as the banker loads his: on the principle of 'much too
much' and 'lots of different things' – from which it follows that the
food is prepared with a view to its effectiveness rather than its
genuine effect, and stimulating drinks are needed to help banish the
heaviness of brain and stomach which results. To the devil with the
dissoluteness and over-excitability which must generally follow
from this! To the devil with the dreams which must also follow! To
the devil with the arts and books which will be the dessert to such

meals! And let them do as they will: pepper and contradiction or world-weariness will reign in all they do! (The wealthy class in England has need of its Christianity in order to endure its indigestion and headaches.) Finally, to mention what is amusing in the thing and not only what is disgusting, these people are by no means gluttons; our century and its way of always keeping busy has more power over their members than their stomach has: what, then, is the purpose of these meals? – *They are representatives!* Representatives of what, in the name of all the saints? Of rank? – No, of *money*: we no longer possess rank! We are 'individuals'! But money is power, fame, dignity, precedence, influence; the amount of money a man has determines his moral prejudices! No one wants to hide it under a bushel, but no one wants to lay it on the table either; consequently money needs a representative which *can* be laid on the table: and hence the meals they eat! –

204

Danäe and god in gold. – Whence comes this immoderate impatience which nowadays turns a man into a criminal under circumstances which would be more compatible with an opposite tendency? For if one man employs false weights, another burns his house down after he has insured it for a large sum, a third counterfeits coins, if three-quarters of the upper classes indulge in permitted fraud and have the stock exchange and speculations on their conscience: what drives them? Not actual need, for they are not so badly off, perhaps they even eat and drink without a care – but they are afflicted day and night by a fearful impatience at the slow way with which their money is accumulating and by an equally fearful pleasure in and love of accumulated money. In this impatience and this love, however, there turns up again that fanaticism of the *lust for power* which was in former times inflamed by the belief one was in possession of the truth and which bore such beautiful names that one could thenceforth venture to be inhuman *with a good conscience* (to burn Jews, heretics and good books and exterminate entire higher cultures such as those of Peru and Mexico). The means employed by the lust for power have changed, but the same volcano continues to glow, the impatience and the immoderate love demand their sacrifice: and what one formerly did 'for the sake of God' one now does for the sake of money, that is to say, for the sake of that which *now* gives the highest feeling of power and good conscience.

205

Of the people of Israel. – Among the spectacles to which the coming
century invites us is the decision as to the destiny of the Jews of
Europe. That their die is cast, that they have crossed their Rubicon, is
now palpably obvious: all that is left for them is either to become the
masters of Europe or to lose Europe as they once a long time ago lost
Egypt, where they had placed themselves before a similar either-or.
In Europe, however, they have gone through an eighteen-century
schooling such as no other nation of this continent can boast of – and
what they have experienced in this terrible time of schooling has
benefited the individual to a greater degree than it has the community
as a whole. As a consequence of this, the psychological and spiritual
resources of the Jews today are extraordinary; of all those who live in
Europe they are least liable to resort to drink or suicide in order to
escape from some profound dilemma – something the less gifted are
often apt to do. Every Jew possesses in the history of his fathers and
grandfathers a great fund of examples of the coldest self-possession
and endurance in fearful situations, of the subtlest outwitting and
exploitation of chance and misfortune; their courage beneath the
cloak of miserable submission, their heroism in *spernere se sperni*,
surpasses the virtues of all the saints. For two millennia an attempt
was made to render them contemptible by treating them with
contempt, and by barring to them the way to all honours and all that
was honourable, and in exchange thrusting them all the deeper into
the dirtier trades – and it is true that they did not grow cleaner in the
process. But contemptible? They themselves have never ceased to
believe themselves called to the highest things, and the virtues which
pertain to all who suffer have likewise never ceased to adorn them.
The way in which they honour their fathers and their children, the
rationality of their marriages and marriage customs, distinguish
them among all Europeans. In addition to all this, they have known
how to create for themselves a feeling of power and of eternal
revenge out of the very occupations left to them (or to which they
were left); one has to say in extenuation even of their usury that
without this occasional pleasant and useful torturing of those who
despised them it would have been difficult for them to have
preserved their own self-respect for so long. For our respect for
ourselves is tied to our being able to practise requital, in good things
and bad. At the same time, however, their revenge does not easily go
too far: for they all possess the liberality, including liberality of soul,
to which frequent changes of residence, of climate, of the customs of

one's neighbours and oppressors educates men; they possess by far the greatest experience of human society, and even in their passions they practise the caution taught by this experience. They are so sure in their intellectual suppleness and shrewdness that they never, even in the worst straits, need to earn their bread by physical labour, as common workmen, porters, agricultural slaves. Their demeanour still reveals that their souls have never known chivalrous noble sentiments nor their bodies handsome armour: a certain importunity mingles with an often charming but almost always painful submissiveness. But now, since they are unavoidably going to ally themselves with the best aristocracy of Europe more and more with every year that passes, they will soon have created for themselves a goodly inheritance of spiritual and bodily demeanour: so that a century hence they will appear sufficiently noble not to make those they dominate *ashamed* to have them as masters. And that is what matters! That is why it is still too soon for a settlement of their affairs! They themselves know best that a conquest of Europe, or any kind of act of violence, on their part is not to be thought of: but they also know that at some future time Europe may fall into their hands like a ripe fruit if they would only just extend them. To bring that about they need, in the meantime, to distinguish themselves in every domain of European distinction and to stand everywhere in the first rank: until they have reached the point at which they themselves determine what is distinguishing. Then they will be called the inventors and signposts of the nations of Europe and no longer offend their sensibilities. And whither shall this assembled abundance of grand impressions which for every Jewish family constitutes Jewish history, this abundance of passions, virtues, decisions, renunciations, struggles, victories of every kind – whither shall it stream out if not at last into great men and great works! Then, when the Jews can exhibit as their work such jewels and golden vessels as the European nations of a briefer and less profound experience could not and cannot produce, when Israel will have transformed its eternal vengeance into an eternal blessing for Europe: then there will again arrive that seventh day on which the ancient Jewish God may *rejoice* in himself, his creation and his chosen people – and let us all, all of us, rejoice with him!

206

The impossible class. – Poor, happy and independent! – these things can go together; poor, happy and a slave! – these things can also go

together – and I can think of no better news I could give to our
factory slaves: provided, that is, they do not feel it to be in general a
disgrace to be thus used, and *used up*, as a part of a machine and as it
were a stopgap to fill a hole in human inventiveness! To the devil
with the belief that higher payment could lift from them the *essence* of
their miserable condition – I mean their impersonal enslavement!
To the devil with the idea of being persuaded that an enhancement
of this impersonality within the mechanical operation of a new
society could transform the disgrace of slavery into a virtue! To the
devil with setting a price on oneself in exchange for which one ceases
to be a person and becomes a part of a machine! Are you
accomplices in the current folly of the nations – the folly of wanting
above all to produce as much as possible and to become as rich as
possible? What you ought to do, rather, is to hold up to them the
counter-reckoning: how great a sum of *inner* value is thrown away in
pursuit of this external goal! But where is your inner value if you no
longer know what it is to breathe freely? if you no longer possess the
slightest power over yourselves? if you all too often grow weary of
yourselves like a drink that has been left too long standing? if you pay
heed to the newspapers and look askance at your wealthy neighbour,
made covetous by the rapid rise and fall of power, money and
opinions? if you no longer believe in philosophy that wears rags, in
the free-heartedness of him without needs? if voluntary poverty and
freedom from profession and marriage, such as would very well suit
the more spiritual among you, have become to you things to laugh
at? If, on the other hand, you have always in your ears the flutings of
the Socialist pied-pipers whose design is to enflame you with wild
hopes? which bid you *to be prepared* and nothing further, prepared
day upon day, so that you wait and wait for something to happen
from outside and in all other respects go on living as you have always
lived – until this waiting turns to hunger and thirst and fever and
madness, and at last the day of the *bestia triumphans* dawns in all its
glory? – In contrast to all this, everyone ought to say to himself:
'better to go abroad, to seek to become *master* in new and savage
regions of the world and above all master over myself; to keep
moving from place to place for just as long as any sign of slavery
seems to threaten me; to shun neither adventure nor war and, if the
worst should come to the worst, to be prepared for death: all this
rather than further to endure this indecent servitude, rather than to
go on becoming soured and malicious and conspiratorial!' This
would be the right attitude of mind: the workers of Europe ought

henceforth to declare themselves *as a class* a human impossibility and
not, as usually happens, only a somewhat harsh and inappropriate
social arrangement; they ought to inaugurate within the European
beehive an age of a great swarming-out such as has never been seen
before, and through this act of free emigration in the grand manner
to protest against the machine, against capital, and against the choice
now threatening them of being *compelled* to become either the slave of
the state or the slave of a party of disruption. Let Europe be relieved
of a fourth part of its inhabitants! They and it will be all the better for
it! Only in distant lands and in the undertakings of swarming trains
of colonists will it really become clear how much reason and fairness,
how much healthy mistrust, mother Europe has embodied in her
sons – sons who could no longer endure it with the dull old woman
and were in danger of becoming as querulous, irritable and
pleasure-seeking as she herself was. Outside of Europe the virtues of
Europe will go on their wanderings with these workers; and that
which was at home beginning to degenerate into dangerous ill-
humour and inclination for crime will, once abroad, acquire a wild
beautiful naturalness and be called heroism. – Thus a cleaner air
would at last waft over old, over-populated and self-absorbed
Europe! No matter if its 'workforce' should be a little depleted!
Perhaps it may then be recalled that we grew accustomed to needing
many things only when these needs became so *easy* to satisfy – we
shall again relinquish some of them! Perhaps we shall also bring in
numerous *Chinese*: and they will bring with them the modes of life
and thought suitable to industrious ants. Indeed, they might as a
whole contribute to the blood of restless and fretful Europe
something of Asiatic calm and contemplativeness and – what is
probably needed most – Asiatic *perseverance*.

207
The German attitude to morality. – A German is capable of great things,
but it is improbable he will do them: for, as befits a sluggish spirit, he
obeys *whenever he can*. If he is brought to the necessity of standing
alone and throwing off his sluggishness, if he no longer finds it
possible to disappear as a cipher in an addition (in this quality he is
not nearly as valuable as a Frenchman or an Englishman) – he
discovers his strength: then he becomes dangerous, evil, profound,
daring and brings into the light of the day the sleeping hoard of
energy he carries within him and in which no one (not even he
himself) had believed. When in such an event a German obeys

himself – this is very exceptional – he does so with the same ponderousness, inexorability and endurance with which he formerly obeyed his prince and his official obligations: so that, as aforesaid, he is then capable of *great* things which stand in no kind of relation to the 'weak character' he supposed he had. Usually, however, he is afraid of depending *on himself alone*, of *improvising*: that is why Germany uses up so many officials and so much ink. – He is a stranger to frivolity, being too timid for it; but in quite novel situations which draw him out of his drowsiness he is almost frivolous; he then enjoys the unfamiliarity of the novel situation as a kind of intoxication, and he understands intoxication! So it is that at present the German is always frivolous in the realm of politics: although it is of course supposed that here too he is, as always, serious and thorough – a supposition of which he amply avails himself in his dealings with other political powers – in secret he is full of high spirits at being for once permitted to be enthusiastic and capricious and innovative, and to exchange persons, parties and prospects as if they were masks. – German scholars, who have hitherto had the reputation of being the most German of Germans, were and perhaps are the equal of German soldiers in their profound, almost childlike tendency to obedience in all external things and in the constraint they are under often to stand alone and be answerable for many things in the realm of scholarship; if they know how to preserve their qualities of pride, simplicity and patience, and their freedom from political folly, in times when the wind blows all in the other direction, great things may still be expected of them: such as they are (or were), they are the embryos of something *higher*. – The advantage and disadvantage of the Germans, and even of their scholars, has hitherto been that they are more inclined to superstition and the desire to believe than are other peoples; their vices are, as they have always been, drunkenness and a tendency to suicide (a sign of the ponderousness of their spirit, which can easily be persuaded to throw down the reins); their danger lies in everything that suppresses the reasoning faculties and unchains the emotions (as, for example, the immoderate use of music and spirituous drinks): for, in a German, emotion is directed against his own advantage and is self-destructive like that of a drunkard. Enthusiasm itself is worth less in Germany than elsewhere, for it is unfruitful. Whenever a German did anything great, he did it because he was obliged to do it, in a state of bravery, with clenched teeth, the tensest reflection and often with magnanimity. – They are certainly worth cultivating – for almost every German has something to *give* if one understands how to make him *find* it, *recover* it (the

German is disorderly in himself). – – Now, if a nation of this sort concerns itself with morality, what morality will it be that will satisfy it? The first thing it will certainly require is that in this morality its heartfelt inclination to obedience shall appear idealised. 'Man has to have something which he can *obey unconditionally*' – that is a German sensation, a German piece of consistency: it is to be encountered at the basis of all German moral teaching. How different an impression we receive from the whole morality of antiquity! All those Greek thinkers, however varied they may appear to us as individuals, seem as moralists like a gymnastics teacher who says to his pupil: 'Come! Follow me! Submit to my discipline! Then perhaps you will succeed in carrying off a prize before all the Hellenes.' Personal distinction – that is antique virtue. To submit, to follow, openly or in secret – that is German virtue. – Long before Kant and his categorical imperative, Luther had, out of the same sensibility, said that there must exist a being in which man could have unconditional trust – it was his *proof of the existence of God*; coarser and grounded more in the people than Kant, he wanted man unconditionally to obey, not a concept, but a person; and Kant, too, made a detour around morality only in order in the end to arrive at *obedience to the person*: precisely this is the cult of the Germans, and is increasingly so the less is left to them of the religious cult. The Greeks and Romans felt differently, and would have mocked at such a statement as '*there must* exist a being': it pertained to their southerly freedom of feeling to ward off any 'unconditional trust' and to keep back in the last recess of their heart a little scepticism for all and everything, whether god or man or concept. Not to speak of the philosopher of antiquity! *Nil admirari* – in this sentence he sees the whole of philosophy. And a German, namely Schopenhauer, went so far in the other direction as to say: *admirari id est philosophari*. – But now, what if the German should for once, as does sometimes happen, get into the state in which he is capable of great things? when the *exceptional* hour, the hour of disobedience, strikes? – I do not believe Schopenhauer was right when he said that the sole advantage the Germans had over other nations was that there were more atheists among them than elsewhere – but I know that, when the German gets into the state in which he is capable of great things, *he always raises himself above morality*! And how should he not? He now has something novel he has to do, namely to command – himself or others! But his German morality has not taught him commanding! German morality forgot to do so!

BOOK IV

208

Question of conscience. – 'And in *summa*: what is it you really want changed?' – We want to cease making causes into sinners and consequences into executioners.

209

The utility of the most rigorous theories. – One overlooks many moral weaknesses in a man, employing in this a coarse sieve, *provided* he is a constant adherent of the most rigorous *theory of morality!* On the other hand, the lives of free-spirited moralists have always been put under the microscope: the rationale of this procedure is that a blunder in life is the surest argument against an unwelcome insight.

210

The 'in itself'. – Formerly we asked: what is the laughable? as though there were things external to us to which the laughable adhered as a quality, and we exhausted ourselves in suggestions (one theologian even opined that it was 'the naivety of sin'.) Now we ask: what is laughter? How does laughter originate? We have thought the matter over and finally decided that there is nothing good, nothing beautiful, nothing sublime, nothing evil in itself, but that there are states of soul in which we impose such words upon things external to and within us. We have again *taken back* the predicates of things, or at least remembered that it was we who *lent* them to them: – let us take care that this insight does not deprive us of the *capacity* to lend, and that we have not become at the same time *richer* and *greedier*.

211

To the dreamers of immortality. – So you want this lovely consciousness of yourself *to last forever*? Is that not immodest? Are you not mindful of all the other things which would then be obliged to *endure you* to all eternity, as they have endured you up to now with a more than Christian patience? Or do you think to inspire them with an everlasting sense of pleasure at your existence? A single immortal man on earth would be enough to drive everything else on earth to a universal rage for death and suicide out of *satiety with him*! And you earth-dwellers, with your petty conception of a couple of thousand little minutes, want to burden eternal existence with yourselves everlastingly! Could anything be more importunate! Finally: let us be indulgent towards a being of a mere seventy years! – he has not been able to imagine the 'everlasting boredom' he *himself* would experience – he has not had enough time to do so!

212

What one knows of oneself. – As soon as one animal sees another it
measures itself against it in its mind, and men in barbarous ages did
likewise. From this it follows that every man comes to know himself
almost solely in regard to his powers of defence and attack.

213

Men whose lives have failed. – Some are of such *material* that society may
be allowed to *make* this or that of them: they will fare well whatever is
done with them and never have to bewail a life of failure. Others are
of so special a material – it does not have to be a specially noble
material, only an unusual one – that they are certain to fare ill unless
they are able to live according to the single purpose of their life: – if
they cannot do that, society will suffer as a consequence. For
whenever the individual feels that his life is a failure, he puts the
responsibility for his burden of ill-humour, paralysis, sickness,
irritability, dissatisfaction on to the shoulders of society – and thus
there forms around it a bad, sultry atmosphere and, in the most
favourable case, a thundercloud.

214

Why forbearance? – You suffer, and demand that we should be
forbearing towards you when as a result of your suffering you do
wrong to things and to men! But what does our forbearance matter!
You, however, ought to be *more cautious* for your own sake! What a
fine way of compensating for your suffering it is to go on and *destroy
your own judgment*! Your revenge rebounds upon you yourself when
you defame something; it is your *own* eye you dim, not that of
another: you accustom yourself to *seeing distortedly*!

215

Morality of sacrificial beasts. – 'Enthusiastic devotion', 'sacrifice of
oneself' – these are the catchwords of your morality, and I can readily
believe that you are, as you say, 'in earnest about it': but I know you
better than you know yourselves when your 'earnestness' is able to
walk arm in arm with such a morality. From the heights of this
morality you look down on that other sober morality which
demands self-control, severity, obedience, and even call it egoistic.
And, to be sure – you *are* being in earnest with yourselves when you
find it disagreeable – you *must* find it disagreeable! for by devoting
yourselves with enthusiasm and making a sacrifice of yourselves you
enjoy the ecstatic thought of henceforth being at one with the

powerful being, whether a god or a man, to whom you dedicate
yourselves: you revel in the feeling of his power, to which your very
sacrifice is an additional witness. The truth of the matter is that you
only *seem* to sacrifice yourselves: in reality you transform yourselves
in thought into gods and enjoy yourselves as such. From the point of
view of this enjoyment – how poor and weak seems to you that
'egoistic' morality of obedience, duty, rationality: it is disagreeable to
you because in this case real sacrifice and devotion are demanded
without the sacrificer supposing himself transformed into a god. In
short, it is *you* who want intoxication and excess, and that morality
you despise raises its finger *against* intoxication and excess – I can
well believe you find it disagreeable!

216
Evil men and music. – Could the full happiness of love, which resides in
unconditional trust, ever have been experienced by anyone who was
not profoundly mistrustful, evil and embittered? For these enjoy in
it the tremendous, unbelieved and unbelievable *exception* in the state
of their soul! One day they are overcome by that limitless, dreamlike
sensation which stands in such contrast to their whole life, hidden
and visible, hitherto: like a precious miracle and enigma, suffused
with a golden glory and quite beyond description. Unconditional
trust makes one dumb; indeed, there is a suffering and an oppression
in this happy dumbness, which is why such souls weighed down with
happiness are usually more grateful to *music* than other and better
people are: for through music, as though through a coloured mist,
they see and hear their love as it were grown *more distant*, more
moving and less oppressive; music is the only means they have of
observing their extraordinary condition and for the first time taking of
it a view informed with a kind of alienation and relief. Everyone who
is in love thinks when he hears music: 'it is speaking of me, it is
speaking in my stead, *it knows everything!*'

217
The artist. – Through the artist the Germans want to achieve a kind of
imagined passion; the Italians want to rest from their real passions;
the French want an opportunity to display their judgment and an
occasion for talking. Therefore let us be fair!

218
To deploy one's weaknesses like an artist. – If we are bound to have
weaknesses, and are also bound in the end to recognise them as a law

set over us, then I would wish that everyone had at any rate sufficient artistic power to set off his weaknesses against his virtues and through his weaknesses make us desire his virtues: the power possessed in so exceptional a degree by the great composers. How frequently there is in Beethoven's music a coarse, obstinate, impatient tone, in Mozart's a joviality of humble fellows who have to be content with little, in Richard Wagner's a convulsive and importunate restlessness at which even the most patient listener begins to lose his composure: at *that* point, however, he reasserts his power, and so with the others; by means of their weaknesses they have all produced in us a ravenous hunger for their virtues and a ten times more sensitive palate for every drop of musical spirit, musical beauty, musical goodness.

219

Deception in self-humiliation. – Through your irrational behaviour you have done your neighbour great harm and destroyed an irrecoverable happiness – and then you subdue your vanity sufficiently to go to him, expose your irrationality to his contempt and believe that after this painful and to you very difficult scene everything has again been put to rights – that your voluntary loss of honour compensates for his involuntary loss of happiness: suffused with this feeling you go away uplifted and restored in your virtue. But your neighbour is still as unhappy as he was before, he derives no consolation from the fact that you are irrational and have admitted it, he even remembers the painful sight of you pouring contempt upon yourself before him as a fresh injury for which he has to thank you – but he has no thought of revenge and cannot grasp how you could in any way *compensate* him. At bottom that scene you performed was performed before yourself and for the sake of yourself: you invited in a witness of it, again for your own sake and not for his – do not deceive yourself!

220

Dignity and timidity. – Ceremonies, garb of rank and office, earnest deportment, solemn stare, slow pace of walking, convoluted speech, and everything else that is called dignity is the form of disguise adopted by those who are at bottom timid – their purpose is to make people afraid (of themselves or of that which they represent). The fearless – that is to say originally the constantly and incontestably fearsome – have no need of dignity and ceremonies; they bring honesty, straightforwardness in word and gesture, into repute, and even more into disrepute, as signs of self-confident fearsomeness.

221
Morality of sacrifice. – The morality which assesses itself according to
degrees of sacrifice is morality at the half-savage stage. Reason here
gains only a hard and bloody victory within the soul, powerful
counter-drives have to be subdued; without such cruelties as the
sacrifices demanded by cannibal gods this victory will not be won.

222
When fanaticism is desirable. – Phlegmatic natures can be inspired to
enthusiasm only by being made into fanatics.

223
The eye that is feared. – Nothing is feared more by artists, poets and
writers than that eye which sees their *petty deceit*, which afterwards
perceives how often they have stood at the crossroads where the way
leads either to an innocent pleasure in themselves or to the
production of effects; which can tell when they have wanted to sell
little in exchange for much, when they have sought to bedeck and
exalt without themselves being exalted; which sees through all the
deception of their art the idea as it was when it first stood before
them, perhaps as an entrancing being of light but perhaps too as a
theft from the rest of the world, an everyday idea which they had to
stretch, shorten, colour, swathe up, season, so as to make something
of it instead of letting it make something of them – oh this eye, which
beholds all the unrest, the greedy spying around, the imitation and
outbidding (this last only an envious imitation) that fills your works,
which knows your blushes as well as it knows the art with which you
conceal this blush and reinterpret it to yourselves!

224
What is 'elevating' in our neighbour's misfortune. – He has experienced a
misfortune, and now the 'compassionate' come along and depict his
misfortune for him in detail   at length they go away content and
elevated: they have gloated over the unfortunate man's distress and
over their own and passed a pleasant afternoon.

225
How to make yourself despised quickly. – A man who says a lot and says it
quickly sinks extraordinarily low in our estimation after even the
briefest acquaintanceship and even if he talks sense – not merely to
the degree that he is burdensome to us but much lower than that.
For we divine to how many men he has already been a burden, and
add to the ill-humour he creates the contempt in which we suppose
he is generally held.

226

On associating with celebrities. – A: But why do you avoid this great man?
– B: I would not want to misunderstand him! Our failings are not
compatible with one another: I am short-sighted, and he is as glad to
wear his false diamonds as he is his genuine ones.

227

The enchained. – Beware of all spirits that lie in chains! Of clever
women, for example, whom fate has confined to a petty, dull
environment, and who grow old there. It is true they lie apparently
sluggish and half-blind in the sunlight: but at every unfamiliar step,
at everything unexpected, they start up and bite; they take their
revenge on everything that has escaped from their dog-kennel.

228

Revenge in praise. – Here is a page written all over with praise, and you
call it shallow: but when you divine that revenge lies concealed
within this praise you will find it almost too subtle and take great
pleasure in the abundance of little bold strokes and figures. It is not
man but his revenge that is so subtle, rich and inventive he himself is
hardly aware of it.

229

Pride. – Ah, none of you knows the feeling the man who has been
tortured has after the torture is over and he is carried back to his cell
and his secret with him! – he is still clinging to it with his teeth. What
do you know of the rejoicing of human pride!

230

'Utilitarian'. – Moral sensibilities are nowadays at such cross-purposes
that to one man a morality is proved by its utility, while to another its
utility refutes it.

231

Of German virtue. – How degenerate in its taste, how slavish before
dignities, classes, decorations, pomp and splendour, must a people
have been when it evaluated the *Schlichte* [the simple] as the *Schlechte*
[the bad], the simple man as the bad man! The moral arrogance of
the Germans should always be confronted with this little word
'schlecht': nothing further is needed.

232

From a disputation. – A: Friend, you have talked yourself hoarse! –
B: Then I am refuted. Let us speak of it no more!

233

The 'conscientious'. – Have you taken note of what kind of people lay most stress on the strictest conscientiousness? Those who are aware within themselves of many pitiable sensations, who think of themselves with anxiety and of others with fear, who want to conceal what they are within as completely as possible – through the impression of severity and harshness which others (especially subordinates) must receive through the strict conscientiousness and rigorous attention to duty they exhibit, they are trying *to impress themselves*.

234

Dread of fame. – A: People have avoided fame, have deliberately offended him who praises them, have shrunk from listening to what is said of them from dread of praise – that, believe it or not, *has actually happened*! – B: I do believe it! Only exercise a little patience, my haughty friend!

235

Refusing gratitude. – One may well refuse a request, but one must never refuse gratitude (or, what comes to the same thing, receive it coldly or conventionally). To do so is very wounding – and why?

236

Punishment. – A strange thing, our kind of punishment! It does not cleanse the offender, it is no expiation: on the contrary, it defiles more than the offence itself.

237

Party in trouble. – A ludicrous difficulty, but one not without peril, arises in almost every party: all those who have for many years been the faithful and honest champions of the party's policy one day suddenly notice that one far mightier than they has taken the trumpet into his hand. How could they endure to be reduced to silence! And so they make a loud noise, and sometimes play a new tune.

238

The striving for charm. – If a strong nature is not inclined to cruelty and is not always occupied with itself, it involuntarily strives after *charm* – this is its characteristic sign. Weak characters, on the other hand, love harsh judgments – they ally themselves with the heroes of misanthropy, with the religious or philosophical blackeners of existence, or withdraw behind stern customs and demanding 'life-tasks': thus they try to create for themselves a character and a kind of strength. And this they likewise do involuntarily.

239

Hint for moralists. – Our composers have made a great discovery: *interesting ugliness* too is possible in their art! And so they throw themselves into this open ocean of ugliness as if drunk, and it has never been so easy to compose music. It is only now that a general dark-coloured background has been gained against which a ray of beautiful music, however paltry, acquires the lustre of gold and emerald, only now does the composer venture to put the listener through storm and tumult, and out of breath, *so as* afterwards to offer him, through a moment of repose, a feeling of happiness which has a favourable influence on his judgment of the music as a whole. Composers have discovered contrast: only now are the most powerful effects possible – and *cheap*: no one asks for good music any more. But you will have to hurry! Every art which has made this discovery has turned out to have only a short time left to live. – Oh, if only our thinkers had ears, that they might hear into the souls of our composers by means of their music! How long it will be before there occurs another such opportunity of catching the inner man in the evil act and in the innocence of this act! For our composers have not the least suspicion that what they are setting to music is their own history, the history of the soul made ugly. Formerly a composer was almost obliged to become a good man for the sake of his art – . And now!

240

On the morality of the stage. – Whoever thinks that Shakespeare's theatre has a moral effect, and that the sight of Macbeth irresistibly repels one from the evil of ambition, is in error: and he is again in error if he thinks Shakespeare himself felt as he feels. He who is really possessed by raging ambition beholds this its image with *joy*; and if the hero perishes by his passion this precisely is the sharpest spice in the hot draught of this joy. Can the poet have felt otherwise? How royally, and not at all like a rogue, does his ambitious man pursue his course from the moment of his great crime! Only from then on does he exercise 'demonic' attraction and excite similar natures to emulation – demonic means here: in defiance *against* life and advantage for the sake of a drive and idea. Do you suppose that Tristan and Isolde are preaching *against* adultery when they both perish by it? This would be to stand the poets on their head: they, and especially Shakespeare,

are enamoured of the passions as such and not least of their *death-welcoming* moods – those moods in which the heart adheres to life no more firmly than does a drop of water to a glass. It is not the guilt and its evil outcome they have at heart, Shakespeare as little as Sophocles (in Ajax, Philoctetes, Oedipus): as easy as it would have been in these instances to make guilt the lever of the drama, just as surely has this been avoided. The tragic poet has just as little desire to take sides *against* life with his images of life! He cries rather: 'it is the stimulant of stimulants, this exciting, changing, dangerous, gloomy and often sun-drenched existence! It is an *adventure* to live – espouse what party in it you will, it will always retain this character!' – He speaks thus out of a restless, vigorous age which is half-drunk and stupefied by its excess of blood and energy – out of a wickeder age than ours is: which is why we need first to *adjust* and *justify* the goal of a Shakespearean drama, that is to say, not to understand it.

241

Fear and intelligence. – If it is true, as is now most definitely asserted, that the cause of black skin pigmentation is *not* to be sought in the action of light, could it perhaps not be the ultimate effect of frequent attacks of rage (and undercurrents of blood beneath the skin) accumulated over thousands of years? While with the other, *more intelligent* races an equally frequent terror and growing pallid has finally resulted in white skin? – For degree of timidity is a measure of intelligence, and frequently to give way to blind rage a sign that animality is still quite close and would like to take over again. – Thus the original colour of man would probably have been a brownish grey – somewhat like the ape and the bear, as seems proper.

242

Independence. – Independence (in its weakest dosage called 'freedom of thought') is the form of renunciation to which the man thirsting to rule at last accedes – the man who has for long been seeking that which he could rule over and has found nothing but himself.

243

The two directions. – When we try to examine the mirror in itself we discover in the end nothing but things upon it. If we want to grasp the things we finally get hold of nothing but the mirror. – This, in the most general terms, is the history of knowledge.

244

Joy in reality. – Our present tendency to feel joy in reality – we almost all of us have it – can be understood only from the fact that in the past we felt joy in unreality for so long we became satiated with it. In itself, and as it appears at present, involuntarily and without refinement, it is a tendency of which it is not possible wholly to approve: – tastelessness is the least of the dangers it presents.

245

Subtlety of the feeling of power. – Napoleon was annoyed at his inability to speak well, and he did not deceive himself in this matter: but his lust for domination, which neglected no opportunity and was subtler than his subtle intellect, persuaded him into speaking worse *than he could.* Thus he revenged himself on his own annoyance (he was jealous of all his affects because they possessed *power*) and felt the enjoyment of exercising his autocratic *pleasure.* And he enjoyed this same pleasure once more in regard to the ears and judgment of his hearers: as though to be spoken to in this way was quite good enough for them. Indeed, he secretly rejoiced in the thought that, through the thunder and lightning of supreme authoritativeness – the authoritativeness which derives from the union of power and genius – he was confusing judgment and misleading taste: while his own judgment and taste adhered coldly and proudly to the truth that he spoke *badly.* – As the personification of a single drive worked through to the end with perfect consistency, Napoleon belongs to the mankind of antiquity: its characteristic signs – the simple construction and the inventive elaboration and variation of a single motif or of a few motifs – can easily be recognised in him.

246

Aristotle and marriage. – In the children of men of great genius madness breaks out, in the children of men of great virtue, stupidity – says Aristotle. Was his object in saying this to persuade exceptional men to get married?

247

Origin of intemperateness. – The lack of just judgment and consistency in the temperament of many people, the disorderliness and immoderation which characterises them, is the ultimate consequence of the countless logical inaccuracies, superficialities and rash conclusions of which their ancestors were guilty. Temperate people, on the other hand, are the descendants of reflective and unsuperficial races who set great store by rationality – whether for praiseworthy or evil ends is of no great moment.

248

Dissimulation as a duty. – Goodness has mostly been developed by the
protracted dissimulation which sought to appear as goodness:
wherever great power existed men saw the necessity for precisely this
kind of dissimulation – it inspired a feeling of trust and security and
multiplied the sum of actual physical power a hundredfold. The lie
is, if not the mother, then the nurse of goodness. Honesty has
likewise been reared mostly by the requirement to seem honest: it
happened within the hereditary aristocracies. What is dissimulated
for a long time at last becomes *nature*: dissimulation in the end
sublimates itself, and organs and instincts are the surprising fruit of
the garden of hypocrisy.

249

Who is ever alone? – The timid man does not know what it is to be
alone: an enemy is always standing behind his chair. – Oh, if there
were someone who could tell us the history of that subtle feeling
called solitude!

250

Night and music. – The ear, the organ of fear, could have evolved as
greatly as it has only in the night and twilight of obscure caves and
woods, in accordance with the mode of life of the age of timidity, that
is to say the longest human age there has ever been: in bright daylight
the ear is less necessary. That is how music acquired the character of
an art of night and twilight.

251

Stoical. – There is a cheerfulness peculiar to the Stoic: he experiences
it whenever he feels hemmed in by the formalities he himself has
prescribed for his conduct; he then enjoys the sensation of himself as
dominator.

252

Reflect! – He who is punished is never he who performed the deed.
He is always the scapegoat.

253

What is manifest. – Oh dear, oh dear! What has to be demonstrated
most clearly and with the most obstinate persistence is what is
manifest. For all too many lack the eyes to see it. But demonstration
is so boring!

254

Anticipators. – The distinguishing, but also perilous quality in poetic natures is their *exhaustive* imagination: they anticipate, enjoy and suffer in advance that which is to come or could come, so that when it finally does come they are already *tired* of it. Lord Byron, who was only too familiar with all this, wrote in his diary: 'If I have a son he shall become something quite prosaic – a lawyer or a pirate.'

255

Conversation about music. – A: What have you to say about this music? – B: It has overcome me, I have nothing at all to say about it. Listen! They are playing it again! – A: So much the better! Let us see to it that this time *we* overcome *it*. May I say a few words about this music? And may I also show you a drama which you may not have noticed at first hearing? – B: Very well! I have two ears, and more if need be. Come up close to me! – A: What we hear now is not yet what *he* wants to say to us: up to now he has only been promising that he will say something and, as by these gestures he intends to indicate, something unheard-of. For they are gestures. How he beckons! draws himself up! throws out his arms! And now he seems to have reached the supreme moment of tension: two more fanfares and he introduces his theme, splendid and adorned, as though jingling with precious stones. Is it a beautiful woman? or a beautiful horse? Enough: he looks around him in delight, for his task is to assemble delighted looks – only now is he wholly satisfied with his theme, only now does he become inventive, venture on bold and novel strokes. How he expands his theme! Ah! Pay attention – he knows not only how to decorate it but also how to *colour* it! Yes, he knows what colour health is, he understands how to make it appear – he is more subtle in his self-knowledge than I thought. And now he is convinced that he has convinced his hearers, he presents his ideas as though they were the most important things under the sun, he points shamelessly at his theme as though it were too good for this world. – Ha, how mistrustful he is! He is afraid we might get tired! So now he showers his melodies with sugar – now he appeals even to our coarser senses so as to excite us and thus again get us into his power. Hear how he conjures up the elemental forces of stormy and thunderous rhythms! And now, when he has seen that these forces have seized hold of us, throttled and almost crushed us, he ventures to introduce his theme into this play of the elements and to *convince* us, half-stupefied and shattered as we are, that our stupefaction and convulsion are the effect of his miraculous theme. And thenceforth his hearers believe it is so: as soon as they hear the theme there arises within them a recollection of that shattering elemental effect – this recollection then benefits the theme, it has now become 'demonic'! How well he understands the soul! He rules over us with the arts of a demagogue! – But the music has stopped! – B: And just as well! For I can no longer endure to listen to *you*! I would ten times rather *let myself be deceived* than *once* know the truth after your fashion! – A: This is what I wanted to hear from you. As you are, so are even the best nowadays: you are content to let yourselves be deceived! You come with coarse and lustful ears, you no longer bring the conscience of the art of hearing with you, on the way here you have thrown away the *finest part of your honesty!* And by doing this you ruin art and artists! Whenever you cheer and clap you have the artists' conscience in your hands – and alas if they notice you are incapable of distinguishing between innocent music and guilty music! I do not mean between 'good' and 'bad' music – both species include both good and bad music. What I mean by *innocent music* is music which thinks wholly and solely of itself, believes in itself and has forgotten the world in contemplation of itself – the self-resounding of the profoundest solitude, which speaks to itself of itself and no longer knows that outside there are hearers and listeners and effects and failures. – Finally: the music we have just heard *is* of this noble and rare species, and everything I said about it was lyingly invented – forgive me my wickedness, if you feel inclined to do so! – B: Oh, then you love *this* music too? Then many sins are forgiven you!

256
Happiness of the evil. – These silent, gloomy, evil men possess something that you cannot deny them, a strange and rare enjoyment of the *dolce far niente*, an evening and sunset repose such as is known only to a heart that is all too often consumed, lacerated and poisoned by passions.

257
Words present in us. – We always express our thoughts with the words that lie to hand. Or, to express my whole suspicion: we have at any moment only the thought for which we have to hand the words.

258
Patting the dog. – This dog needs to be stroked only once: he is

145

immediately ignited and throws off sparks, like any other flatterer –
and he is clever in his own way. Why should we not put up with him?

259

The former panegyrist. – 'He has ceased to talk about me, although he
now knows the truth and could tell it. But it would sound like
revenge – and he has such respect for truth, the honourable man!'

260

Amulet of the dependent. – He who is unavoidably dependent on a
patron ought to have something by means of which he inspires fear
in his patron and keeps him in check: integrity, for instance, or
sincerity, or a wicked tongue.

261

Why so exalted! – Oh, I know these beasts! To be sure, they like
themselves better when they stalk around on two legs 'like a god' –
but when they have fallen back on to their four legs *I* like them better:
this posture is so incomparably more natural!

262

The demon of power. – Not necessity, not desire – no, the love of power is
the demon of men. Let them have everything – health, food, a place
to live, entertainment – they are and remain unhappy and low-
spirited: for the demon waits and waits and will be satisfied. Take
everything from them and satisfy this, and they are almost happy – as
happy as men and demons can be. But why do I repeat this? Luther
has said it already, and better than I, in the verses: 'Let them take
from us our body, goods, honour, children, wife: let it all go – the
kingdom [*Reich*] must yet remain to us!' Yes! Yes! The *'Reich'*!

263

Contradiction in body and soul. – There exists a physiological contradiction
in the so-called genius: on the one hand he is informed with much
wild, disorderly, involuntary agitation, and on the other with much
purposiveness in this agitation – at the same time he represents a
mirror which reflects both kinds of agitation side by side and
intertwined, but also often enough in conflict. As a consequence of
this spectacle he is often unhappy, and when he is feeling at his best,
when he is creating, he does so because he forgets that he is at
precisely this time doing – and is bound to be doing – something
fantastic and irrational (which is what all art is) but with the highest
degree of purposiveness.

264

The desire to be mistaken. – Envious people with subtler sensibilities try to avoid getting to know their rival more closely so as to be able to feel superior to him.

265

There is a time for the theatre. – If a people's imagination grows weak there arises in it the inclination to have its legends presented to it on the stage: it can now *endure* these crude substitutes for imagination. But for those ages to which the epic rhapsodist belongs the theatre and the actor disguised as a hero is a hindrance to imagination rather than a means of giving it wings: too close, too definite, too heavy, too little in it of dream and bird-flight.

266

Without charm. – He lacks charm and knows it: oh, how well he understands how to mask this fact with strict virtue, with gloomy aspect, with affected mistrust of men and existence, with hollow jests, with contempt for a more refined mode of life, with pathos and pretensions, with cynical philosophy – constant awareness of his lack has, indeed, made of him a character.

267

Why so proud! – A noble character is distinguished from a common one in *not possessing* a number of habits and points of view which the latter does possess: he chances not to have inherited or acquired them.

268

The Scylla and Charybdis of the speaker. – How difficult it was in Athens to speak in such a way as to win one's hearers *for* one's cause without repelling them *through the form* in which one spoke or drawing them *away* from one's cause with it! How difficult it still is in France to write in this way!

269

Art and the sick. – To counter any kind of affliction or distress of soul one ought in the first instance to try change of diet and hard physical labour. But in these cases men are accustomed to resort to means of intoxication: to art, for example – to the detriment of themselves and of art as well! Do you not realise that if you demand art when you are sick you make sick the artists?

270

Apparent toleration. – You speak fair words about science, but! – I see *behind* your toleration of science! In a corner of your heart you believe, all this notwithstanding, that *you do not need it*, that you are being magnanimous in according it recognition, in being indeed its advocate, especially since science does not exhibit the same magnanimity in regard to your views on life. Do you realise that you have no right whatever to this exercise of toleration? that this gracious demeanour is a cruder insult to science than the open mockery of it which some arrogant priest or artist permits himself? You lack the strict conscience for what is true and actual, it does not torment you to find science in conflict with your feelings, you do not know a greedy longing for knowledge as a law ruling over you, you do not feel it as a duty to desire to be present as a witness *wherever* knowledge is present and to let nothing already known escape again. You *do not know* that which you treat so tolerantly! And it is only *because* you do not know it that you are able to adopt so gracious a demeanour! You, precisely you would glare in bitter and fanatical hostility if science should ever look you straight in the face with *its* eyes! – What do we care, then, if you practise toleration – towards a *phantom*! and not even towards us! And what do we matter!

271

The festive mood. – It is to precisely those people who strive most hotly after power that it is indescribably pleasant to feel themselves *overcome*! Suddenly and deeply to sink into a feeling as into a whirlpool! To let the reins be torn from one's grasp and to look on at a movement going who knows where! Whoever it may be, whatever it may be, that does us this service – it is a great service: we are so happy and breathless and feel around us an exceptional silence, as though we were at the midpoint of the earth. For once quite without power! A plaything of primeval forces! There is in this happiness a relaxation of tension, a throwing-off of the great burden, an effortless falling as though by the pull of gravity. It is the dream of the mountaineer who, though his *goal* may be above him, goes wearily to sleep on his way and dreams of the *happiness of the opposite course* – of effortless falling. – I am describing happiness as I imagine it to exist in the agitated, power-hungry society of present-day Europe and America. Now and then they want for once to fall back into *powerlessness* – wars, arts, religions, geniuses offer them this enjoyment. When one has surrendered oneself for a time to an impression which consumes and crushes everything – this is the modern *festive mood*! – one is again freer, more refreshed, colder, more severe, and again resumes one's unwearying quest for its opposite: for *power*. –

272

The purification of the race. – There are probably no pure races but only races that have become pure, even these being extremely rare. What is normal is crossed races, in which, together with a disharmony of physical features (when eye and mouth do not correspond with one another, for example), there must always go a disharmony of habits and value-concepts. (Livingstone heard someone say: 'God created white and black men but the Devil created the half-breeds.') Crossed races always mean at the same time crossed cultures, crossed moralities: they are usually more evil, crueller, more restless. Purity is the final result of countless adaptations, absorptions and secretions, and progress towards purity is evidenced in the fact that the energy available to a race is increasingly *restricted* to individual selected functions, while previously it was applied to too many and often contradictory things: such a restriction will always seem to be an *impoverishment* and should be assessed with consideration and caution. In the end, however, if the process of purification is successful, all that energy formerly expended in the struggle of the dissonant qualities with one another will stand at the command of the total organism: which is why races that have become pure have always also become *stronger* and *more beautiful*. – The Greeks offer us the model of a race and culture that has become pure: and hopefully we shall one day also achieve a pure European race and culture.

273

Praise. – Here is one who, you can plainly see, is going to *praise* you: you bite your lip, your heart contracts: ah, that *this* cup might pass from me! But it does not pass, it approaches! Let us therefore drink down the sweet impudence of the panegyrist, let us overcome our nausea and profound disgust at the essence of his praise, let us twist our face into an expression of joyful gratitude! – for, after all, he meant to do us a favour! And now, after it is all over, we realise that he feels very exalted, he has achieved a victory over us – yes! and over himself too, the dog! – for he did not find it easy to wring this praise from himself.

274

Human right and privilege. – We human beings are the only creatures

149

who, if they have turned out unsatisfactorily, can cross themselves out like an unsatisfactory sentence – whether we do so for the honour of mankind or out of pity for it, or from displeasure at ourselves.

275
A man transformed. – Now he is becoming virtuous, but only so as to hurt others with his virtue. Do not pay him so much attention!

276
How often! How unforeseen! – How many married men there are who have experienced the morning when it has dawned on them that their young wife is tedious and believes the opposite. Not to speak of those women whose flesh is willing but whose spirit is weak!

277
Hot and cold virtues. – Courage as cold valorousness and intrepidity, and courage as hotheaded, half-blind bravery – both are called by the same name! Yet how different from one another are the *cold virtues* and the *hot*! And he would be a fool who believed that 'being good' happens only when heat is applied: and no less a fool he who wanted to ascribe it only to coldness! The truth is that mankind has found hot and cold courage very useful and, moreover, of sufficient rarity to count it in both colours as among the precious stones.

278
The courteous memory. – He who is of high rank would do well to furnish himself with a courteous memory: that is to say, to notice everything good about other people and after that to draw a line; in this way one keeps them in a state of pleasant dependence. A man may deal with himself in the same way: whether or not he has a courteous memory in the end determines his own attitude towards himself; it determines whether he regards his own inclinations and intentions with a noble, benevolent or mistrustful eye; and it determines, finally, the nature of these inclinations and intentions themselves.

279
Wherein we become artists. – He who makes an idol of someone tries to justify himself in his own eyes by elevating this person to an ideal; in the process he becomes an artist so as to have a good conscience. If he suffers, he suffers not from *not knowing* but from self-deception, from the pretence of not knowing. – The inner distress and joy of such a person – and all passionate lovers are of their number – is not to be measured with an ordinary measure.

280

Childlike. – He who lives as children live – who does not struggle for his bread and does not believe that his actions possess any ultimate significance – remains childlike.

281

The ego wants everything. – It seems that the sole purpose of human action is possession: this idea is, at least, contained in the various languages, which regard all past action as having put us in possession of something ('I *have* spoken, struggled, conquered': that is to say, I am now in possession of my speech, struggle, victory). How greedy man appears here! He does not want to extricate himself even from the past, but wants to continue to *have* it!

282

Danger in beauty. – This woman is beautiful and clever: but how much cleverer she would have become if she were not beautiful!

283

Domestic peace and peace of soul. – The mood in which we usually exist depends upon the mood in which we maintain our environment.

284

Presenting the new as old. – Many seem irritated when they are told something new: they sense the advantage which what is new bestows on him who knows it first.

285

Where does the ego cease? – Most people take a thing that they *know* under their protection, as if knowledge of it sufficed to make it their property. The ego's desire for appropriation is boundless: great men speak as though all time stood behind them and they were the head of this long body; and the dear ladies count the beauty of their children, their clothes, their dog, their physician, their town to their own credit and only stop short of saying 'all this am I'. *Chi non ha, non è* – they say in Italy.

286

Domestic animals, pets and the like. – Is there anything more nauseous than the sentimentality exhibited towards plants and animals by a creature who from the very first dwelt among them as a raging foe and who in the end claims to feel affection for his exhausted and mutilated victims! In the face of this kind of 'nature' the proper attitude of a man rational in other respects is before all one of *seriousness*.

287

Two friends. – They were friends but have ceased to be, and they both severed their friendship at the same time: the one because he thought himself too much misunderstood, the other because he thought himself understood too well – and both were deceiving themselves! – for neither understood himself well enough.

288

Comedy of the nobility. – Those to whom a warm and noble intimacy is impossible try to display the nobility of their nature through reserve and severity and a certain deprecation of intimacy: as though their feeling of intimate trust were so strong it was ashamed to show itself.

289

Where one may not speak against a virtue. – Among cowards it is not the done thing to say anything against bravery, and to do so excites contempt: and inconsiderate people exhibit annoyance if anything is said against pity.

290

A waste. – In the case of excitable and abrupt natures their first words and actions are usually *not indicative* of their real character (they are prompted by the circumstances prevailing at the time and are as it were imitations of the spirit of these circumstances), but since they have been spoken and done the subsequent words and actions actually characteristic of the person frequently have to be *wasted* in counterbalancing or withdrawing them or ensuring they are forgotten.

291

Presumption. – Presumption is a pretended and hypocritical pride; an essential quality of pride, however, is that it is not and cannot be a pretence, a dissimulation or hypocrisy: to this extent, then, presumption is the hypocritical pretence of incapacity for hypocrisy – something very difficult and usually a failure. If, however, as is usually the case, it does fail, the presumptuous person may expect three pieces of unpleasantness: we are angry with him because he wants to deceive us, and are also angry because he wants to show himself superior to us – and finally we laugh at him because he has failed in both. How inadvisable it is, then, to attempt presumption!

292

A kind of misunderstanding. – When we hear someone speak, the sound of a single consonant (for example an r) often suffices to make us doubt the honesty of his feelings: *we* are not accustomed to this sound and would have to *affect* it deliberately – it sounds to us 'affected'. This is a domain of the crudest misunderstanding: and the same goes for the style of a writer who has habits that are not the habits of everybody. The 'naturalness' of his style is felt to be so only by him; and it is perhaps precisely by means of what he himself feels as 'affected' – because with it he has for once given in to fashion and to so-called 'good taste' – that he gives pleasure and inspires confidence.

293

Grateful. – One grain of gratitude and piety too much: – and one suffers from it as from a vice and, for all one's honesty and independence, falls prey to a bad conscience.

294

Saints. – It is the *most sensual* men who *have* to flee from women and torment their body.

295

Refinement of service. – Within the great art of serving one of the most refined tasks is to serve a man of unbounded ambition who, while being an absolute egoist in everything, absolutely desires not to appear so (this precisely is an aspect of his ambition), who demands that everything shall take place in accordance with his will and pleasure, yet always in such a way as to make it seem that he is a model of self-sacrifice who rarely wants anything for himself.

296

The duel. – I regard it as an advantage, somebody said, to be able to have a duel if I absolutely need one; for I always have brave comrades about me. The duel is the last remaining wholly honourable path to suicide, though unfortunately a circuitous path and not even a completely certain one.

297

Ruinous. – The surest way of ruining a youth is to teach him to respect those who think as he does more highly than those who think differently from him.

298

The hero-cult and its fanatics. – The fanatic of an ideal which has flesh and blood is usually in the right so long as he *denies*, and in this he is dreadful: he knows that which he denies as well as he knows himself, for the simple reason that he comes from there, is at home there, and lives in the secret dread of having to go back there – he wants to make it impossible for him to return by the way in which he denies. But as soon as he affirms he half-closes his eyes and begins to idealise (often only so as to hurt those who have stayed at home –); one might call this something artistic – very well, but there is also something dishonest in it. He who idealises a person sets this person at so great a distance from himself that he can no longer see him clearly – and then he reinterprets what he still sees into the 'beautiful', that is to say the symmetrical, soft-lined, indefinite. Since he henceforth wants also to worship his distant ideal he needs to construct a temple to guard it from the *profanum vulgus.* Into this temple he fetches all the revered and consecrated objects he otherwise possesses, so that their magic may rub off on to his ideal and, thus *nourished*, it shall grow and become ever more divine. At last he has actually succeeded in completing his god – but alas! there is one who knows how this has been brought about, his intellectual conscience – and there is also one who, quite unconsciously, protests at it, namely the deified being himself, who in consequence of the cult, worship and incense surrounding him has now become insupportable and in a horrible fashion betrays himself as being very obviously not a god and all too much a human. Here a fanatic such as we have described is now left with only one recourse: he patiently submits himself and his kind to mistreatment and interprets the whole misery still *ad majorem dei gloriam* by means of a new species of self-deception and noble falsehood: he takes sides against himself and, as the one mishandled and as interpreter, feels as he does so something like a martyrdom – thus he mounts to the peak of his arrogance. – Men of this kind lived about Napoleon, for example: perhaps, indeed, it was precisely he who implanted into the soul of our century the romantic prostration before 'genius' and the 'hero' which is so contrary to the spirit of the Enlightenment; he of whom a Byron was not ashamed to say he was 'a worm compared with such a being'. (The formula for this kind of prostration was invented by that presumptuous old grumbler and muddle-head Carlyle, who employed a long life in trying to turn romantic the reasonableness of his Englishmen: in vain!)

299

Apparent heroism. – To throw oneself into the thick of the battle can be a sign of cowardice.

300

Gracious towards the flatterer. – The ultimate piece of prudence exercised by the insatiably ambitious is to conceal the contempt for man they feel at the sight of flatterers and to appear gracious towards them too, like a god who cannot be other than gracious.

301

'Possessing character'. – 'Once I have said I will do a thing, I do it' – this mode of thinking counts as a sign of possessing character. How many actions have been done, not because they were chosen as the most rational, but because when they occurred to us they in some way tickled our vanity and ambition, so that we stuck with them and blindly carried them out! In this way they increase our belief in our own character and our good conscience, and thus in general our *strength*: while the choice of the most rational course keeps alive scepticism towards us and to this extent a feeling of weakness.

302

Once, twice and three times true! – People lie unspeakably often, but afterwards they do not remember it and on the whole do not believe it.

303

Psychologist's pastime. – He believes he knows me and feels very grand when he treats me thus and thus: I take care not to undeceive him. For I should have to pay for it, while now he is *well disposed* towards me because I evoke in him a feeling of superiority. – There is another: he is afraid I imagine I know him, and feels debased by this fear. Thus he behaves towards me in a chilly and offhand manner and tries to mislead me about himself – so as again to gain ascendancy over me.

304

The world-destroyers. – This man fails in something; finally he exclaims in rage: 'Then let the whole world perish!' This revolting feeling is the summit of envy, which argues: because there is *something* I cannot have, the whole world shall have *nothing*! the whole world shall *be* nothing!

305

Greed. – Our greed when we are buying increases with the cheapness of the article – why? Is it that the little price-differences actually *constitute* the little eye of greed?

306

Greek ideal. – What did the Greeks admire in Odysseus? Above all, his capacity for lying, and for cunning and terrible retribution; his being equal to contingencies; when need be, appearing nobler than the noblest; the ability to be *whatever he chose*; heroic perseverence; having all means at his command; possession of intellect – his intellect is the admiration of the gods, they smile when they think of it – : all this is the Greek *ideal*! The most remarkable thing about it is that the antithesis of appearance and being is not felt at all and is thus of no significance morally. Have there ever been such consummate actors!

307

Facta! Yes, Facta ficta! – A historian has to do, not with what actually happened, but only with events supposed to have happened: for only the latter have *produced an effect*. Likewise only with supposed heroes. His theme, so-called world history, is opinions about supposed actions and their supposed motives, which in turn give rise to further opinions and actions, the reality of which is however at once vaporised again and produces an *effect* only as vapour – a continual generation and pregnancy of phantoms over the impenetrable mist of unfathomable reality. All historians speak of things which have never existed except in imagination.

308

To know nothing about trade is noble. – To sell one's virtue only for the highest price, let alone to carry on usury with it, as teacher, official, artist – makes of genius and talent a shopkeeper's affair. One should not want to employ one's *wisdom* in being *clever*!

309

Fear and love. – Fear has promoted knowledge of men more than love has, for fear wants to divine who the other is, what he can do, what he wants: to deceive oneself in this would be disadvantageous and dangerous. On the other hand, love contains a secret impulse to see as much beauty as possible in the other or to elevate him as high as possible: to deceive oneself here would be a joy and an advantage – and so one does so.

310

The good-natured. – The good-natured have acquired their good-nature through the constant fear of attack in which their forefathers lived – they treated with their enemies, humbled and prostrated themselves, entertained and flattered, concealed their distress, smoothed their features – and in the end they bequeathed this whole delicate and well-tested mechanism to their children and grand-children. A more favourable fate gave these no occasion for that constant fear: nonetheless they constantly continue to play the same instrument.

311

The so-called soul. – The sum of the inner movements which a man *finds easy*, and as a consequence performs gracefully and with pleasure, one calls his soul; – if these inner movements are plainly difficult and an effort for him, he is considered soulless.

312

The forgetful. – In outbursts of passion, and in the fantasising of dreams and insanity, a man rediscovers his own and mankind's prehistory: *animality* with its savage grimaces; on these occasions his memory goes sufficiently far back, while his civilised condition evolves out of a forgetting of these primal experiences, that is to say out of a relaxation of his memory. He who, as a forgetter on a grand scale, is wholly unfamiliar with all this *does not understand man* – but it is to the general advantage that there should appear here and there such individuals as 'do not understand us' and who are as it were begotten by the seed of the gods and born of reason.

313

The friend we no longer desire. – The friend whose hopes one cannot satisfy one would rather have for an enemy.

314

From the company of thinkers. – In the midst of the ocean of becoming we awake on a little island no bigger than a boat, we adventurers and birds of passage, and look around us for a few moments: as sharply and as inquisitively as possible, for how soon may a wind not blow us

157

away or a wave not sweep across the little island, so that nothing more is left of us! But here, on this little space, we find other birds of passage and hear of others still who have been here before – and thus we live a precarious minute of knowing and divining, amid joyful beating of wings and chirping with one another, and in spirit we adventure out over the ocean, no less proud than the ocean itself.

315
To divest oneself. – To let some of one's property go, to relinquish one's rights – gives pleasure when it indicates great wealth. Magnanimity belongs here.

316
Weak sects. – Sects which feel they will remain weak hunt after individual intelligent adherents and try to make up in quality what they lack in quantity. This represents no small danger for the intelligent.

317
The judgment of the evening. – He who reflects on the work he has done during the day and during his life, but does so when he has finished it and is tired, usually arrives at a melancholy conclusion: this however is not the fault of his day or his life, but of his tiredness. – In the midst of our work we usually have no leisure to pass judgment on life and existence, nor in the midst of our pleasures: but if we should happen to do so, we should no longer agree with him who waited for the seventh day and its repose before he decided that everything was very beautiful – he had let the *better* moment go by.

318
Beware of systematisers! – Systematisers practise a kind of play-acting: in as much as they want to fill out a system and round off its horizon, they have to try to present their weaker qualities in the same style as their stronger – they try to impersonate whole and uniformly strong natures.

319
Hospitality. – The meaning of the usages of hospitality is the paralysing of enmity in the stranger. Where the stranger is no longer felt to be first and foremost an enemy, hospitality decreases; it flourishes as long as its evil presupposition flourishes.

320
Weather. – Very uncertain and incalculable weather makes people

mistrustful of one another too; they also become greedy for novelties, for they are obliged to depart from their usual habits. That is why despots love those regions where the weather is moral.

321

Danger in innocence. – The innocent will always be the victims because their ignorance prevents them from distinguishing between measure and excess and from keeping themselves in check in good time. Thus innocent, that is to say ignorant young wives become accustomed to the frequent enjoyment of sex and miss it very greatly later if their husbands become ill or prematurely feeble; it is precisely this innocent and credulous idea that frequent intercourse is thoroughly right and proper that produces in them a need which later exposes them to the most violent temptations and worse. But speaking quite generally: he who loves a person or a thing without knowing him or it falls prey to something that he would not love if he could see it. Wherever experience, caution and measured steps are needed, it is the innocent person who will be most thoroughly ruined, for he has blindly to drink the dregs and the bottommost poison of everything. Consider the practice of every prince, church, sect, party, corporation: is the innocent person not always employed as the sweetest bait in really dangerous and infamous cases? – as Odysseus employed the innocent Neoptolemus to trick the sick old hermit and monster of Lemnos out of his bow and arrows. – Christianity, with its contempt for the world, made a *virtue* of ignorance, Christian innocence, perhaps because the most frequent result of this innocence is, as aforesaid, guilt, the feeling of guilt and despair, and thus a virtue which leads to Heaven via a detour through Hell: for only then can the gloomy propylaea of Christian salvation open up, only then will there be any point to the promise of a posthumous *second innocence* – it is one of Christianity's fairest inventions!

322

If possible live without a physician. – It seems to me that an invalid is more frivolous when he has a physician than when he takes care of his health himself. In the former case, it is sufficient if he adheres strictly to what has been prescribed; in the latter, we take a more conscientious view of that which these prescriptions are designed to serve, that is to say our health, and notice much more, order and forbid ourselves much more, than would happen at the instigation of the physician. – All rules have the effect of drawing us away from the purpose behind them and making us more frivolous. – And to what heights of abandonment and destructiveness the frivolity of men would have ascended if they had ever with complete sincerity left everything in the hands of the divinity as their physician, in accordance with the words 'as God ordains'! –

323

Darkening of the sky. – Do you know the revenge of shy people who behave in society as though they had stolen their limbs? The revenge of humble, Christian-like souls who can do no more than creep through the world? The revenge of those who always judge quickly and are always quickly judged wrong? The revenge of the drunkards of every species for whom the morning is the most dismal time of day? That of the invalids of every species, the sickly and depressed, who no longer possess the courage to get well? The number of these revengeful little people is tremendous, not to speak of that of their little revengeful acts; the whole air is continually whizzing with the arrows of their malice, so that the sun and the sky of life are darkened by them – not only their sky but ours too: which is worse than the scratches they often make on our heart and skin. Do we not sometimes *deny* that there is such a thing as sun and sky, simply because we have not seen them for so long? – Therefore: solitude! Solitude for this reason too!

324

Psychology of actors. – Great actors have the happy delusion that the historical personages they play really felt as they do when they play them – but they are strongly in error: their power of imitation and divination, which they would dearly love to pretend is a capacity for clairvoyance, penetrates only sufficiently far to understand gestures, tones of voice, facial expressions and the superficial in general; that is to say, they catch the shadow of the soul of a great hero, statesman, warrior, man of ambition, jealousy or despair, they press close to the soul but not into the spirit of their object. That it requires only the clairvoyant actor, and not the labours of thinkers, experts, professionals, to illumine the *essence* of an object would, to be sure, be a fine discovery! Whenever a piece of presumption of this sort becomes audible, however, let us never forget that the actor is no more than an ideal ape, and so much of an ape that he is incapable of believing in 'essence' or the 'essential': with him everything becomes play, word, gesture, stage, scenery and public.

325

Living and believing apart. – The means of becoming the prophet and miracle-worker of one's age is the same today as it has always been: one lives apart, with little knowledge, a few ideas and a very great deal of arrogance – finally there arises in us the belief that mankind cannot get on without us *because we ourselves quite clearly* can get on without mankind. As soon as we have this belief we find that others believe in us. Lastly, a piece of advice for those who would like to use it (it was given to Wesley by his spiritual teacher, Böhler): 'Preach the faith until you have it, and then you will preach it because you have it!' –

326

Knowing one's circumstances. – We can estimate our powers but not our *power.* Our circumstances do not only conceal and reveal it to us – no! they magnify and diminish it. One should regard oneself as a variable quantity whose capacity for achievement can under favourable circumstances perhaps equal the highest ever known: one should thus reflect on one's circumstances and spare no effort in observing them.

327

A fable. – The Don Juan of knowledge: no philosopher or poet has yet discovered him. He does not love the things he knows, but has spirit and appetite for and enjoyment of the chase and intrigues of knowledge – up to the highest and remotest stars of knowledge! – until at last there remains to him nothing of knowledge left to hunt down except the absolutely *detrimental*; he is like the drunkard who ends by drinking absinthe and *aqua fortis.* Thus in the end he lusts after Hell – it is the last knowledge that *seduces* him. Perhaps it too proves a disillusionment, like all knowledge! And then he would have to stand to all eternity transfixed to disillusionment and himself become a stone guest, with a longing for a supper of knowledge which he will never get! – for the whole universe has not a single morsel left to give to this hungry man.

328

What idealist theories seem to indicate. – The place one is most certain to find idealist theories is with unreflective practical men; for their reputation requires an idealist lustre. They reach for them instinctively and have no feeling of hypocrisy as they do so: as little as an Englishman feels a hypocrite with his Christianness and his sancti-monious Sunday. Conversely: contemplative natures who have to keep a rein on their imagination and avoid the reputation of being dreamers are satisfied only with rigorous realistic theories: they reach for them with the same instinctive need and without any loss of honesty.

329

The slanderers of cheerfulness. – People who have been deeply injured by life are all suspicious of cheerfulness, as though it were childlike and childish and betrayed a kind of irrationality at the sight of which one can only be moved to pity, as one would be at the sight of a dying child continuing to play with its toys. Such people discover under every rose a disguised and hidden grave; festivities, carousels, joyful music seem to them like the determined self-deception of a man fatally sick determined to consume one last minute of the intoxication of life. But this judgment of cheerfulness is nothing other than its refraction on the dark background of sickness and weariness: it is itself something moving, irrational, inspiring of pity, indeed even something childlike and childish, but deriving from that *second childhood* which succeeds old age and is the forerunner of death.

330

Not enough! – It is not enough to prove something, one has also to seduce or elevate people to it. That is why the man of knowledge should learn how to *speak* his wisdom: and often in such a way that it *sounds* like folly!

331

Rights and limits. – Asceticism is the right discipline for those who have to exterminate their sensual drives because the latter are raging beasts of prey. But only for those!

332

The inflated style. – An artist who wants, not to discharge his high-swollen feelings in his work and so unburden himself, but rather to communicate precisely this feeling of swollenness, is bombastic, and his style is the inflated style.

333

'Humanity'. – We do not regard the animals as moral beings. But do you suppose the animals regard us as moral beings? – An animal which could speak said: 'Humanity is a prejudice of which we animals at least are free.'

334

The benefactor. – The benefactor satisfies a need of his nature when he does good. The stronger this need is, the less he enters into the feelings of that other person who serves to still his need, he becomes rough and, on occasion, offensive. (This has been asserted of Jewish benefaction and charity, which, as is well known, is somewhat more effusive than that of other nations.)

335

That love may be felt as love. – We need to be honest with ourselves and know ourselves very well if we are to be able to practise towards others that philanthropic dissimulation called goodness and love.

336

What are we capable of? – A man was so tormented the whole day long by his undutiful and ill-humoured son that in the evening he struck him and, turning to the rest of the family, said with a sigh of relief: 'So! now we can go quietly to bed!' – Who knows to what we *could* be driven by circumstances!

337

'Natural'. – That he is *natural* at least in his faults – is perhaps the ultimate praise that can be bestowed on an artificial and in all other respects theatrical and half-genuine artist. That is why such a creature will boldly give rein precisely to his faults.

338

Substitute conscience. – One man is another's conscience: and this is especially important if the other has no other conscience.

339

Metamorphosis of duties. – When duty ceases to be a burden but, after long practice, becomes a joyful inclination and a need, the rights of those others to whom our duties, now our inclinations, refer, become something different: namely occasions of pleasant sensations for us. From then onwards, the other becomes, by virtue of his rights, lovable (instead of feared and revered, as heretofore). We are now seeking *pleasure* when we recognise and sustain the sphere of his power. When the Quietists came to feel their Christianity no longer a burden and experienced only pleasure in God, they adopted as their motto 'All for the honour of God': whatever they did under this banner was no longer a sacrifice; their motto came to the same thing as 'all for our own pleasure!' To demand that duty must *always* be something of a burden – as Kant does – means to demand that it should never become habit and custom: in this demand there is concealed a remnant of ascetic cruelty.

340

Appearance is against the historian. – It is a well proven fact that human beings emerge from the body of their mother: nonetheless, when grown-up children stand beside their mother they make the hypothesis seem very absurd; it has appearance against it.

341

Advantage in misunderstanding. – Someone said that as a child he felt such contempt for the coquettish whims of the melancholic temperament that until he was middle-aged he failed to realise what his own temperament was: namely melancholic. He declared this to be the best of all possible pieces of ignorance.

342

Beware of confusion! – Yes! He considers the matter from all sides, and you think he is a genuine man of knowledge. But he only wants to lower the price – he wants to buy it.

343

Supposedly moral. – You refuse ever to be dissatisfied with yourselves, ever to suffer from yourselves – and you call this being moral! Very well – another, however, might call it being cowardly. But one thing is certain: you will never travel round the world (which you yourself are!) but will remain an impenetrable enigma to yourselves! For do you imagine that it is out of pure folly that we who think differently expose ourselves to our own deserts, swamps and icy mountains, and voluntarily choose pain and self-satiety, as the stylites did?

344

Subtle blunders. – If, as they say he did, Homer sometimes nodded, he acted more sagely than do artists whose ambition never sleeps. One must allow one's admirers to catch their breath by turning them into critics from time to time; for no one can endure an uninterruptedly brilliant and wakeful gift; and instead of conferring benefit, a master of this kind becomes a taskmaster whom one hates as he goes on before us.

345

Happiness is no argument, for or against. – Many people are able to be only moderately happy: it is no more an objection to their degree of wisdom that it can offer them no more happiness than it does than it is an objection to medicine that many people cannot be cured and others are always unwell. May each of us be fortunate enough to discover that philosophy of life which enables him to realise *his* greatest measure of happiness: even so, his life can still be miserable and little to be envied.

346

Misogynists. – 'Woman is our enemy' – out of the man who says that to other men there speaks an immoderate drive which hates not only itself but its means of satisfaction as well.

347

A school for speakers. – If one stays silent for a year one unlearns chattering and learns to speak. The Pythagoreans were the finest statesmen of their age.

348

Feeling of power. – Be sure you mark the difference: he who wants to acquire the feeling of power resorts to any means and disdains nothing that will nourish it. He who has it, however, has become very fastidious and noble in his tastes; he now finds few things to satisfy him.

349

Not all that important. – When one witnesses a death there regularly arises a thought which, out of a false sense of decency, one immediately suppresses: that the act of dying is not as significant as it is generally regarded as being, and that the dying man has probably lost more important things in his life than that which he is about to lose. Here the end is certainly not the goal. –

350

How best to promise. – When a promise is made, it is not the words that are said which constitute the promise but what remains unspoken behind the words that are said. Indeed, the words even weaken the promise, in as much as they discharge and use up strength which is a part of the strength which makes the promise. Therefore extend your hand and lay your finger on your lips – thus will you take the surest vows.

351

Usually misunderstood. – In a conversation you can watch one of the participants busy setting a trap into which the other then falls – but he does it, not out of malice, as might be thought, but out of pleasure at his own artfulness. Then again, you will see one set up a joke so

165

that the other can make it, tie a loop so that the other can unknot it:
but he does it, not out of benevolence, as might be thought, but out
of malice and contempt for cruder intellects.

352

Centre. – The feeling 'I am the mid-point of the world!' arises very
strongly if one is suddenly overcome with shame; one then stands
there as though confused in the midst of a surging sea and feels
dazzled as though by a great eye which gazes upon us and through
us from all sides.

353

Freedom of speech. – 'The truth must be told though the world
crumble!' – thus in a great voice cried the great Fichte! – Yes! Yes! But
one would have to know it before one could tell it! – But what he
means is that everyone ought to be allowed to express his own
opinion though the result should be turmoil: and that proposition is
disputable.

354

Courage to suffer. – As we are now, we are able to endure a fairly large
amount of unpleasure, and our stomach is designed to take this
heavy fare. Perhaps without it we would find life's repast insipid: and
without our ready tolerance of pain we should have to give up too
many pleasures!

355

Admirers. – He who admires to such a degree as to crucify those who
do not admire is one of the executioners of his party – beware of
offering him your hand, even if you belong to his party.

356

Effect of happiness. – The first effect of happiness is the *feeling of power*:
this wants to *express itself*, either to us ourselves, or to other men, or to
ideas or imaginary beings. The most common modes of expression
are: to bestow, to mock, to destroy – all three out of a common basic
drive.

357

Moral sting-flies. – Those moralists who lack a love of knowledge and
know only the pleasure of causing pain have the minds and the
tedious pastimes of provincials; their way of passing the time, as
cruel as it is pathetic, is to observe their neighbour as closely as they
can and then, unnoticed, stick a pin into him in such a way that he

cannot help but scratch himself. They retain the naughtiness of little boys who are never happy unless they are chasing and mistreating something living or dead.

358
Grounds and their groundlessness. – You dislike him and present many grounds for this dislike – but I believe only in your dislike, not in your grounds! You flatter yourself in your own eyes when you suggest to yourself and to me that what has happened through instinct is the result of a process of reasoning.

359
Approval. – One approves of marriage firstly because one does not yet know it, secondly because one has got used to the idea of it, thirdly because one is married – in almost every case, that is to say. And yet none of this is proof that marriage as such is a good thing.

360
No utilitarians. – 'Power which is attacked and defamed is worth more than impotence which is treated only with kindness' – that is how the Greeks felt. That is to say: they valued the feeling of power more highly than any kind of utility or good name.

361
Ugly-looking. – Moderation sees itself as beautiful; it is unaware that in the eye of the immoderate it appears black and sober, and consequently ugly-looking.

362
Different kinds of hatred. – Some hate only when they feel weak and tired: at other times they are fair-minded and forgiving. Others hate only when they see the possibility of revenge: at other times they guard against all secret or open anger and when an occasion for it arises they overlook it.

363
Men of chance. – The essential part of every invention is the work of chance, but most men never encounter this chance.

364
Choice of environment. – One should take care not to live in an environment in which one can neither preserve a dignified silence nor communicate what is of most moment to us, so that our complaints and needs and the whole story of our distress must

remain untold. In this condition one grows dissatisfied with oneself and with one's environment – indeed, the displeasure we feel at seeming always to be the complainant is added to the distress which originally caused us to complain. One ought to live where one *is ashamed* to speak of oneself and does not need to. – But who gives thought to such things, to possessing a *choice* in such things! One speaks of one's 'destiny', spreads one's broad back, and sighs: 'what an unhappy Atlas I am!'

365
Vanity. – Vanity is the fear of appearing original: it is thus a lack of pride, but not necessarily a lack of originality.

366
Grief of the criminal. – The man detected as a criminal suffers, not from his crime, but from shame, or from annoyance at a piece of stupidity, or at being deprived of his customary way of life, and it requires a rare subtlety of discernment to distinguish between these kinds of suffering. Those who frequent prisons and penitentiaries are astonished at how rarely an unmistakable 'pang of conscience' is to be met with in them: what is found much more frequently is homesickness for the old, beloved, wicked crime.

367
Always to seem happy. – When philosophy became a matter of public competition, in Greece in the third century, there were not a few philosophers who were happy at the thought that others who lived according to different principles and were tormented by them were bound to be annoyed at the sight of their own happiness: they believed that their happiness was the best refutation of other ways of life, and in pursuit of that all they needed to do was always to seem happy: but by doing that they were bound in the long run to *become* happy! This, for example, was the fate of the Cynics.

368
Cause of much misunderstanding. – The morality that goes with an increase in nervous energy is joyful and restless; the morality that goes with a decrease in nervous energy, as in the evening or in the case of invalids and old people, is suffering, calming, patient, sorrowful, indeed often gloomy. According to whether we have the former or the latter we fail to understand the one we do not have, and we often interpret it as immorality and weakness.

369

Raising oneself above one's own wretchedness. – There are proud fellows who, to produce in themselves a feeling of dignity and importance, always require others whom they can dominate and rape: others, that is to say, whose impotence and cowardice permits with impunity a display of anger and haughtiness in their presence! – so that they require their environment to be wretched in order to raise themselves for a moment above their own wretchedness! – To this end, one person has need of a dog, a second a friend, a third a wife, a fourth a party, and a very rare type a whole era.

370

To what extent the thinker loves his enemy. – Never keep back or bury in silence that which can be thought against your thoughts! Give it praise! It is among the foremost requirements of honesty of thought. Every day you must conduct your campaign also against yourself. A victory and a conquered fortress are no longer your concern, your concern is truth – but your defeat is no longer your concern, either!

371

The evil of the strong. – The act of violence as a consequence of passion, of anger for example, is to be understood physiologically as an attempt to prevent a threatening attack of suffocation. Countless acts of arrogance vented on other people have been diversions of a sudden rush of blood through a vigorous action of the muscles: and perhaps the whole phenomenon of the 'evil of the strong' belongs in this domain. (The evil of the strong harms others without giving thought to it – it *has* to discharge itself; the evil of the weak *wants* to harm others and to see the signs of the suffering it has caused.)

372

To the honour of the expert. – As soon as anyone who is not an expert starts to play the judge we should at once protest: whether the person concerned is a little man or a little woman. Enthusiasm for and delight in a thing or a person are no arguments: nor are repugnance and hatred for them, either.

373

Revelatory censure. – 'He does not know men' – in the mouth of one person this means: 'he does not know what is common to men', in the mouth of another: 'he does not know what is exceptional, and what is common he knows all too well'.

374

Value of sacrifice. – The more one denies to states and princes the right to sacrifice individuals (as in the administration of justice and the army, etc.), the greater will be the value of self-sacrifice.

375

Speaking too clearly. – One can for different reasons speak with too great articulation: from mistrust of oneself in a new, unfamiliar language, but also from mistrust of others on account of their stupidity or slowness of apprehension. And so it is in the most spiritual things: we sometimes communicate too clearly, with too great exactitude, because those we are communicating to would otherwise not understand us. Consequently, the perfect and easy style is *permissible* only before a perfect audience.

376

Plenty of sleep. – What can one do to arouse oneself when one is tired and has had enough of oneself? One person recommends the casino, another Christianity, a third electricity. The best thing, however, my melancholy friend, is *plenty of sleep*, real and metaphorical! Thus one will again awake to a new morning! The art in the wisdom of life lies in knowing how to fall asleep in either sense at the proper time.

377

What fantastic ideals seem to indicate. – It is where our deficiencies lie that we indulge in our enthusiasms. The command 'love your enemies!' had to be invented by the Jews, the best haters there have ever been, and the fairest glorification of chastity has been penned by such as in their youth lived in dissoluteness.

378

Clean hands and clean wall. – Paint neither God nor the Devil on your wall. If you do so you ruin both your wall and your company.

379

Probable and improbable. – A woman was secretly in love with a man, raised him high above her, and said a hundred times in the most secret recesses of her heart: 'if such a man loved me, it would be something I so little deserve I would have to humble myself in the dust!' – And the man felt in the same way, and in regard to the same woman, and he said the same thing in the most secret recesses of his heart. When at last their tongues were loosed and they told one another everything they had kept hidden, there followed a silence; then, after she had been sunk in thought for a time, the woman said in a cold voice: 'but everything is now clear! neither of us is what we have loved! If you are that which you say, and no more, I have debased myself and loved you in vain; the demon seduced me, as he did you.' – This story, which is not at all an improbable one, never happens – why not?

380

Tried and tested advice. – For those who need consolation no means of consolation is so effective as the assertion that in their case no consolation is possible: it implies so great a degree of distinction that they at once hold up their heads again.

381

Knowing one's 'individuality'. – We are too prone to forget that in the eyes of people who are seeing us for the first time we are something quite different from what we consider ourselves to be: usually we are nothing more than a single individual trait which leaps to the eye and determines the whole impression we make. Thus the gentlest and most reasonable of men can, if he wears a large moustache, sit as it were in its shade and feel safe there – he will usually be seen as no more than the *appurtenance* of a large moustache, that is to say a military type, easily angered and occasionally violent – and as such he will be treated.

382

Gardener and garden. – Out of damp and gloomy days, out of solitude, out of loveless words directed at us, *conclusions* grow up in us like fungus: one morning they are there, we know not how, and they gaze upon us, morose and grey. Woe to the thinker who is not the gardener but only the soil of the plants that grow in him!

383

The comedy of pity. However much we may sympathise with an unfortunate, in his presence we always play a little comedy: much that we think and the way we think it we do not say, like a physician at the bedside of a serious invalid.

384

Strange saints. – There are faint-hearted people who rate low their own best works and present and produce them badly: but out of a kind of revenge they also rate low the sympathy of others or even go so far as to believe that no such sympathy exists; they are ashamed to appear to be carried away by themselves and take a defiant pleasure in becoming ludicrous. – These states are to be found in the souls of melancholy artists.

385

The vain. – We are like shop windows in which we are continually arranging, concealing or illuminating the supposed qualities others ascribe to us – in order to deceive *ourselves*.

386

The pathetic and the naive. – To neglect no opportunity of exhibiting pathos can be a very ignoble habit: its purpose is to enjoy the thought of the spectator beating his breast and feeling small and miserable. To make fun of pathetic situations and to behave badly in them can therefore be a sign of a noble mind. The ancient, warlike aristocracy of France possessed this kind of nobility and refinement.

387

Sample of reflection before marriage. – Supposing she loves me, how burdensome she would become to me in the long run! And supposing she does not love me, how really burdensome she would become to me in the long run! – It is only a question of two different kinds of burdensomeness – therefore let us get married!

388

Knavery with a good conscience. – To be cheated in some small transaction – in some regions, in Tirol for instance, this is so unpleasant because in addition to the bad bargain we also get the cheating salesman's evil face and coarse thirst for gain, together with his bad conscience and the crude hostility he feels for us. In Venice, on the other hand, the cheater is heartily delighted at his successful trickery and feels in no way hostile towards the person he has cheated, indeed ,he is inclined to be very amiable with him, and especially to have a good laugh with him if he should happen to feel so inclined. – In short, successful knavery requires spirit and a good conscience: they almost reconcile the dupe to being duped.

389

Somewhat too grave. – There are very excellent people who are too grave to be amiable or polite, and whenever they encounter a piece of civility they at once try to answer it with an earnest act of service or with a contribution from their store of energy. It is touching to see how they diffidently produce their gold pieces when another has offered them his gilded pennies.

390

Concealing mind. – When we catch someone concealing his mind from us we call him evil: and all the more so, indeed, if we suspect that he has done so out of politeness and philanthropy.

391

The evil moment. – Lively natures lie only for a moment: immediately afterwards they lie to themselves and are convinced and honest.

392

Condition for politeness. – Politeness is a very good thing and in fact one of the four cardinal virtues (if the last of them): but if it is not to make us burdensome to one another, he with whom I have to do has to be a degree more or a degree less polite than I am – otherwise we shall get nowhere, and the salve will not only salve us but stick us together.

393

Dangerous virtues. – 'He forgets nothing but he forgives everything' – In that case he will be doubly hated, for he makes doubly ashamed – with his memory and with his magnanimity.

394

Without vanity. – Passionate people think little of what others are thinking: the condition they are in raises them above vanity.

395

Contemplation. – With one thinker the reflective state peculiar to the thinker always succeeds a state of fear, with another it always succeeds a state of desire. In the one case, therefore, reflectiveness seems to be associated with a feeling of *security*, in the other with a feeling of *satiety* – that is to say: the former is in a happy and courageous mood, the latter in a weary and neutral mood.

396

Hunting. – This one is hunting pleasant truths, that one unpleasant. But even the former takes more pleasure in the hunt than in the booty.

397

Education. – Education is a continuation of procreation, and often a kind of supplementary beautification of it.

398

How to recognise the more ardent. – Of two people who are fighting one another, or are mutual admirers, or are in love, he who is the more ardent is always in the less comfortable position. The same also applies to two nations.

399

Defending oneself. – Many people have the best possible right to act in such and such a manner, but as soon as they begin to defend that right we cease to believe in it – and are mistaken.

400

Moral tenderness. – There are morally tender natures which feel ashamed at every success and pangs of conscience at every failure.

401

The most dangerous kind of unlearning. – One begins by unlearning how to love others and ends by no longer finding anything lovable in oneself.

402

This too is tolerance. – 'To have lain a minute too long on the glowing coals and have got a little *burned* – that does no harm, to men or to chestnuts! It is only this little bit of hardening and bitterness which will let us taste how sweet and soft the kernel is'. – Yes! That is your judgment, you who intend to enjoy these things! You sublime cannibals!

403

Different kinds of pride. – Women grow pale at the thought that their beloved may not be worthy of them; men grow pale at the thought that they may not be worthy of their beloved. I am speaking of whole women, whole men. Such men, as men who are *customarily* confident and full of the feeling of power, acquire in a state of passion a sense of shame and doubt; such women, however, who normally feel themselves the weak and devoted sex, acquire in the *exceptional* state of passion their pride and their feeling of power – which asks: who is worthy *of me?*

404

To whom one is rarely just. – Many people cannot become enthusiastic for something great and good without doing a great injustice to something else: this is *their* kind of morality.

405

Luxury. – An inclination for luxury extends into the depths of a man: it betrays the fact that superfluity and immoderation is the water in which his soul most likes to swim.

406

Making immortal. – He who intends to kill his enemy should consider whether this is not precisely the way to make his enemy immortal to him.

407

Contrary to our character. – If the truth we have to tell is contrary to our character – as often happens – we behave as though we were lying badly and excite mistrust.

408

Where much restraint is needed. – Some natures have only the choice of being either public wrong-doers or secret mourners.

409

Sickness. – 'Sickness' is: the premature approach of old age, ugliness and pessimism: which things go together.

410

The timid. – It is precisely the clumsy, timid natures who easily become killers: they do not understand how to defend or revenge themselves in a measure appropriate to the case; lacking intelligence and presence of mind, their hatred knows no expedient other than destruction.

411

Without hatred. – Do you want to say farewell to your passion? Do so, but *without hatred* of it! Otherwise you will have acquired a second passion. – The soul of the Christian who has freed himself from sin is usually afterwards ruined by hatred of sin. Regard the faces of great Christians! They are the faces of great haters.

412

Ingenious and limited. – He does not know how to love anyone but himself; and when he wants to love others he always has first to transform them into himself. But in that he is ingenious.

413

Private and public prosecutors. – Take a close look at anyone who prosecutes and investigates – he reveals his character in so doing:

and often, indeed, it is a worse character than that of the victim whose crime he is pursuing. The prosecutor believes in all innocence that the assailant of a crime and a criminal must of necessity be of good character or count as such – and so he lets himself go, that is to say: he *discloses* himself.

414

Voluntarily blind. – There is a kind of excessive devotion to a person or a party which betrays that we secretly feel superior to it and are angry with ourselves about the fact. We as it were blind ourselves voluntarily as a punishment for having seen too much.

415

Remedium amoris. – The cure for love is still in most cases that ancient radical medicine: love in return.

416

Where is our worst enemy? – He who can promote his cause well, and is aware of the fact, is usually conciliatory towards his opponent. But to believe one's cause is a good cause and to know one is *not* skilled in defending it – that inspires a wrathful and unconciliatory hatred of the opponent of one's cause. – Let everyone judge from this where his worst enemies are to be sought!

417

The limit of humility. – Many have no doubt attained to that humility which says: *credo quia absurdum est* and sacrificed their reason to it: but, so far as I know, no one has yet attained to that humility which says: *credo quia absurdus sum*, though it is only one step further.

418

Playing at truth. – Many a man is truthful – not because he detests hypocrisy but because hardly anyone would believe in his hypocrisy. In short, he does not trust his acting talents and prefers honesty, 'playing at truth'.

419

Party courage. – The poor sheep say to their shepherd: 'go on ahead and we shall never lack the courage to follow you'. The poor shepherd, however, thinks to himself: 'follow me and I shall never lack the courage to lead you'.

420

Cunning of the sacrificial beast. – It is a sad piece of cunning if we want to deceive ourself over someone to whom we have sacrificed ourself and create for him the occasion in which he has to appear to us as we wish he were.

421

Through others. – There are people who want to be seen in no other way than shining through others. And there is a great deal of prudence in that.

422

Making others joyful. – Why is making joyful the greatest of all joys? – Because we thereby give joy to our fifty separate drives all at once. Individually they may be very little joys: but if we take them all into one hand, our hand is fuller than at any other time – and our heart too! –

BOOK V

423

In the great silence. – Here is the sea, here we can forget the city. The bells are noisily ringing the angelus – it is the time for that sad and foolish yet sweet noise, sounded at the crossroads of day and night – but it will last only for a minute! Now all is still! The sea lies there pale and glittering, it cannot speak. The sky plays its everlasting silent evening game with red and yellow and green, it cannot speak. The little cliffs and ribbons of rock that run down into the sea as if to find the place where it is most solitary, none of them can speak. This tremendous muteness which suddenly overcomes us is lovely and dreadful, the heart swells at it. – Oh the hypocrisy of this silent beauty! How well it could speak, and how evilly too, if it wished! Its tied tongue and its expression of sorrowing happiness is a deception: it wants to mock at your sympathy! – So be it! I am not ashamed of being mocked by such powers. But I pity you, nature, that you have to be silent, even though it is only your malice which ties your tongue; yes, I pity you on account of your malice! – Ah, it is growing yet more still, my heart swells again: it is startled by a new truth, *it too cannot speak*, it too mocks when the mouth calls something into this beauty, it too enjoys its sweet silent malice. I begin to hate speech, to hate even thinking; for do I not hear behind every word the laughter of error, of imagination, of the spirit of delusion? Must I not mock at my pity? Mock at my mockery? – O sea, O evening! You are evil instructors! You teach man to cease to be man! Shall he surrender to you? Shall he become as you now are, pale, glittering, mute, tremendous, reposing above himself? Exalted above himself?

424

For whom truth exists. – Up to now errors have been forces of *consolation*: now we expect the same effect from known truths, and have been waiting for it for some little time. How if this effect – the effect of consolation – were precisely what truths are incapable of? – Would this then constitute an objection to truths? What have they in common with the inner states of suffering, stunted, sick human beings that they must necessarily be of use to them? For to determine that a plant makes no contribution to the treatment of sick human beings is no argument against the *truth* of the plant. In earlier times, however, the conviction that mankind was the goal of nature was so strong that it was assumed without question that nothing could be disclosed by knowledge that was not salutary and useful to man,

181

indeed that things other than this *could* not, *ought* not to *exist*. –
Perhaps all this leads to the proposition that truth, *as a whole* and
interconnectedly, exists only for souls which are at once powerful
and harmless, and full of joyfulness and peace (as was the soul of
Aristotle), just as it will no doubt be only such souls as these that will
be capable of *seeking it*: for, no matter how proud they may be of their
intellect and its freedom, the others are seeking *cures* for themselves –
they are *not* seeking truth. This is why these others take so little real
pleasure in science, and make of the coldness, dryness and inhumanity
of science a reproach to it: it is the sick passing judgment on the
games of the healthy. – The Greek gods, too, were unable to offer
consolation; when Greek mankind at last one and all grew sick, this
was a reason for the abolition of such gods.

425

We gods in exile! – It is through *errors* as to its origin, its uniqueness, its
destiny, and through the *demands* that have been advanced on the
basis of these errors, that mankind has raised itself on high and again
and again 'excelled itself': but through these same errors an
unspeakable amount of suffering, mutual persecution, suspicion,
misunderstanding, and even greater misery for the individual in and
for himself, have come into the world. Men have become *suffering*
creatures as a consequence of their moralities: what they have
purchased with them is, all in all, a feeling that at bottom they are too
good and too significant for the earth and are paying it only a passing
visit. For the present, the 'proud sufferer' is still the highest type of
man.

426

Colourblindness of thinkers. – How different nature must have appeared
to the Greeks if, as we have to admit, their eyes were blind to blue and
green, and instead of the former saw deep brown, instead of the
latter yellow (so that they used the same word, for example, to
describe the colour of dark hair, that of the cornflower, and that of
the southern sea; and again the same word for the colour of the
greenest plants and that of the human skin, honey, and yellow resins:
it has been shown that their greatest painters reproduced their world
using only black, white, red and yellow) – how different and how
much more like mankind nature must have appeared to them, since
in their eyes the coloration of mankind also preponderated in nature
and the latter as it were floated in the atmosphere of human

coloration! (Blue and green dehumanise nature more than anything else does.) It is on this *deficiency* that there grew up in the Greeks the playful facility which distinguishes them for seeing natural events as gods and demi-gods, that is to say as human-like forms. – But let this be no more than a metaphor for a further supposition. Every thinker paints his world in fewer colours than *are actually there*, and is blind to certain individual colours. This is not merely a deficiency. By virtue of this approximation and simplification he introduces harmonies of colours *into the things themselves*, and these harmonies possess great charm and can constitute an enrichment of nature. Perhaps it was only in this way that mankind first learned to take *pleasure* in the sight of existence: existence, that is to say, was in the first instance presented to them in one or two colours, and thus presented harmoniously: mankind then as it were practised on these few shades before being able to go over to several. And even today many an individual works himself out of a partial colourblindness into a richer seeing and distinguishing: in which process, however, he not only discovers new enjoyments but is also *obliged to give up and relinquish* some of his earlier ones.

427

The beautification of science. – As rococo horticulture arose from the feeling 'nature is ugly, savage, boring – come! let us beautify it!' (*embellir la nature*) – so there again and again arises from the feeling 'science is ugly, dry, cheerless, difficult, laborious – come! let us beautify it!' something that calls itself *philosophy*. It wants, as all art and poetry want – above all to *entertain*: but, in accordance with its inherited pride, it wants to do this in a more sublime and exalted fashion and before a select audience. To create for these a horticulture whose principal charm is, as with the 'more common' kind, a *deception of the eyes* (with temples, distant prospects, grottos, mazes, waterfalls, to speak in metaphors), to present science in extract and with all kinds of strange and unexpected illuminations and to involve it in so much indefiniteness, irrationality and reverie that one can wander in it 'as in wild nature' and yet without effort or boredom – that is no small ambition: he who has this ambition even dreams of thereby making superfluous religion, which with earlier mankind constituted the highest species of the art of entertainment. – This then takes its course and will one day attain the height of its achievement: and already voices begin to be raised against philosophy, crying 'back to science! To the nature and naturalness of science!' –

428 DAYBREAK

and with that an age may perhaps *begin* which will discover the mightiest beauty in precisely the 'wild, ugly' sides of science, just as it was only from the time of Rousseau that one discovered a sense for the beauty of high mountains and the desert.

428

Two kinds of moralist. – To perceive for the first time a law of nature and to perceive it whole, that is to say to *demonstrate* it (for example that of gravity, of the reflection of light and sound), is something different from *explaining* such a law, and is a matter for a different kind of mind. In the same way those moralists who perceive and exhibit the laws and habits of mankind – men with subtle eyes, ears and noses – differ altogether from those who explain what has been observed. The latter have to be above all *inventive* and possess an imagination *unchained* by acuteness and knowledge.

429

The new passion. – Why do we fear and hate a possible reversion to barbarism? Because it would make people unhappier than they are? Oh no! The barbarians of every age were *happier*: let us not deceive ourselves! – The reason is that our *drive to knowledge* has become too strong for us to be able to want happiness without knowledge or the happiness of a strong, firmly rooted delusion; even to imagine such a state of things is painful to us! Restless discovering and divining has such an attraction for us, and has grown as indispensable to us as is to the lover his unrequited love, which he would at no price relinquish for a state of indifference – perhaps, indeed, we too are *unrequited* lovers! Knowledge has in us been transformed into a passion which shrinks at no sacrifice and at bottom fears nothing but its own extinction; we believe in all honesty that all mankind must believe itself more exalted and comforted under the compulsion and suffering of *this* passion than it did formerly, when envy of the coarser contentment that follows in the train of barbarism had not yet been overcome. Perhaps mankind will even perish of this passion for knowledge! – even this thought has no power over us! But did Christianity ever shun such a thought? Are love and death not brothers? Yes, we hate barbarism – we would all prefer the destruction of mankind to a regression of knowledge! And finally: if mankind does not perish of a *passion* it will perish of a *weakness*: which do you prefer? This is the main question. Do we desire for mankind an end in fire and light or one in the sand? –

184

430

This too is heroic. – To do things of the vilest odour of which one hardly ventures even to speak but which are useful and necessary – this too is heroic. The Greeks were not ashamed to include among the great labours of Heracles the cleansing of a stable.

431

The opinions of one's opponents. – To assess the natural quality of even the cleverest heads – to see whether they are naturally subtle or feeble – one should take note of how they interpret and reproduce the opinions of their opponents: for how it does this betrays the natural measure of every intellect. – The perfect sage without knowing it elevates his opponent into the ideal and purifies his contradictory opinion of every blemish and adventitiousness: only when his opponent has by this means become a god with shining weapons does the sage fight against him.

432

Investigators and experimenters. – There are no scientific methods which alone lead to knowledge! We have to tackle things experimentally, now angry with them and now kind, and be successively just, passionate and cold with them. One person addresses things as a policeman, a second as a father confessor, a third as an inquisitive wanderer. Something can be wrung from them now with sympathy, now with force; reverence for their secrets will take one person forwards, indiscretion and roguishness in revealing their secrets will do the same for another. We investigators are, like all conquerors, discoverers, seafarers, adventurers, of an audacious morality and must reconcile ourselves to being considered on the whole evil.

433

Seeing with new eyes. – Supposing that beauty in art is always to be understood as the *imitation of happiness* – and this I hold to be the truth – in accordance with how an age, a people, a great, self-regulating individual imagines happiness: what does the so-called *realism* of contemporary artists give us to understand as to the happiness of our own age? *Its* kind of beauty is undoubtedly the kind of beauty we can most easily grasp and enjoy. Is one not then obliged to believe that *our* happiness lies in realism, in possessing the sharpest possible senses and in the faithful interpretation of actuality – thus not in reality but in *knowledge of reality?* The influence of science has already acquired such depth and breadth that the artists of our century have, without intending to do so, already become glorifiers of the 'delights' of science!

434

Making intercession. – Unprepossessing landscapes exist for the great landscape painters, remarkable and rare ones for the petty. For the great things of nature and mankind have to intercede for all the petty, mediocre and ambitious among their admirers – but the *great man* intercedes for the *simple* things.

435

Do not perish unnoticed. – Our greatness and efficiency crumbles away not *all at once* but continually; the little plants which grow up in and around everything and know how to cling everywhere, it is these which ruin that which is great in us – the everyday, hourly pitiableness of our environment which we constantly overlook, the thousand tendrils of this or that little, fainthearted sensation which grows out of our neighbourhood, out of our job, our social life, out of the way we divide up the day. If we neglect to notice this little weed, we shall ourselves perish of it unnoticed! – And if you absolutely must perish, do so *all at once* and suddenly: then perhaps there may remain of you some *sublime ruin*! And not, as there is now some reason to fear, a molehill! And grass and weeds upon it, little victors, modest as ever and too pitiable even to celebrate their triumph!

436

Casuistical. – There is a wicked dilemma to which not everyone's courage and character are equal: as a passenger on a ship to discover that the captain and steersman are making dangerous mistakes and that one is their superior in nautical knowledge – and then to ask oneself: how if you should incite a mutiny against them and have them both seized? Does your superiority not give you the right to do so? And would they not also be in the right if they locked you up for undermining discipline? – This is a metaphor for more elevated and more agonising situations: in which the question in the end is always what guarantees our superiority, and justifies our faith in ourself, in such cases. Success? But one has already had to *do* the thing which bears within itself all the dangers – and not only dangers for us but for the ship as well.

437

Privileges. – He who really possesses himself, that is to say he who has definitively *conquered himself*, henceforth regards it as his own privilege to punish himself, to pardon himself, to take pity on himself: he does not need to concede this to anyone else, but he can freely relinquish it to another, to a friend for example – but he knows that he therewith confers a *right* and that one can confer rights only out of the possession of *power*.

438

Man and things. – Why does man not see things? He is himself standing in the way: he conceals things.

439

Signs of happiness. – All sensations of happiness have two things in common: *abundance* of feeling and *high spirits*, so that, like a fish, we feel our element around us and leap about in it. Good Christians will understand what Christian exuberance is.

440

Do not renounce: – To forego the world without knowing it, like a *nun* – that leads to a fruitless, perhaps melancholy solitude. It has nothing in common with the solitude of the *vita contemplativa* of the thinker: when he chooses *that* he is renouncing nothing; on the contrary, it would be renunciation, melancholy, destruction of himself if he were obliged to persist in the *vita practica*: he foregoes this because he knows it, because he knows himself. Thus he leaps into *his* element, thus he gains *his* cheerfulness.

441

Why what is closest grows more and more distant. – The more we think about all that has been and will be, the paler grows that which is. If we live with the dead and die with them in their death, what are our 'neighbours' to us then? We grow more solitary – and we do so *because* the whole flood of humanity is surging around us. The fire within us, which is for *all* that is human, grows brighter and brighter – and *that* is why we gaze upon that which immediately surrounds us as though it had grown more shadowy and we had grown more indifferent to it. – But the coldness of our glance *gives offence*!

442

The rule. – 'I always find the rule more interesting than the exception' – he who feels like that is far advanced in the realm of knowledge and is among the initiated.

443

On education. – I have gradually seen the light as to the most universal deficiency in our kind of cultivation and education: no one learns, no one strives after, no one teaches – *the endurance of solitude.*

444

Surprise at resistance. – Because something has become transparent to us, we think it will no longer offer us any resistance – and are then amazed when we discover we can see through it but cannot go through it! It is the same folly and amazement as overcomes the fly in face of a pane of glass.

445

Where the noblest go wrong. – We give somebody the best that we have – until at last love has nothing left to give: but he who receives it has certainly not received in it the best that *he* has, and consequently fails to evidence that completeness of gratitude which the giver counted upon.

446

Order of rank. – There are, first of all, superficial thinkers; secondly, deep thinkers – those who go down into the depths of a thing; thirdly, thorough thinkers, who thoroughly explore the grounds of a thing – which is worth very much more than merely going down into its depths! – finally, those who stick their heads into the swamp: which ought not to be a sign either of depth or of thoroughness! They are the dear departed underground.

447

Master and pupil. – It is part of the humanity of a master to warn his pupil about himself.

448

Honouring reality. – How can one see this rejoicing crowd without feeling with them and being moved to tears! Previously we thought little of the object of their rejoicing and would still think little of it *if* we had not now experienced it! To what, then, may our experiences not impel us! What really are our opinions! If we are not to lose ourselves, if we are not to lose our *reason*, we have to flee from experiences! Thus did Plato flee from reality and desire to see things only in pallid mental pictures; he was full of sensibility and knew how easily the waves of his sensibility could close over his reason. – Would the wise man consequently have to say to himself: 'I shall honour *reality*, but I shall turn my back on it *because* I know and fear it'? – ought he to do as African tribes do in the presence of their princes: approach them only backwards and thus show their respect and at the same time their fear?

449

Where are the needy in spirit? – Ah! How reluctant I am to *force* my own ideas upon another! How I rejoice in any mood and secret transformation within myself which means that the ideas *of another* have prevailed over my own! Now and then, however, I enjoy an even higher festival: when one is for once *permitted* to *give away* one's spiritual house and possessions, like a father confessor who sits in his corner anxious for *one in need* to come and tell of the distress of his mind, so that he may again fill his hands and his heart and *make light* his troubled soul! He is not merely not looking for fame: he would even like to escape gratitude, for gratitude is too importunate and lacks respect for solitude and silence. What he seeks is to live nameless and lightly mocked at, too humble to awaken envy or hostility, with a head free of fever, equipped with a handful of knowledge and a bagful of experience, as it were a poor-doctor of the spirit aiding those whose head is *confused by opinions* without their being really aware who has aided them! Not desiring to maintain his own opinion or celebrate a victory over them, but to address them in such a way that, after the slightest of imperceptible hints or contradictions, they themselves arrive at the truth and go away proud of the fact! To be like a little inn which rejects no one who is in need but which is afterwards forgotten or ridiculed! To possess no advantage, neither better food nor purer air nor a more joyful spirit – but to give away, to give back, to communicate, to grow poorer! To be able to be humble, so as to be accessible to many and humiliating to none! To have much injustice done him, and to have crept through the worm-holes of errors of every kind, so as to be able to reach many hidden souls on their secret paths! For ever in a kind of love and for ever in a kind of selfishness and self-enjoyment! To be in possession of a dominion and at the same time concealed and renouncing! To lie continually in the sunshine and gentleness of grace, and yet to know that the paths that rise up to the sublime are close by! – That would be a life! That would be a reason for a long life!

450

The allurement of knowledge. – A glance through the portals of science affects passionate spirits as the magic of all magic; and it will probably turn them into fantasists and, in the most favourable case, into poets: so vehement is their craving for the happiness of those with knowledge. Does it not thrill through all your senses – this sound of sweet allurement with which science has proclaimed its glad tidings, in a hundred phrases and in the hundred-and-first and fairest: 'Let delusion vanish! Then "woe is me!" will vanish too; and with "woe is me!" woe itself will be gone.' (Marcus Aurelius)

451

To whom a court jester is a necessity. – The very beautiful, the very good, the very powerful almost never learn the full and universal truth about anything – for in their presence one always involuntarily lies a little, because one ·is always subject to their influence and in accordance with this influence presents the truth one might communicate in the form of an *adaptation* (by falsifying the facts in some degree and colour, omitting or adding details, and keeping back that which absolutely resists being adapted). If people of this kind are nonetheless determined to hear the truth they have to maintain their *court jester* – a being with the madman's privilege of being unable to adapt himself.

452

Impatience. – People both active and contemplative may be subject to a degree of impatience which, when they experience a failure, at once bids them go over to an antithetical domain of endeavour, take a passionate interest in it and pursue new undertakings – until a delay in achieving success drives them out of this new domain too: thus they wander, reckless and adventurous, through the practices of many domains and natures and, through the knowledge of man and things they have accumulated on their tremendous travels and with a little amelioration of their impatient drive, at last become mighty practitioners. Thus a defect of character becomes a school of genius.

453

Moral interregnum. – Who would now be in a position to describe that which will one day *do away with* moral feelings and judgments! – however sure one may be that the foundations of the latter are all defective and their superstructure is beyond repair: their obligatory force must diminish from day to day, so long as the obligatory force of reason does not diminish! To construct anew the laws of life and action – for this task our sciences of physiology, medicine, sociology and solitude are not yet sufficiently sure of themselves: and it is from them that the foundation-stones of new ideals (if not the new ideals themselves) must come. So it is that, according to our taste and talent, we live an existence which is either a *prelude* or a *postlude*, and the best we can do in this *interregnum* is to be as far as possible our own *reges* and found little *experimental states*. We are experiments: let us also want to be them!

454
Digression. – A book such as this is not for reading straight through or reading aloud but for dipping into, especially when out walking or on a journey; you must be able to stick your head into it and out of it again and again and discover nothing familiar around you.

455
First nature. – The way in which we are educated nowadays means that we acquire a *second nature*: and we have it when the world calls us mature, of age, employable. A few of us are sufficiently snakes one day to throw off this skin, and to do so when beneath its covering their *first nature* has grown mature. With most of us, its germ has dried up.

456
A virtue in process of becoming. – Such assertions and promises as those of the antique philosophers concerning the unity of virtue and happiness, or the Christian 'But seek ye first the kingdom of God, and his righteousness; and all these things shall be added unto you' have never been made with total honesty and yet always without a bad conscience: one has advanced such propositions, which one very much desires to be true, boldly as the truth in the face of all appearance and has felt in doing so no religious or moral pang of conscience – for one had transcended reality *in honorem majorem* of virtue or of God and without any selfish motive! Many worthy people still stand at this *level of truthfulness*: when they *feel* themselves selfless they think they are permitted to *trouble themselves less* about truth. Notice, however, that *honesty* is among neither the Socratic nor the Christian virtues: it is the youngest virtue, still very immature, still often misjudged and taken for something else, still hardly aware of itself – something in process of becoming which we can advance or obstruct as we think fit.

457
Ultimate silence. – Some act like treasure-seekers: they light by accident

upon things which the soul of another has kept hidden and acquire a
knowledge of it which is often hard to bear! There are circumstances
under which one can know and understand the living and the dead
to such a degree that it is painful to speak about them to others: one is
constantly afraid of being indiscreet. – I can imagine the wisest
historian suddenly falling silent.

458

The grand destiny. – This is something very rare but a thing to take
delight in: a man with a finely constituted intellect who has the
character, the inclinations and *also the experiences* appropriate to such
an intellect.

459

The magnanimity of the thinker. – Rousseau and Schopenhauer – both
were sufficiently proud to inscribe upon their existence the motto:
vitam impendere vero. And both again – how they must have suffered in
their pride when they failed to make *verum impendere vitae! – verum* as
each of them understood it – when their life ran along beside their
knowledge like a wayward bass which refuses to harmonise with the
melody! – But knowledge would be in a bad way if it were
apportioned to every thinker only as it happened to fit his person!
And things would be in a bad way with thinkers if their vanity were so
great they could endure only this! The fairest virtue of the great
thinker is the magnanimity with which, as a man of knowledge, he
intrepidly, often with embarrassment, often with sublime mockery
and smiling – offers himself and his life as a sacrifice.

460

Making use of hours of danger. – We get to know a man or a state of affairs
far differently when they represent a danger to our possessions,
honour, life and death, or to those of our loved ones: as Tiberius, for
example, must have reflected more profoundly on the nature of the
Emperor Augustus and that of his system of government, and
known more about them, than the wisest historian possibly could.
Now, we all live, comparatively speaking, in far too great security for
us ever to acquire a sound knowledge of man: one person studies
him from a desire to do so, another from boredom, a third from
habit: it is never a case of: 'study or perish!'. As long as truths do not
cut into our flesh with knives, we retain a secret contempt for them:
they still appear to us too much like 'winged dreams', as though we
were free to have them or not have them – as though there were

something in them which stood at our discretion, as though we could *awaken* from these truths of ours!

461

Hic Rhodus, hic salta. – Our music, which can transform itself into everything and has to transform itself because, like the demon of the sea, it has in itself no character: in the past this music followed the *Christian scholar* and was able to translate his ideal into sounds; why should it not in the end discover that brighter, more joyful and universal sound which corresponds to the *ideal thinker?* – a music which knows how to *be at home* only floating up and down among the broad soaring vaulted arches of *his* soul? – Our music has hitherto been so great, so good: nothing has been impossible to it! So let it then show that it is possible to feel these three things at the same time: sublimity, deep and warm illumination, and the joy of perfect consistency.

462

Slow cures. – Like those of the body, the chronic sicknesses of the soul arise very rarely from one single gross offence against the rationality of body and soul but usually from countless little unheeded instances of neglect. – He, for example, who day by day breathes too weakly and thus takes too little air into his lungs, even though it be to an infinitesimal degree, finally falls victim to a chronic lung infection: in such a case, the only cure is to take countless little exercises in the opposite direction; to make it a rule, for example, to take strong and deep breaths every quarter of an hour (when possible lying flat on the floor; a watch which chimes the quarters must then become a permanent companion). All these cures are petty and *slow*; and he who wishes to cure his soul must also consider making changes to the very pettiest of his habits. Many a man curses his environment ten times a day and pays little heed to the fact, and especially not to the fact that after a few years he has created for himself a *law* of habit which henceforth *compels* him to put his environment out of temper ten times a day. But he can also acquire the habit of conferring a benefit upon it ten times a day!

463

On the seventh day. – 'You praise that as my *creation?* I have only put from me what was a burden to me! My soul is above the vanity of creators. – You praise this as my *resignation?* Have I only put from me what was a burden to me? My soul is above the vanity of the resigned.'

464

The shame of those who bestow. – It is so unmagnanimous always to play
the bestower and giver and to show one's face when doing so! But to
give and bestow and to conceal one's name and awareness one is
bestowing a favour! Or to have no name, like nature, in which the
most refreshing thing of all is that here we at last no longer encounter
a giver and bestower, a 'gracious countenance'! – To be sure, you
have frivolously sacrificed even this refreshment, for you have put a
god into nature – and now everything is again tense and unfree!
What? Never to be allowed to be alone with oneself? Never again to
be unobserved, unprotected, free of leading-reins and gifts? If we are
always surrounded by another, the best of courage and goodness in
this world is rendered impossible. Is this importunity from Heaven,
this inescapable supernatural neighbour, not enough to drive one to
the Devil! – But there is no need for that, it has been only a dream!
Let us wake up!

465

A meeting. – A: What are you gazing at? You have been standing here
such a long time. – B: The same old thing and the same new thing!
The helplessness of a thing draws me so far and so deep into it that I
finally reach its bottom and discover that it is not worth so very
much. At the end of all such events there arises in me a kind of
sorrow and fixity. I experience this on a small scale three times every
day.

466

Fame brings a loss. – What an advantage to be allowed to address men
as an unknown! The gods take from us 'half our virtue' when they
take from us our incognito and make us famous.

467

Twofold patience. – 'In doing this you will cause pain to many people.' –
I know; and I know also that I shall have to suffer twofold for it: once
from pity at their suffering, and then through the revenge they will
take on me. Nonetheless it is no less necessary that I should do as I
do.

468

The realm of beauty is bigger. – As we go about in nature, with joy and
cunning, bent on discovering and as it were catching in the act the
beauty proper to everything; as we try to see how that piece of

coastline, with its rocks, inlets, olive trees and pines, attains to its perfection and mastery whether in the sunshine, or when the sky is stormy, or when twilight has almost gone: so we ought to go about among men, viewing and discovering them, showing them their good and evil, so that they shall behold their own proper beauty which unfolds itself in one case in the sunlight, in another amid storms, and in a third only when night is falling and the sky is full of rain. Is it then forbidden to *enjoy* the *evil* man as a wild landscape possessing its own bold lineaments and effects of light, if the same man appears to our eyes as a sketch and caricature and, as a blot in nature, causes us pain, when he poses as good and law-abiding? – Yes, it is forbidden: hitherto we have been permitted to seek beauty only in the *morally good* – a fact which sufficiently accounts for our having found so little of it and having had to seek about for imaginary beauties without backbone! – As surely as the wicked enjoy a hundred kinds of happiness of which the virtuous have no inkling, so too they possess a hundred kinds of beauty: and many of them have not yet been discovered.

469

The inhumanity of the sage. – Since the progress of the sage, who, as the Buddhist hymn says, 'walks alone like the rhinoceros', is heavy and crushes all in its path – there is need from time to time of a sign of a conciliatory and gentler humanity: and by that I mean, not only a swifter progress, a politeness and companionableness, not only a display of wit and a certain self-mockery, but a self-contradiction and an occasional regression into the nonsense currently in vogue. If he is not to resemble a steamroller which advances like fatality, the sage who wants to teach has to employ his *faults* as an extenuation, and when he says 'despise me!' he pleads for permission to be the advocate of a presumptuous truth. He wants to lead you into the mountains, he wants perhaps to put your life in danger: in return he is willing, before and afterwards, to let you take revenge on such a leader – it is the price at which he purchases for himself the pleasure of *going on ahead*. – Do you recall what went through your mind when once he led you by slippery paths through a dark cavern? How your heart, beating and discouraged, said to itself: 'this leader might do something better than crawl about here! He is one of those inquisitive kinds of idlers: – does it not already do him too much honour that we should appear to accord him any value at all by *following* him?'

470

At the banquet of many. – How happy one is when one is fed like the birds, out of the hand of someone who scatters food to the birds without looking too closely at them or assessing their worthiness! To live like a bird who comes and flies away and bears no name in its beak! Thus it is my delight to eat my fill at the banquet of many.

471

A different kind of neighbour-love. – Behaviour that is excited, noisy, inconsistent, nervous constitutes the antithesis of *great passion*: the latter, dwelling within like a dark fire and there assembling all that is hot and ardent, leaves a man looking outwardly cold and indifferent and impresses upon his features a certain impassivity. Such men are, to be sure, occasionally capable of *neighbour-love* – but it is a kind different from that of the sociable and anxious to please: it is a gentle, reflective, relaxed friendliness; it is as though they were gazing out of the windows of their castle, which is their fortress and for that reason also their prison – to gaze into what is strange and free, into *what is different*, does them so much good!

472

Not to justify oneself. – A: But why will you not justify yourself? – B: I could do so, in this and in a hundred other things, but I despise the self-satisfied pleasure that lies in justification: for I do not find these things of sufficient importance, and I would rather bear a few blemishes than give these petty people the spiteful joy of saying: 'how seriously he takes these things!' For this is not the case! Perhaps I would have to take myself more in earnest to feel it a duty to correct erroneous ideas about me – I am too indifferent and lazy with regard to myself and thus also with regard to the effect I produce.

473

Where one should build one's house. – If you feel yourself great and fruitful in solitude, a life in society will diminish you and make you empty: and *vice versa*. Powerful gentleness, like that of a father: – where you are seized by this mood, there found your house, whether it be in the midst of the crowd or in a silent retreat. *Ubi pater sum, ibi patri.*

474

The only ways. – 'Dialectics is the only way of attaining the divine being and getting behind the veil of appearance' – this is asserted by Plato as solemnly and passionately as Schopenhauer asserts it of the antithesis of dialectics – and both are wrong. For that to which they want to show us the way does not *exist*. – And have all the great passions of mankind not hitherto been as these are, passions for a nothing? And all their solemnities – solemnities about a nothing?

475

Growing heavy. – You do not know him: though he hang many weights on himself he can nonetheless lift them with him into the heights. And you, judging him by the beating of your own petty wings, conclude that, *because* he hangs these weights on himself, he wants to stay *below*!

476

At the harvest-festival of the spirit. – From day to day they accumulate and well up, experiences, events, thoughts about them and dreams about these thoughts – an immeasurable, overwhelming property! One grows dizzy at the sight of it; I no longer understand how one can call the poor in spirit *blessed*! – But sometimes, when I am tired, I envy them: for the *administration* of such a property is a heavy task, and its heaviness not seldom weighs down all happiness. – If only it were enough just to stand and gaze at it! If only one were a miser of one's knowledge!

477

Redeemed from scepticism. – A: Others emerge out of a general moral scepticism ill-humoured and feeble, gnawed-at and worm-eaten, indeed half-consumed – but I do so braver and healthier than ever, again in possession of my instincts. Where a sharp wind blows, the sea rises high and there is no little danger to be faced, that is where I feel best. I have not become a worm, even though I have often had to work and tunnel like a worm. – B: You have just *ceased* to be a sceptic! For you *deny*! – A: And in doing so I have again learned to *affirm*.

478

Let us pass by! – Spare him! Leave him in his solitude! Do you want to break him completely to pieces? He has sprung a leak, like a glass into which something too hot has suddenly been poured – and he was such a precious glass!

479

Love and truthfulness. – For the sake of love we are inveterate transgressors against truth and habitual thieves and receivers, who allow more to be true than appears to us true – that is why the thinker must always from time to time drive away those people he loves (they will not be precisely those who love him), so that they may display their sting and their malice and cease to *seduce* him. Consequently the thinker's goodness will have its waxing and waning moon.

480

Unavoidable. – Whatever you may experience, he who is ill-disposed towards you will always find in your experience an occasion for diminishing you! Experience the profoundest convulsion of heart and of knowledge and emerge at last like a convalescent, with a sorrowful smile, into freedom and luminous silence – someone will still say: 'he regards his sickness as an argument, his impotence as proof that all are impotent; he is vain enough to become sick so as to feel the sense of superiority enjoyed by the sufferer'. – And supposing someone burst his own chains and deeply wounded himself in doing so: there will always be another to point at him in mockery. 'How clumsy he is!' he will say; 'but that is how a man is bound to be when he has got used to his chains and is fool enough to break them!'

481

Two Germans. – If you compare Kant and Schopenhauer with Plato, Spinoza, Pascal, Rousseau, Goethe in respect of their soul and not of their mind, then the former are at a disadvantage: their thoughts do not constitute a passionate history of a soul; there is nothing here that would make a novel, no crises, catastrophes or death-scenes; their thinking is not at the same time an involuntary biography of a soul but, in the case of Kant, the biography of a *head*, in the case of Schopenhauer the description and mirroring of a *character* ('that which is unalterable') and pleasure in the 'mirror' itself, that is to say in an excellent intellect. When he does shine through his thoughts, Kant appears honest and honourable in the best sense, but insignificant: he lacks breadth and power; he has not experienced very much, and his manner of working deprives him of the *time* in which to experience things – I am thinking, of course, not of crude 'events' impinging from without, but of the vicissitudes and convulsions which befall the most solitary and quietest life which possesses leisure and burns with the passion of thinking. Schopenhauer has one advantage over him: he at least possesses a certain *vehement ugliness* in hatred, desire, vanity, mistrust; his disposition is somewhat more ferocious and he had time and leisure for this ferocity. But he lacked 'development': just as development is lacking in the domain of his ideas; he had no 'history'.

482

Seeking one's company. – Are we then seeking too much if we seek the company of men who have grown gentle, well-tasting and nutritious, like chestnuts which have been put on to the fire and taken from it again at the proper time? Who expect little from life, and would rather take this as a gift than as something they have earned, as though the birds and the bees had brought it to them? Who are too proud ever to be able to feel themselves rewarded? And are too serious in their passion for knowledge and for honesty to have time or inclination for fame? – Such men we should call philosophers; and they themselves will always find a more modest name.

483

Satiety with mankind. – A: Learn to know! Yes! But always as a man! What? Always to sit before the same comedy, act in the same comedy? Never to be able to see into things out of any other eyes but *these*? And what uncountable kinds of beings may there not be whose organs are better equipped for knowledge! What will mankind have come to know at the end of all their knowledge? – their organs! And that perhaps means: the impossibility of knowledge! Misery and disgust! – B: This is a serious attack – *reason* is attacking you! But tomorrow you will be again in the midst of knowledge and therewith also in the midst of unreason, which is to say in *delight* in the human. Let us go down to the sea! –

484

One's own path. – If we take the decisive step and enter upon the path which is called our 'own path', a secret is suddenly revealed to us: all those who have hitherto been our friends and familiars have imagined themselves superior to us, and are now offended. The best of them are lenient with us and wait patiently for us soon to find our way back to the 'right path' – they know, it seems, what the right path is! The others resort to mockery and act as though one had become temporarily insane, or they make spiteful allusions to the person they suppose to have misled us. The more malicious declare us to be vain fools and seek to blacken our motives, while the worst former friend of all sees in us his worst enemy and one thirsting for revenge for a protracted dependence – and is afraid of us. – What are we to do? My advice is: to inaugurate our sovereignty by promising all our acquaintances a year's amnesty in advance for all their sins.

485

Distant perspectives. – A: But why this solitude? – B: I am not at odds with anyone. But when I am alone I seem to see my friends in a clearer and fairer light than when I am with them; and when I loved and appreciated music the most, I lived far from it. It seems I need a distant perspective if I am to think well of things.

486
Gold and hunger. – Now and then there comes along a man who changes everything he touches to gold. One fine evil day he will discover that this gift means he is going to starve to death. Everything around him is glittering, glorious, ideally unapproachable, and now he longs for things which are *altogether impossible for him* to change to gold – and *how* ardently he longs! As a starving man longs for food! – What will he reach for?

487
Shame. – Here stands the handsome steed and paws the ground: it snorts, longs for the gallop and loves him who usually rides him – but oh shame! his rider cannot mount up on to his back today, he is weary. – This is the shame of the wearied philosopher before his own philosophy.

488
Against the squandering of love. – Do we not blush when we detect ourselves in the act of feeling a violent aversion? But we ought to do the same in the case of violent affections too, on account of the injustice which they too involve! More, indeed: there are people who feel as though hedged in, and whose heart grows tight, when anyone favours them with his affection only by *withdrawing* something of his affection from others. When we hear from his voice that *we* are chosen and preferred! Ah, I am not grateful for this favour, I notice in myself a grudge against him who wants to favour me in this way: he ought not to love me at the *expense* of others! I want to see how I can endure myself at my own expense! And often I find that my heart is full and I feel in high spirits – to a man who possesses such things one should give nothing that *others* stand in need, sorely in need of!

489
Friends in need. – Sometimes we notice that one of our friends belongs more to another than he does to us, and that his delicacy is troubled by and his selfishness inadequate to this decision: we then have to make things easier for him and *estrange* him from us. – This is likewise necessary when we adopt a way of thinking which would be ruinous to him: our love for him has to drive us, through an injustice which

we take upon ourself, to create for him a good conscience in renouncing us.

490

These petty truths! – 'You know all this, but you have never experienced it – I do not accept your evidence. These "petty truths"! – you think them petty because you have not paid for them with your blood!' – But are they then great because one has paid *too much* for them? And blood is always too much! – 'Do you think so? How niggardly you are with blood!'

491

Another reason for solitude! – A: So you intend to return to your desert? – B: I am not quick moving, I have to wait for myself – it is always late before the water comes to light out of the well of my self, and I often have to endure thirst for longer than I have patience. That is why I gc into solitude – so as not to drink out of everybody's cistern. When I am among the many I live as the many do, and I do not think as I really think; after a time it always seems as though they want to banish me from myself and rob me of my soul – and I grow angry with everybody and fear everybody. I then require the desert, so as to grow good again.

492

Among south winds. – A: I no longer understand myself! Only yesterday I felt so wild and stormy and at the same time so warm, so sunny – and bright in the extreme. And today! All is now motionless, flat, dejected, gloomy, like the lagoon of Venice: – I want nothing and draw a deep breath of relief at that, and yet I am secretly vexed at this wanting nothing. Thus do the waves splash back and forth in the lake of my melancholy. – B: You have described a pleasant little illness. The next north-east wind will blow it away! – A: Why should it!

493

On one's own tree. – A: The thoughts of no thinker give me so much pleasure as my own do: that, of course, says nothing as to their value, but I would be a fool to refuse the fruit I find most tasty simply because it happens to grow on *my* tree! – And I was such a fool at one time. – B: With others it is the reverse: but this too says nothing as to the value of their thoughts, and especially nothing against their value.

494

Final argument of the brave. – 'There are snakes in these bushes.' –

Good, I shall go into the bushes and kill them. – 'But perhaps you will be their victim, and not they yours!' – What do I matter!

495

Our teachers. – In our youth we take our teachers and guides from the time in which we happen to live and the circle in which we happen to move: we are thoughtlessly confident that the times we live in are bound to have teachers better suited to us than to anyone else and that we are bound to find them without much trouble. For this childishness we have in later years to pay a heavy price: *we have to expiate our teachers in ourself.* We then perhaps go in search of our true guides throughout the whole world, the world of the past included – but perhaps it is too late. And in the worst case we discover that they were living when we were young – and that we missed them.

496

The evil principle. – Plato has given us a splendid description of how the philosophical thinker must within every existing society count as the paragon of all wickedness: for as critic of all customs he is the antithesis of the moral man, and if he does not succeed in becoming the lawgiver of new customs he remains in the memory of men as 'the evil principle'. From this we may gather what the city of Athens, tolerably freeminded and avid for innovation though it was, did with the reputation of Plato during his lifetime: is it any wonder if, filled with the 'political drive' as he himself says he was, he attempted three times to settle in Sicily, where at that time a Pan-Hellenic Mediterranean city seemed to be in process of formation? In this city, and with its help, Plato intended to do for all the Greeks what Mohammed later did for his Arabs: to determine customs in things great and small and especially to regulate everyone's day-to-day mode of life. His ideas were as surely *practical* as those of Mohammed were practical: after all, far more incredible ideas, those of Christianity, have proved practical! A couple of accidents more and a couple of other accidents fewer – and the world would have seen the Platonisation of the European south; and if this state of things still persisted, we should presumably be honouring in Plato the 'good principle'. But success eluded him: and he was thus left with the reputation of being a fantasist and utopian – the more opprobrious epithets perished with ancient Athens.

497

The purifying eye. – 'Genius' is most readily to be ascribed to those men in whom, as with Plato, Spinoza and Goethe, the spirit seems to be only *loosely attached* to the character and temperament, as a winged being who can easily detach itself from these and then raise itself high above them. On the other hand, it is precisely those who could *never get free* from their temperament and knew how to endow it with the most spiritual, expansive, universal, indeed sometimes cosmic expression (Schopenhauer, for example) who have been given to speaking most freely of their 'genius'. These geniuses were unable to fly above and beyond themselves, but they believed that wherever they flew they would discover and rediscover *themselves* – that is *their* 'greatness', and it *can* be greatness! – The others, who better deserve the name, possess the *pure, purifying eye* which seems not to have grown out of their temperament and character but, free from these and usually in mild opposition to them, looks down on the world as on a god and loves this god. But even they have not acquired this eye at a single stroke: seeing needs practice and preschooling, and he who is fortunate enough will also find at the proper time a teacher of pure seeing.

498

No demands! – You do not know him! Yes, he does *submit* to men and things, freely and easily, and is well disposed to both; all he asks is to be left in peace – but only *as long as* men and things do not *demand* submission. When anything is demanded of him he becomes proud, retiring and warlike.

499

The evil man. – 'Only the solitary man is evil!' cried Diderot: and Rousseau at once felt mortally offended. Which means that he admitted to himself that Diderot was right. It is, indeed, a fact that, in the midst of society and sociability every evil inclination has to place itself under such great restraint, don so many masks, lay itself so often on the Procrustean bed of virtue, that one could well speak of a martyrdom of the evil man. In solitude all this falls away. He who is evil is at his most evil in solitude: which is where he is also at his best – and thus to the eye of him who sees everywhere only a spectacle also at his most beautiful.

500

Against the grain – A thinker can for years on end force himself to think against the grain: that is to say, to pursue not the thoughts which offer themselves from within him but those to which an office, a

prescribed schedule, an arbitrary kind of industriousness seem to
oblige him. In the end, however, he will fall sick: for this apparently
moral overcoming of himself will ruin his nervous energy just as
thoroughly as any regularly indulged in excess could do.

501

Mortal souls. – So far as the promotion of knowledge is concerned,
mankind's most useful achievement is perhaps the abandonment of
its belief in an immortal soul. Now mankind can wait, now it no
longer needs to rush precipitately forward or gulp down ideas only
half-tasted, as it formerly had to do. For in the past the salvation of
the 'eternal soul' depended on knowledge acquired during a brief
lifetime, men had to *come to a decision* overnight – 'knowledge'
possessed a frightful importance. We have reconquered our courage
for error, for experimentation, for accepting provisionally – none of
it is so very important! and it is for precisely this reason that
individuals and generations can now fix their eyes on tasks of a
vastness that would to earlier ages have seemed madness and a
trifling with Heaven and Hell. We may experiment with ourselves!
Yes, mankind now has a right to do that! The greatest sacrifices have
not yet been offered to knowledge – indeed, merely to *have an inkling*
of such ideas as nowadays determine our actions would in earlier
times have been blasphemy and the loss of one's eternal salvation.

502

One word for three different conditions. – In passion, one person
experiences an outbreak of the savage, dreadful and unendurable
beast; another experiences an elevation of himself into a height and
grandeur and splendour compared with which his normal state of
being appears insipid. A third, who is noble through and through,
also experiences the noblest storm and stress, and in this condition
of passion he becomes *nature in its wild beauty* and only one degree
more profound than nature in its quiet beauty that he usually
represents: but men understand him more when he is in passion,
and revere him more, precisely on account of these moments – they
bring him a step closer and make him more akin to them. At such a
sight they experience delight and terror, and it is *precisely then* that
they call him – divine.

503

Friendship. – The objection to the philosophical life that it makes one
useless to one's friends would never occur to a modern man: it

belongs to antiquity. Antiquity lived and reflected on friendship to the limit, and almost buried friendship in its own grave. This is its advantage over us: we in turn can show idealised sexual love. All great achievements on the part of the man of antiquity were supported by the fact that *man stood beside man*, and that a woman was not allowed to claim to be the nearest or highest, let alone sole object of his love – as sexual passion teaches us to feel. Perhaps our trees fail to grow as high on account of the ivy and the vines that cling to them.

504

Reconciliation: – Ought it to be the task of philosophy to *reconcile* that which the *child* has learned and the *man* has come to know? Ought philosophy to be the special task of youths, since these stand midway between child and man and have needs common to both? It almost seems so, if one considers at what age philosophers nowadays usually produce their grand idea: at an age when it is too late for belief and still too early for knowledge.

505

The practical. – It is we thinkers who first have to determine the *palatableness* of things and, if necessary, decree it. Practical people in the end take it from us, their dependence on us is inconceivably great and the most ludicrous spectacle in the world, however little they may realise it and however proudly they may love to ignore us impractical people: indeed, they would deprecate their practical life if we should choose to deprecate it: – a thing to which a little desire for revenge might now and then incite us.

506

The necessary drying-out of everything good. – What! Does one have to understand a work in precisely the way in which the age that produced it understood it? But one takes more pleasure in a work, is more astonished by it, and learns more from it, if one does not understand it in that way! Have you not noticed that every new good work is at its least valuable so long as it lies exposed to the damp air of its own age? – the reason being that there still adheres to it all too much of the odour of the market-place and of its opponents and of the latest opinions and everything that changes from today to tomorrow. Later on it dries out, its 'timeboundness' expires – and only then does it acquire its deep lustre and pleasant odour and, if that is what it is seeking, its quiet eye of eternity.

507

Against the tyranny of the true. – Even if we were mad enough to consider all our opinions true, we should still not want them alone to exist – : I cannot see why it should be desirable that truth alone should rule and be omnipotent; it is enough for me that it should possess *great power*. But it must be able to *struggle* and have opponents, and one must be able to *find relief* from it from time to time in untruth – otherwise it will become boring, powerless and tasteless to us, and make us the same.

508

Not with pathos. – That which we do for our own *benefit* ought not to entail for us any moral praise, either from others or from ourself; the same goes for that which we do for our own *pleasure*. Not to take such things with pathos, and to eschew pathos ourselves in such cases, is *good form* among all higher human beings: and he who has accustomed himself to this has recovered *naivety*.

509

The third eye. – What! You still need the theatre! Are you still so young? Grow wise, and seek for tragedy and comedy where they are better acted! Where things are more interesting and interested! It is not altogether easy, I know, to remain a mere spectator in these cases – but learn it! And then, in almost every situation you find hard and painful you will have a little portal to joy and a refuge even when your own passions assail you. Open your theatre-eye, the great third eye which looks out into the world through the other two!

510

Escaping from one's virtues. – What is a thinker worth if he does not know how to escape from his own virtues occasionally! For he ought not to be 'only a moral being'!

511

The temptress. – Honesty is the great temptress of all fanatics. That which seemed to approach Luther in the shape of the Devil or a beautiful woman, and which he warded off in so uncouth a manner, was no doubt honesty, and perhaps, in rarer cases, even truth.

512

Courageous against causes. – He who is by nature considerate or timid with regard to people but is courageous against causes, shuns new and closer acquaintanceships and circumscribes his old ones: so that his incognito and his ruthlessness for truth may increase together.

513

Beauty and limits. – Are you seeking men of *beautiful* culture? But in that case, as when you are seeking beautiful scenery, you must be willing to be content with *circumscribed* views and prospects. – Certainly there are panoramic men too, and certainly they are, like panoramic scenery, instructive and astonishing: but not beautiful.

514

To the stronger. – You stronger and arrogant spirits, I ask of you but one thing: lay no new burden on to us others, but take something of our burden on to yourselves, since you are, after all, the stronger! But you like so much to do the reverse: for *you* want to fly, and thus we are supposed to bear your burden in addition to our own: that is to say, *we* are supposed to crawl!

515

Increase of beauty. – Why does beauty increase as civilisation increases? Because civilised man has less and less experience of the three occasions for ugliness: firstly, the emotions in their wildest outbursts; secondly, physical exertions in their extremest degree; thirdly, the need to inspire fear through one's appearance which is at lower and imperilled cultural levels so great and frequent that it even prescribes demeanour and ceremonial and makes of ugliness a *duty*.

516

Do not let your devil enter into your neighbour! – Let us for the time being agree that benevolence and beneficence are constituents of the good man; only let us add: 'presupposing that he is first benevolently and beneficently inclined *towards himself*!' For *without this* – if he flees from himself, hates himself, does harm to himself – he is certainly not a good man. For in this case all he is doing is rescuing himself from himself *in others*: let these others look to it that they suffer no ill effects from him, however well disposed he may want to appear! – But it is precisely this: to flee from the ego, and to hate it, and to live in others and for others – that has hitherto, with as much thoughtlessness as self-confidence, been called *'unegoistic' and consequently 'good'*.

517

Seducing into love. – We have cause to fear him who hates himself, for we shall be the victims of his wrath and his revenge. Let us therefore see if we cannot seduce him into loving himself!

518

Resignation. – What is resignation? It is the most comfortable position of an invalid who, having tossed and turned in his torment in an endeavour to *find* it, at last *grew tired* through this tossing and turning – and therewith found it!

519

Being deceived. – If you want to act you have to close the door on doubt – said a man of action. – And aren't you afraid of thus being *deceived?* – replied a man of contemplation.

520

Everlasting funeral rites. – Beyond the realm of history, one could fancy one hears a continuous funeral oration: men have always buried, and are still burying, that which they love best, their thoughts and hopes, and have received, and are still receiving, in exchange pride, *gloria mundi*, that is to say the pomp of the funeral oration. This is supposed to make up for everything! And the funeral orator is still the greatest public benefactor!

521

Vain of an exception. – This man has the consolation of possessing one supreme quality: over the rest of his being – and it is almost all the rest! – he casts his eye with contempt. But he finds relief from himself whenever he enters as though into his sanctuary; even the path thither seems to him an ascent on broad and gentle steps: – and you are cruel enough to call him vain on that account!

522

Wisdom without ears. – Daily to hear what is said of us, let alone to speculate as to what is thought of us – that would annihilate the strongest man. For the rest of them let us go on living only so as daily to get the better of us! They would not endure us if we were to get the better of them, or even *wanted to*! In short, let us act in a spirit of conciliation, let us not listen when we are spoken of, praised, blamed, when something is desired or hoped of us, let us not even think about it!

523

Subsequent questions. – Whenever a person reveals something, one can ask: what is it supposed to conceal? From what is it supposed to divert the eyes? What prejudice is it supposed to arouse? And additionally: how far does the subtlety of this dissimulation go? And in what way has it failed?

524

Jealousy of the solitary. – Between sociable and solitary natures there

exists this distinction (presupposing they both possess spirit!): the
former will be happy, or almost happy with a thing, whatever it may
be, from the moment they have found in their spirit a communicable
and pleasing way of expressing it – this will reconcile them to the
Devil himself! The solitary, however, have their enjoyment or their
torment of a thing in silence, they hate a clever and glittering display
of their innermost problems as they hate to see their beloved too
carefully dressed: they gaze at her with melancholy eyes, as though
becoming prey to the suspicion she wants to appear pleasing to
others! This is the jealousy which all solitary thinkers and passionate
dreamers feel towards *esprit*.

525

Effect of praise. – Some are made modest by great praise, others
insolent.

526

Not willing to be a symbol. – I commiserate with princes: they are not
permitted to vanish into society from time to time, and so they come
to know mankind only from an uncomfortable and dissimulated
position; the continual compulsion to signify something in the end
makes of them solemn nullities. – And so it is with all who see it their
duty to be symbols.

527

The hidden. – Have you never yet encountered those people who hold
fast to their heart and keep it close even when it is rejoicing, and who
would rather become dumb than relinquish the modesty of moderation? – And have you never yet encountered either those uncomfortable and often so good-natured people who do not want to be
recognised, and who always efface their footprints in the sand and
are, indeed, deceivers, of others and of themselves, in order to
remain hidden?

528

Rare abstemiousness. – It is often no small sign of humanity not to wish
to judge another and to refrain from thinking about him.

529

How men and nations acquire glory. – How many actions stamped with
genuine *individuality* do not *remain undone* because one sees or
suspects before one does them that they will be misunderstood! –
and these actions are precisely those which alone *possess value* for
good and evil. Thus the more respect an age or a nation accords the

individual, the more the individual is allowed to predominate and is seen as self-justified, the greater will be the number of actions of this kind which will venture to come forth – and so in the end a shimmer of honesty, of genuineness in good and evil, will spread over entire ages and nations; so that, like the Greeks for example, they will continue to shine on for many millennia after they have perished, as many stars do.

530

Thinker's digressions. – With many thinkers, the course of their thought as a whole is rigorous and inexorably bold, indeed sometimes cruel towards themselves, while in detail they are gentle and flexible; with benevolent hesitation they circle around a thing ten times, though in the end they resume their rigorous path. They are rivers with many meanderings and secluded hermitages; there are places in their course where the river plays hide-and-seek with itself and creates for itself a brief idyll, with islands, trees, grottos and waterfalls: and then it goes on again, past rocky cliffs and breaking its way through the hardest stone.

531

A different feeling for art. – From the time when one retires a little from social life, becomes more solitary and lives, consuming and consumed, in the company of profound fruitful ideas and only with them, one comes to desire of art either nothing at all or something quite different from what one desired before – that is to say, one's taste alters. For that element into which one formerly wanted to drive for a few moments through the gateway of art is the element in which one now continually dwells; formerly one dreamed through art of possessing something which one now possesses in fact. Indeed, to throw aside for a while that which one now has, and to dream oneself a child, beggar and fool – can from now on occasionally give us pleasure.

532

'Love makes the same'. – Love wants to spare the person to whom it dedicates itself every feeling of *being other*, and consequently it is full of dissimulation and pretence of similarity, it is constantly deceiving and feigning a sameness which in reality does not exist. And this happens so instinctively that women in love deny this dissimulation and continual tender deceit and boldly assert that love *makes the same* (that is to say, that it performs a miracle!). – This process is simple

when one party *lets himself be loved* and does not find it necessary to dissimulate but leaves that to the other, loving party; but there is no more confused or impenetrable spectacle than that which arises when both parties are passionately in love with one another and both consequently abandon themselves and want to be the same as one another: in the end neither knows what he is supposed to be imitating, what dissimulating, what pretending to be. The beautiful madness of this spectacle is too good for this world and too subtle for human eyes.

533

We beginners! – How much an actor sees and divines when he watches another act! He knows when a muscle employed in some gesture fails in its duty; he segregates those little, artificial things which have been practised one by one cold-bloodedly before the mirror and then refuse to integrate themselves into the whole; he feels it when the actor is surprised by his own inventiveness on the stage and then *spoils* it through being surprised. – Again, how differently a painter observes a person moving before him! For he at once visualises many more things *in addition*, so as to make a complete picture of what is presently before his eyes and to realise its whole effectiveness; in his mind he illuminates the same object in several different ways; he divides the effect of the whole by adding to it an antithetical contrast. – If only we possessed the eye of this actor and this painter for the domain of human souls!

534

Small doses. – If a change is to be as profound as it can be, the means to it must be given in the smallest doses but unremittingly over long periods of time! Can what is great be created at a *single stroke?* So let us take care not to exchange the state of morality to which we are accustomed for a new evaluation of things head over heels and amid acts of violence – no, let us continue to live in it for a long, long time yet – until, probably a long while hence, we become aware that *the new evaluation* has acquired predominence within us and that the little doses of it *to which we must from now on accustom ourselves* have laid down a new nature in us. – It is now, indeed, also beginning to become apparent that the most recent attempt at a great change in evaluations, and that in the political field – the 'Great Revolution' – was nothing *more* than a pathetic and bloody *piece of quackery* which knew how, through the production of sudden crises, to inspire in credulous Europe the hope of a *sudden* recovery – and which therewith made all political invalids up to the present moment *impatient and dangerous*.

535

Truth has need of power. – In itself truth is no power at all – whatever its flatterers of the Enlightenment may be accustomed to say to the contrary! – It has, rather, to draw power over to its side, or go over to the side of power, or it will perish again and again! This has been proved sufficiently and more than sufficiently!

536

The thumbscrew. – One finally grows indignant to see again and again how cruelly everyone reckons up the couple of private virtues he happens to possess to the prejudice of others who happen not to possess them, how he plagues and teases others with them. And so let us act humanely with our 'sense of honesty' – even though we do possess in it a thumbscrew which we could fasten on to all those great self-opinionated believers who even now still want to impose their belief on the whole world and torment them to the quick: – we have tested this thumbscrew on ourselves!

537

Mastery. – One has attained to mastery when one neither goes wrong *nor hesitates* in the performance.

538

Moral insanity of the genius. – In the case of a certain species of great spirits one may observe a painful, in part dreadful spectacle: their most productive moments, their flights upwards and into the distance, seem to be disproportionate to their constitution as a whole and somehow to exceed their strength, so that each time a defect, and in the long run the *defectiveness of the machine*, remains behind, which then, in the case of such highly intellectual natures as we are speaking of here, manifests itself much more regularly in all kinds of moral and mental symptoms than in physical distress. Thus the incomprehensible anxiety, vanity, odiousness, enviousness and tightlacedness which suddenly leaps out of them, all that is excessively personal and unfree in natures such as those of Rousseau and Schopenhauer, could well be the result of periodic heart-attacks: these, however, are the result of nervous disease, and this, finally, the result – –. So long as genius dwells within us, we are courageous, as if mad, indeed, and are heedless of life, health and honour; we fly through the day freer than an eagle and in the dark we are more

certain than the owl. But all at once it deserts us, and just as suddenly
we are assailed by a profound timidity: we no longer understand
ourselves, we suffer from all we experience, from all we do not
experience, we are as though among naked rocks in the face of a
storm, and at the same time like pitiable childish souls afraid of a
rustling and a shadow. – Three-quarters of all the evil done in the
world happens out of timidity: and this is above all a physiological
phenomenon!

539

Do you know what you want? – Have you never been plagued by the fear
that you might be completely incapable of knowing the truth? The
fear that your mind may be too dull and even your subtle faculty of
seeing still much too coarse? Have you not noticed what kind of will
rules behind your seeing? For example, how yesterday you wanted
to see *more* than another, today *differently* from another, or how from
the very first you longed to find what others fancied they had found
or the opposite of that! Oh shameful craving! How you sometimes
looked for something which affected you strongly, sometimes for
what soothed you – because you happened to be tired! Always full of
secret predeterminations of *how* truth would have to be constituted if
you would consent to accept it! Or do you believe that today, since
you are frozen and dry like a bright morning in winter and have
nothing weighing on your heart, your eyes have somehow improved?
Are warmth and enthusiasm not needed if a thing of thought is to
have *justice* done to it? – *and that precisely is seeing!* As though you *were
able* to traffic with things of thought any differently from the way you
do with men! In this traffic too there is the same morality, the same
honourableness, the same reservations, the same slackness, the
same timidity – your whole lovable and hateful ego! When you are
physically tired you will bestow on things a pale and tired coloration,
when you are feverish you will turn them into monsters! Does your
morning not shine upon things differently from your evening? Do
you not fear to re-encounter in the cave of every kind of knowledge
your own ghost – the ghost which is the veil behind which truth has
hidden itself from you? Is it not a horrible comedy in which you so
thoughtlessly want to play a role? –

540

Learning. – Michelangelo saw in Raphael study, in himself nature:
there *learning*, here *talent*. This, with all deference to the great pedant,
is pedantic. For what is talent but a name for an *older* piece of

213

learning, experience, practice, appropriation, incorporation, whether at the stage of our fathers or an even earlier stage! And again: he who learns *bestows talent upon himself* – only it is not so easy to learn, and not only a matter of having the will to do so; one has to be *able* to learn. In the case of an artist learning is often prevented by envy, or by that pride which puts forth its sting as soon as it senses the presence of something strange and involuntarily assumes a defensive instead of a receptive posture. Raphael, like Goethe, was without pride or envy, and that is why both were *great learners* and not merely exploiters of those veins of ore washed clean from the siftings of the history of their forefathers. Raphael vanishes as a learner in the midst of appropriating that which his great competitor designated as *his* 'nature': he took away a piece of it every day, this noblest of thieves; but before he had taken over the whole of Michelangelo into himself, he died – and his last series of works is, as the *beginning* of a new plan of study, less perfect and absolutely good precisely because the great learner was interrupted in his hardest curriculum and took away with him the justificatory ultimate goal towards which he looked.

541

How one ought to turn to stone. – Slowly, slowly to become hard like a precious stone – and at last to lie there, silent and a joy to eternity.

542

The philosopher and age. – It is not wise to let the evening judge the day: for it means all too often that weariness sits in judgment on strength, success and good will. And great caution is likewise in order with regard to *age* and its judgment of life, especially as, like evening, age loves to dress itself in a new and enticing morality and knows how to put the day to shame through twilight and solemn or passionate silence. The reverence we accord the aged man, especially when he is an aged thinker and sage, easily blinds us to the *aging of his mind*, and it is always necessary to draw forth the *signs* of such an aging and weariness out of their hiding-place – draw forth, that is to say, the *physiological* phenomenon behind the moral predispositions and prejudices – so as not to become the fools of reverence and injurers of knowledge. For it not infrequently happens that the aged man is subject to the illusion of a great moral renewal and rebirth and from the sensibility thus engendered in him passes judgment on the work and the course of his life, as though it was only now that he had been endowed with clear sight: and yet the inspirer behind this feeling of wellbeing and these confident judgments is not wisdom but *weariness*. Its most dangerous characteristic is probably *belief in their own genius*, which usually assails great and semi-great men of the spirit only at this frontier of their life: the belief they occupy an exceptional position and enjoy exceptional rights. The thinker visited by this belief henceforth considers himself permitted to *take things easier* and, as genius, to promulgate decrees rather than demonstrate: yet it is probably the drive to seek *relief* for weariness of mind which is the most potent source of this belief; it precedes the latter, even though the reverse may seem to be the case. Then: at this time of life one wants, in accordance with the thirst for enjoyment which characterises the weary and aged, to *enjoy* the results of one's thinking instead of testing and sowing them out again, and to that end needs to make them palatable and enjoyable and to get rid of their dryness, coldness and lack of spice; and so it happens that the aged thinker appears to elevate himself above the work of his life, though in reality he ruins it through infusing it with enthusiasms, sweetness, spices, poetic mists and mystic lights. This is what happened in the end to Plato, this is what happened in the end to that great honest Frenchman beside whom, as embracer and conqueror of the strict sciences, the Germans and English of this century can place no rival, Auguste Comte. A third sign of weariness: that ambition which burned in the great thinker's breast when he was young, and at that time could find satisfaction in nothing, has also grown old; now, like one who can afford to lose no more time, he reaches for coarser and broader means of satisfaction, that is to say for the satisfactions of active, dominant, violent, conquering natures: from now on he wants to found, not structures of thought, but institutions which will bear his name; what does he care now for ethereal victories and honours in the realm of demonstrations and refutations! what do being eternalised in books, a tremble of exaltation in the soul of a reader, mean to him! The institution, on the other hand, is a temple – that he knows well; and a temple of enduring stone will keep its god alive more surely than will the sacrificial gifts of rare and tender souls. Perhaps he will also encounter at this time for the first time that love which is more appropriate to a god than to a man, and his whole being will grow gentler and sweeter beneath the rays of such a sun, like fruit in autumn. Indeed, he will in fact grow more divine and more beautiful, this great aged man – and nonetheless it is age and weariness which *permit* him to ripen out in this way, to grow silent, and to repose in the radiant idolatry of a woman. It is all over now with the self-surpassing desire that filled him in earlier years for genuine pupils, that is to say genuine continuators of his thought, that is to say genuine opponents: that desire proceeded from the unweakened power, the conscious pride, of being able at any time himself to become the opponent and mortal enemy of his own teachers – what he desires now is resolute party followers, unhesitating comrades, auxiliaries, a pompous processional train. Now he can no longer endure at all the dreadful isolation in which every spirit lives who flies on out ahead; he henceforth surrounds himself with objects of veneration, communality, emotion and love; he wants at long last to enjoy what all the religious enjoy and celebrate within the *community* that which he values; indeed, in order to possess this community he will invent a religion. Thus does the aged sage live, and in doing so drifts imperceptibly into so wretchedly close an approximation to the excesses of priests and poets that one hardly dares to remember his wise and rigorous youth, the strict intellectual morality he then practised, and his truly manly dread of inspirations and fantasies. When in earlier years he compared himself with other, older thinkers, it was so as seriously to measure his weakness against their strength and to grow colder and freer towards himself: now he does it only so as to intoxicate himself in his own delusions. In earlier years he thought with confidence of the thinkers yet to come, indeed he joyfully saw himself extinguished by their more perfect light: now it torments him that he cannot be the last thinker; he ponders how, with the inheritance he will bestow upon mankind, he can also impose upon them a limitation of independent thinking, he fears and reviles the pride and thirst for freedom felt by individualist spirits – : after him none shall have full power over his own intellect, he wants to stand as the bulwark against which the surges of thought in general shall ever afterwards break – these are his secret, and perhaps not always secret desires! The hard fact behind such desires, however, is that he himself has *come to a halt* before his teaching and has erected in it his boundary-stone, his 'thus far and no farther'. By *canonising* himself he has also displayed above himself his own death certificate: from now on his spirit *may* not develop farther, time has run out for him, the clock stands still. Whenever a great thinker wants to make of himself a binding institution for future mankind, one may be certain that he is past the peak of his powers and is very weary, very close to the setting of his sun.

543

Do not make passion an argument for truth! – O you good-natured and even noble enthusiasts, I know you! You want to win your argument against us, but also against yourself, and above all against yourself! – and a subtle and tender bad conscience so often incites you *against* your enthusiasm! How ingenious you then become in the outwitting and deadening of this conscience! How you hate the honest, the simple, the pure, how you avoid their innocent eyes! That *knowing better* whose representatives *they* are and whose voice you hear all too loudly within you, how it casts doubt on your belief – how you seek to make it suspect as a bad habit, as a sickness of the age, as neglect and infection of your own spiritual health! You drive yourself to the point of hating criticism, science, reason! You have to falsify history so that it may bear witness for you, you have to deny virtues so that they shall not cast into the shade those of your idols and ideals! Coloured pictures where what is needed is rational grounds! Ardour and power of expression! Silvery mists! Ambrosial nights! You understand how to illuminate and how to obscure, and how to obscure *with light*! And truly, when your passion rises to the point of frenzy, there comes a moment when you say to yourself: now I have *conquered* the good conscience, now I am light of heart, courageous, self-denying, magnificent, now I am honest! How you thirst for those moments when your passion bestows on you perfect self-justification and as it were innocence; when in struggle, intoxication, courage, hope, you are beside yourself and beyond all doubting; when you decree: 'he who is not beside himself as we are can in no way know what and where truth is!' How you thirst to discover people of your belief in this condition – it is that of *intellectual vice* – and ignite your flame at their torch! Oh your deplorable martyrdom! Oh your deplorable victory of the sanctified lie! Must you inflict so *much* suffering upon yourself? – *Must* you?

544

How philosophy is done today. – I have observed that our philosophising youths, women and artists of today want of philosophy precisely *the opposite* of that which the Greeks derived from it! He who does not hear the continual rejoicing which resounds through every speech and counter-speech of a Platonic dialogue, the rejoicing over the new invention of *rational* thinking, what does he understand of Plato, of the philosophy of antiquity? In those days, souls were filled with drunkenness at the rigorous and sober game of concept, generalisation, refutation, limitation – with that drunkenness which the great ancient rigorous and sober contrapuntal composers perhaps also knew. In those days there still lingered on the palate of the Greeks that other, more ancient and formerly all-powerful taste: and the new taste presented so magical a contrast to this that they sang and stammered of dialectics, the 'divine art', as though in a delirium of love. That ancient way, however, was thinking under the spell of custom, for which there was nothing but established judgments, established causes, and no other reasons than those of authority: so that thinking was an *imitation* and all pleasure in speech and language had to lie in the *form*. (Wherever the content is thought of as eternal and universally valid, there is only *one* great magic: that of changing form, that is to say of fashion. In their poets, too, from the time of Homer onwards, and later in their sculptors, what the Greeks enjoyed was not originality but its opposite.) It was Socrates who discovered the antithetical magic, that of cause and effect, of ground and consequence: and we modern men are so accustomed to and brought up in the necessity of logic that it lies on our palate as the normal taste and, as such, cannot help being repugnant to the lustful and conceited. These take delight in that which stands out in opposition to it: their more refined ambition would all too gladly have them believe that their souls are exceptions, not dialectical or rational beings but – well, 'intuitive beings', for instance, gifted with an 'inner sense' or with 'intellectual intuition'. Above all, however, they want to be 'artistic natures', with a genius in their head and a demon in their body and consequently enjoying special rights in both worlds, and especially the divine privilege of being incomprehensible. – *That* is what now does philosophy! I fear they will one day see that they have made a mistake – what they want is religion!

545

But we do not believe you! – You would dearly like to pass as being well versed in the ways of men, but we shall not let you do so! Do we not notice that you represent yourselves as being more experienced, profounder, more passionate, more complete than you are? Just as well as we feel the presumptuousness of that painter even in the way he wields his brush: just as well as we hear how that composer wants to make his theme appear more elevated than it is by the way he introduces it. Have you experienced *history* in yourselves, convulsions, earthquakes, sadness wide and protracted, happiness that strikes like lightning? Have you been foolish with fools great and small? Have you really borne the delusion and the burden of good men? And the burden and singular happiness of the most evil as well? If so, speak of morality: but not otherwise!

546

Slave and idealist. – The human being after the model of Epictetus would certainly not be to the taste of those who strive after the ideal nowadays. The constant tension of his being, the unwearied glance turned inward, the reserve, caution, uncommunicativeness of his eye if it should even turn to view the outer world; not to speak of his silence or near-silence: all signs of the most resolute bravery – what could this mean to our idealists, who are above all greedy for *expansion*! In addition to all this, he is not fanatical, he hates the display and vainglory of our idealists: his arrogance, great though it is, has nonetheless no desire to disturb others, it admits a certain mild intimacy and wants to spoil no one's good humour – it can, indeed, even smile! there is very much of the humanity of antiquity in this ideal! The fairest thing about it is, however, that it lacks all fear of God, that it believes strictly in reason, that it is no penitential preacher. Epictetus was a slave: his ideal human being is without class and possible in every class, but is to be sought above all in the depths of the masses as the silent, self-sufficient man within a universal enslavement who defends himself against the outside world and lives in a constant state of supreme bravery. He differs from the *Christian*, above all in that the Christian lives in hope, in the promise of 'inexpressible glories', in that he accepts gifts and expects and receives the best he knows at the hands of divine love and grace and not at his own hands: while Epictetus does not hope and does not accept the best he knows as a gift – he possesses it, he holds it bravely in his own hand, he defends it against the whole world if the world wants to rob him of it. Christianity was made for a different species of antique slave, for those weak in will and mind, that is to say for the great mass of slaves.

547

The tyrants of the spirit. – The march of science is now no longer crossed by the accidental fact that men live for about seventy years, as was for all too long the case. Formerly, a man wanted to reach the far end of knowledge during this period of time and the methods of acquiring knowledge were evaluated in accordance with this universal longing. The small single questions and experiments were counted contemptible: one wanted the shortest route; one believed that, because everything in the world seemed to be *accommodated to man*, the knowability of things was also accommodated to a human time-span. To solve everything at a stroke, with a single word – that was the

secret desire: the task was thought of in the image of the Gordian
knot or in that of the egg of Columbus; one did not doubt that in the
domain of knowledge too it was possible to reach one's goal in the
manner of Alexander or Columbus and to settle all questions with a
single answer. 'There is a *riddle* to be solved': thus did the goal of life
appear to the eye of the philosopher; the first thing to do was to find
the riddle and to compress the problem of the world into the
simplest riddle-form. The boundless ambition and exultation of
being the 'unriddler of the world' constituted the thinker's dreams:
nothing seemed worth-while if it was not the means of bringing
everything to a conclusion *for him*! Philosophy was thus a kind of
supreme struggle to possess the tyrannical rule of the spirit – that
some such very fortunate, subtle, inventive, bold and mighty man
was in reserve – one only! – was doubted by none, and several, most
recently Schopenhauer, fancied themselves to be that one. – From
this it follows that by and large the sciences have hitherto been kept
back by the *moral narrowness* of their disciples and that henceforth
they must be carried on with a higher and *more magnanimous* basic
feeling. 'What do I matter!' – stands over the door of the thinker of
the future.

548
Victory over strength. – If we consider all that has hitherto been revered
as 'superhuman mind', as 'genius', we come to the sad conclusion
that the intellectuality of mankind must on the whole have been
something very low and paltry: it has hitherto required so little mind
to feel at once considerably superior to it! Oh, the cheap fame of the
'genius'! How quickly his throne is established, how quickly worship
of him becomes a practice! We are still on our knees before *strength* –
after the ancient custom of slaves – and yet when the degree of
worthiness to be revered is fixed, only the *degree of rationality in strength* is
decisive: we must assess to what extent precisely strength has been
overcome by something higher, in the service of which it now stands
as means and instrument! But for such an assessment there are still
far too few eyes, indeed the assessment of the genius is still usually
regarded as a sacrilege. And so perhaps the most beautiful still
appears only in the dark, and sinks, scarcely born, into eternal night
– I mean the spectacle of that strength which employs genius *not for
works* but for *itself as a work*; that is, for its own constraint, for the
purification of its imagination, for the imposition of order and
choice upon the influx of tasks and impressions. The great human

being is still, in precisely the greatest thing that demands reverence, invisible like a too distant star: his *victory over strength* remains without eyes to see it and consequently without song and singer. The order of rank of greatness for all past mankind has not yet been determined.

549

'Flight from oneself'. – Those men given to intellectual spasms – Byron and Alfred de Musset are examples – who are impatient and gloomily inclined towards themselves and in all they do resemble rampaging horses, and who derive from their own works, indeed, only a shortlived fire and joy which almost bursts their veins and then a desolation and sourness made more wintry by the contrast it presents – how should such men endure to remain within *themselves*! They long to dissolve into something *'outside'*; if one is a Christian and is possessed by such a longing one's goal is to be dissolved into God, to 'become wholly at one with him'; if one is Shakespeare one is satisfied only with being dissolved into images of the most passionate life; if one is Byron one longs for *action*, because action draws us away from ourself even more than do thoughts, feelings or works. And so could all impulse to action perhaps be at bottom flight from oneself? – Pascal would ask. And the proposition might indeed be demonstrated in the case of the supreme examples known to us of the impulse to action: for consider – in the light of the experience of psychiatry, as is only proper – that four of the most active men of all time were epileptics (namely Alexander, Caesar, Mohammed and Napoleon), just as Byron was also subject to this complaint.

550

Knowledge and beauty. – If, as they still do, people as it were reserve their reverence and feeling of happiness for works of imagination and dissembling, we ought not to wonder if the opposite of imagination and dissembling makes them feel cold and disconsolate. The delight produced by even the smallest definite piece of real progress in knowledge, which science as it is now bestows so abundantly and already upon so many – this delight is for the present not *credited* by all those who have accustomed themselves to finding delight only in relinquishing reality and plunging into the depths of appearance. These believe reality is ugly: but they do not reflect that knowledge of even the ugliest reality is itself beautiful, nor that he who knows much is in the end very far from finding ugly the greater part of that reality whose discovery has always brought him happiness. For is anything 'beautiful in itself'? The happiness of the man of knowledge enhances the beauty of the world and makes all that exists sunnier; knowledge casts its beauty not only over things but in the long run into things – may future mankind bear witness to the truth of this proposition! In the meantime let us recall an experience of olden time: two men as fundamentally different as Plato and Aristotle were in agreement as to what constituted *supreme happiness*, not only for them or for mankind but in itself, even for gods of the highest empyrean: they found it *in knowledge*, in the activity of a well-trained inquisitive and inventive *mind* (*not*, that is to say, in 'intuition', as German theologians and semi-theologians do; *not* in visions, as mystics do; and likewise *not* in creating, as all practical people do). Descartes and Spinoza came to a similar conclusion: how they must all have *enjoyed* knowledge! And what a danger their honesty faced of becoming a panegyrist of things! –

551
Of future virtues. – How comes it that the more comprehensible the world has grown the more solemnities of every kind have decreased? Is it that fear was so much the basic element of that reverence which overcame us in the presence of everything unknown and mysterious and taught us to fall down before the incomprehensible and plead for mercy? And has the world not lost some of its charm for us because we have grown less fearful? With this diminution of our fearfulness has our own dignity and solemnity, our own *fearsomeness*, not also diminished? Perhaps we have less respect for the world and for ourselves since we have come to think of it and of ourselves more courageously? Perhaps there will come a time when this courage in thinking will have grown so great that, as the supreme form of arrogance, it will feel itself *above* man and things – when the sage will, as the most courageous man, also be the man who sees himself and existence farthest beneath him? – This species of courage, which is not far from being an extravagant generosity, has hitherto been *lacking* in mankind. – Oh if the poets would only be again what they were once supposed to have been: – *seers* who tell us something of the *possible*! Now that actuality and the past are and have to be taken more and more out of their hands – for the age of harmless false-coinage is at an end! If only they would let us feel in advance something of the *virtues of the future*! Or of virtues that will never exist on earth, though they could exist somewhere in the universe – of purple-glowing galaxies and whole Milky Ways of beauty! Astronomers of the ideal, where are you?

552

Ideal selfishness. – Is there a more holy condition than that of pregnancy? To do all we do in the unspoken belief that it has somehow to benefit that which is coming to be within us! – has to *enhance* its mysterious worth, the thought of which fills us with delight! In this condition we avoid many things without having to force ourself very hard! We suppress our anger, we offer the hand of conciliation: our child shall grow out of all that is gentlest and best. We are horrified if we are sharp or abrupt: suppose it should pour a drop of evil into the dear unknown's cup of life! Everything is veiled, ominous, we know nothing of what is taking place, we wait and try to be *ready*. At the same time, a pure and purifying feeling of profound irresponsibility reigns in us almost like that of the auditor before the curtain has gone up – *it* is growing, *it* is coming to light: *we* have no right to determine either its value or the hour of its coming. All the influence we can exert lies in keeping it safe. 'What is growing here is something greater than we are' is our most secret hope: we prepare everything for it so that it may come happily into the world: not only everything that may prove useful to it but also the joyfulness and laurel-wreaths of our soul. – It is in this *state of consecration* that one should live! It is a state one can live in! And if what is expected is an idea, a deed – towards every bringing forth we have essentially no other relationship than that of pregnancy and ought to blow to the winds all presumptuous talk of 'willing' and 'creating'. This is *ideal selfishness*: continually to watch over and care for and to keep our soul still, so that our fruitfulness shall *come to a happy fulfilment*! Thus, as intermediaries, we watch over and care for to the *benefit of all*; and the mood in which we live, this mood of pride and gentleness, is a balm which spreads far around us and on to restless souls too. – But the pregnant are *strange*! So let us be strange too, and let us not hold it against others if they too have to be so! And even if the outcome is dangerous and evil: let us not be less reverential towards that which is coming to be than worldly justice is, which does not permit a judge or an executioner to lay hands on one who is pregnant!

553

By circuitous paths. – Whither does this whole philosophy, with all its circuitous paths, want to go? Does it do more than translate as it were into reason a strong and constant drive, a drive for gentle sunlight, bright and buoyant air, southerly vegetation, the breath of the sea, fleeting meals of flesh, fruit and eggs, hot water to drink, daylong silent wanderings, little talking, infrequent and cautious reading, dwelling alone, clean, simple and almost soldierly habits, in short for all those things which taste best and are most endurable precisely to me? A philosophy which is at bottom the instinct for a personal diet? An instinct which seeks my own air, my own heights, my own kind of health and weather, by the circuitous path of my head? There are many other, and certainly many much loftier sublimities of philosophy, and not only those which are gloomier and make more claims for themselves than mine – perhaps they too are one and all nothing other than the intellectual circuitous paths of similar personal drives? – In the meantime I have come to look with new eyes on the secret and solitary fluttering of a butterfly high on the rocky seacoast where many fine plants are growing: it flies about unconcerned that it has but *one* day more to live and that the night will be too cold for its winged fragility. For it too a philosophy could no doubt be found: though it would no doubt not be mine. –

554

Going on ahead. – When one lauds *progress*, one is lauding only the movement and those who refused to let us stand still – and in certain circumstances much is to be thereby achieved, especially if one is living among Egyptians. In volatile Europe, however, where movement 'goes without saying' as they say – ah, if only *we* knew what to say about it! – I prefer *going on ahead* and those who do so: those, that is to say, who again and again leave themselves behind and give no thought to whether anyone else is following behind them. 'Wherever I stop I find myself alone: so why should I stop! The desert still stretches away!' – that is the feeling of one who in this way goes on ahead.

555

The least are sufficient. – We ought to avoid experiences when we know that the *least* of them will make a sufficiently strong impression on us – and these we cannot avoid. – The thinker must possess within him a rough canon of those things which he still *wants to experience* at all.

556

The good four. – *Honest* towards ourselves and whoever *else* is a friend to us; *brave* towards the enemy; *magnanimous* towards the defeated; *polite* – always: this is what the four cardinal virtues want us to be.

557

Off to fight an enemy. – How fine bad music and bad reasons sound when one marches off to fight an enemy!

558

But do not hide your virtues either. – I love those who are transparent
water and who, as Pope puts it, 'do not hide from view the turbid
bottom of their stream'. But for them too there is a species of vanity,
if a very rare and sublimated species: some of them desire to display
precisely this turbidity and count as nothing the transparency of the
water that makes this possible. No less a person than Gautama
Buddha invented this rare kind of vanity in the formula: 'let your sins
be seen before the people and hide your virtues!' But to do this
means to present the world with an ill spectacle – it is a sin against
taste.

559

'Nothing too much!' – How often the individual is advised to set himself
a goal that he cannot reach and is beyond his strength, so that he will
at least reach that which his strength is capable of *when put to the
farthest stretch*! But is this really so desirable? Must even the best
performers who live according to this teaching, and their best
performances, not acquire something exaggerated and distorted
precisely because there is too much tension in them? And when as a
result one sees nothing but struggling athletes, tremendous efforts,
and nowhere a laurel-crowned and triumphant victor, does that not
envelop the world in a grey veil of *failure*?

560

What we are at liberty to do. – One can dispose of one's drives like a
gardener and, though few know it, cultivate the shoots of anger, pity,
curiosity, vanity as productively and profitably as a beautiful fruit
tree on a trellis; one can do it with the good or bad taste of a gardener
and, as it were, in the French or English or Dutch or Chinese fashion;
one can also let nature rule and only attend to a little embellishment
and tidying-up here and there; one can, finally, without paying any
attention to them at all, let the plants grow up and fight their fight out
among themselves – indeed, one can take delight in such a
wilderness, and desire precisely this delight, though it gives one
some trouble, too. All this we are at liberty to do: but how many
know we are at liberty to do it? Do the majority not *believe* in *themselves*
as in complete *fully-developed facts*? Have the great philosophers not
put their seal on this prejudice with the doctrine of the unchange-
ability of character?

561

Let your happiness too shine out. – As painters, being quite unable to reproduce the radiant colour of the real sky, are obliged to employ in their landscapes all the colours they need a couple of tones deeper than they are in nature: as by means of this artifice they do then attain a similarity of texture and harmony of tones corresponding to those in nature: so poets and philosophers too have to resort to a similar expedient when they are unable to reproduce the radiance of real happiness; by painting all things a couple of degrees darker than they are, they can make their lighter touches seem almost sunny and, by contrast, similar to actual happiness. – The pessimist, who gives to all things the blackest and gloomiest colours, employs only flames and flashes of lightning, celestial radiance, and anything whose light is glaring and confuses the eyes; with him the function of brightness is only to enhance terror and to make us feel there is more horror in things than there really is.

562

The settled and the free. – It is only in the underworld that we are shown something of the gloomy background to all those adventurer's joys which shine around Odysseus and his kind like an eternal shimmering of the sea – and once we are shown that background we never again forget it: the mother of Odysseus died of grief and of longing for her child! One person moves restlessly from place to place, and the heart of another who is *settled* and tender breaks as a consequence: so it has always been! Sorrow breaks the heart of those to whom it happens that he whom they love best deserts their faith – this is part of the tragedy which free spirits *produce* and of which they are sometimes aware! Then they too have at some time or other to go down to the dead, like Odysseus, to assuage their grief and soothe their tenderness.

563

The delusion of a moral world-order. – *There is absolutely no eternal necessity* which decrees that every guilt will be atoned and paid for – that such a thing exists has been a dreadful and to only a minuscule extent useful delusion – : just as it is a delusion that everything is guilt which is *felt as such*. It is not *things*, but opinions *about things that have absolutely no existence*, which have so deranged mankind!

564

Just beyond experience! – Even great spirits have only their five-fingers' breadth of *experience* – just beyond it their thinking ceases and their endless empty space and stupidity begins.

565

Dignity and ignorance in union. – When we understand we become polite, happy, inventive, and when we have only learned enough and have *created* eyes and ears for ourselves our souls exhibit more charm and pliability. But we understand very little, and are poorly instructed, and so it rarely happens that we embrace a thing and thus make ourselves lovable too: what we are much more likely to do is move stiffly and insensitively through city, nature, history, and we are somewhat proud of this deportment and coldness, as though it were the effect of superiority. Indeed, our ignorance and our lack of desire for knowledge are very adept at stalking about as dignity, as character.

566

Living cheaply. – The cheapest and most inoffensive way of living is that of the thinker: for, to get at once to the main point, the things he needs most are precisely those which others despise and throw away – . Then: he is easily pleased and has no expensive pleasures; his work is not hard but as it were southerly; his days and nights are not spoiled by pangs of conscience; he moves about, eats, drinks and sleeps in proportion as his mind grows ever calmer, stronger and brighter; he rejoices in his body and has no reason to be afraid of it; he has no need of company, except now and then so as afterwards to embrace his solitude the more tenderly; as a substitute for the living he has the dead, and even for friends he has a substitute: namely the best who have ever lived. – Consider whether it is not the opposite desires and habits that make the life of men expensive and consequently arduous and often insupportable. – In another sense, to be sure, the life of the thinker is the most expensive – nothing is too good for him; and to be deprived of *the best* would here be an *unendurable* deprivation.

567

In the field. – 'We must take things more cheerfully than they deserve; especially since we have for a long time taken them more seriously than they deserve.' – So speak brave soldiers of knowledge.

568

Poet and bird. – The phoenix showed the poet a scroll which was burning to ashes. 'Do not be dismayed!' it said, 'it is your work! It does not have the spirit of the age and even less the spirit of those who are against the age: consequently it must be burned. But this is a good sign. There are many kinds of daybreaks.'

569

To the solitary. – If we are not as considerate of the honour of other people in our private soliloquies as we are in public, we are not behaving decently.

570

Losses. – There are losses which communicate a sublimity to the soul which makes it refrain from lamentation and go about in silence as though among tall black cypress-trees.

571

Field-dispensary of the soul. – What is the strongest cure? – Victory.

572

Life must offer us a rest. – If, as the thinker does, one usually dwells in a great stream of thought and feeling, and pursues this stream even in nocturnal dreams: then what one desires of *life* is rest and silence – while others, conversely, want to take a rest from life when they give themselves over to meditation.

573

Sloughing one's skin. – The snake that cannot slough its skin, perishes. Likewise spirits which are prevented from changing their opinions; they cease to be spirits.

574

Do not forget! – The higher we soar, the smaller we seem to those who cannot fly.

575

We aeronauts of the spirit! – All those brave birds which fly out into the distance, into the farthest distance – it is certain! somewhere or other they will be unable to go on and will perch on a mast or a bare cliff-face – and they will even be thankful for this miserable accommodation! But who could venture to infer from that, that there was *not* an immense open space before them, that they had flown as far as one *could* fly! All our great teachers and predecessors have at last come to a stop and it is not with the noblest or most graceful of gestures that weariness comes to a stop: it will be the same with you and me! But what does that matter to you and me! *Other birds will fly farther!* This insight and faith of ours vies with them in flying up and away; it rises above our heads and above our impotence into the heights and from there surveys the distance and sees before it the flocks of birds which, far stronger than we, still strive whither we have striven, and where everything is sea, sea, sea! – And whither then would we go? Would we *cross* the sea? Whither does this mighty longing draw us, this longing that is worth more to us than any pleasure? Why just in this direction, thither where all the suns of humanity have hitherto *gone down*? Will it perhaps be said of us one day that we too, *steering westward, hoped to reach an India* – but that it was our fate to be wrecked against infinity? Or, my brothers. Or? –

Notes

Preface

1 **Trophonius**: a Boeotian oracular god, whose oracle was highly valued. Pausanius, a Greek traveler and geographer, who had been to see the oracle, describes how Trophonius would lead the inquirer to the underworld itself for direct revelations.

3 **Circe of the Philosophers**: an allusion to Circe, daughter of Helios and Perse (*Odyssey*, x, 210 ff.). In Greek mythology, a seductress and deity who, in the *Odyssey*, magically transforms half of Odysseus' crew into beasts.

3 **"aere perennius"**: "more enduring than bronze," from Horace, *Odes* 3.30.1, on his poetic achievement. "Bronze" here refers to the bronze tablets on which Roman laws were inscribed for preservation. They were proverbially long-lasting (several still survive).

3 **Robespierre, Maximilien F. M. I. de** (1758–94): leading figure in the French Revolution and an ardent believer in Rousseau's doctrines. His genuine and incessant praise of "virtue," which won him the surname of "the Incorruptible," was instrumental in the execution of the Reign of Terror.

3 **"de fonder sur la terre l'empire de la sagesse, de la justice et de la vertu"**: "to found the empire of wisdom, justice and virtue on earth."

3 **Luther, Martin** (1483–1546): German leader of the Reformation and founder of Protestantism. Preached the doctrine of salvation by faith rather than by works. Denied freedom of the will in *De servo arbitrio* (1525).

3 **dialectical principle**: the central method in Hegel's work in which one starts from a given position (a thesis – say, ancient Greek ethics); this thesis itself generates its own destruction by contradiction (the Socratic questioning of Greek ethics), until it is replaced by something else (a Reformation morality based on individual conscience). This new anti-thesis – morality in this case – is also unstable and so

230

must yield to a third position that combines the positive points of the two predecessors (a rational community). The classic formulation is one of movement from *thesis* to *antithesis* to *synthesis* (though Hegel does not use these terms), although in some cases the synthesis of one stage serves as the thesis of another. See M. N. Forster, "Hegel's Dialectical Method," in F. Beiser (ed.), *The Cambridge Companion to Hegel* (1993).

3   *credo quia absurdum*: "I believe because it is absurd."

5   *lento*: "prolongation" (of time).

5   **philologist**: literally, "lover of words." One who studies literature, esp. of classical antiquity. Classical philology, the discipline in which Nietzsche was trained, was viewed as a *Wissenschaft* (a science) in the nineteenth century.

Book I

8   **Raphael**: Raffaello Santi, or Sanzio (1483–1520): Italian painter, one of the greatest of the Italian Renaissance. Among his most famous paintings are the *Sistine Madonna*, the *Marriage of the Virgin* and the *School of Athens*.

9   **Brahmin**: one of the priestly class of the orthodox Hindus, the highest of the four *varnas*, or castes. Since they had almost exclusive access to the *Rig Veda*, they were responsible for transmission of the Sanskritic sacred traditions and for executing the sacrificial rituals.

14   **Solon** (*c.* 630 BC – *c.* 560 BC): Athenian poet, lawgiver and statesman, one of the Seven Wise Men of Greece. Recited a martial poem that inspired the Athenians to capture Salamis from the Magarians *c.* 600 BC. The Athenians ejected the Magarians, whose presence on the island threatened Athenian approaches by sea.

14   **angekok (or angakok)**: an Eskimo medicine man or shaman.

22   **Protestant doctrine of faith**: refers to one of the chief characteristics of all denominations of Protestantism: that justification before God comes by faith alone. Protestants hold that salvation is a gift, and since God has "acquitted" his creation, no one can "earn" it. God, on this view, has merely decided to bestow his grace.

27   *pia fraus*: "a pious (noble) lie": a deception practiced from the holiest of motives.

38   **Hesiod** (*fl. c.* 800 BC): Greek poet whose poem *Works and Days* described life on his farm, and contained avuncular advice. His *Theogony* describes the beginning of the world and the birth of the gods.

38   **Eris**: Greek goddess of strife and discord: daughter of Zeus and Hera. She called forth war, while her brother, Ares, carried out its destruction.

41 *Vita contemplativa, vita activa*: a Latin dualism: literally, "the contemplative life," as opposed to the "active life" (e.g., of politics).

42 *pudenda origo*: "[O] shameful origin."

43 **dialectics**: refers to Socrates' elenctic questioning, a method whereby Socrates and his interlocutor engaged in a search for the true meaning of a word (justice, courage, piety, beauty, etc.). Marked by severe and relentless cross-examination and refutation.

46 **Montaigne** (1533–82): French essayist, author of *Essais*, which reflects a spirit of skepticism and inspiration from the study of the classics.

46 **Pascal** (1623–62): French philosopher and scientist. Wrote the *Pensées* and contributed to probability theory, number theory, and geometry, among other fields. The reference to the need for the pillow probably stems from Pascal's well-known painful preoccupation with God and religion, death and immortality, concerns that have overshadowed his other contributions.

49 *nihil humani a me alienum puto*: "[I am human], I consider nothing human alien to me." From the Roman playwright Terence's play, the *Heautontimorumenos*, or "The Self-Tormenter."

53 **Lenten preachers**: refers to the admonitions of preachers during Lent, a period in the Ecclesiastical calendar in which the faithful must atone for their sins.

56 *spernere se sperni* and *spernere se ipsum*: "to scorn scorning oneself" and "to scorn oneself."

63 **Nero** (AD 37–68): Roman Emperor from AD 54, said to have murdered his own mother, stepfather, wives and others. Persecuted Christians wantonly after the fire of Rome in 64 AD, because he suspected they caused it. He committed suicide before the Senate could carry out its execution orders.

63 **Tacitus** (*c.* AD 55 – *c.* 120): Roman historian who wrote of the Roman Empire in his *Annales* and *Historiae*.

63 *odium generis humani*: "Hatred of humankind." This was a stock charge leveled at the early Christians by traditional pagans, who believed the Christians sacrificed babies and drank blood.

68 **Paul's writings in the Bible**: Paul, born at approximately the beginning of the common era into a strict Pharisaic Jewish family under the Hebrew name Saul, so zealously pious that he was called "The Pharisee of the Pharisees," is famous for his conversion to Christianity. Ten epistles are credited to him, including the hymn on love (I. Cor. xiii), the talk of the battle between flesh and spirit in the mortal frame (Romans vii), and the chapter on resurrection (I Cor. xv). In Galatians, Paul decries a return to legalism as the path to salvation, espousing instead a kind of "inward" freedom that marks the true Christian. In Ephesians, he urges a reconciliation of all humans in order that there might be achieved a "household of God," and a breaking down of all barriers that separate them. Romans may be considered his most mature work.

The events to which Nietzsche refers are recounted in the books of Acts and Galatians. Saul, a passionate Jew and persecutor of Christians, was confronted on the road to Damascus by Jesus of Nazareth, stricken from his horse to the earth and left sightless for three days: thus the conversion of Paul.

71 **Horace** (65 BC – 8 BC): Roman lyric poet and satirist whose works include *Satires*.

72 **Epicurus** (341 BC – 271 BC): Greek philosopher who taught in Athens from 306 BC. An atomist, Epicurus embraced hedonism: pleasure is a natural, innate goal, to which all other virtues are subordinated. The only alternative to pleasure for this philosopher was pain, with no intermediate states. To minimize pain, he exhorted others to relieve themselves of the fear of death and of the gods, and see Hell as only an illusion.

72 **Lucretius** (99 or 94 BC – 55 BC): Roman philosopher, author of *De rerum natura* (On the Nature of Things), an explication of Epicurean atomism. In it, Lucretius attempts to demonstrate, *inter alia*, that there is nothing but an infinite number of atoms moving in a void; that all finite worlds are doomed to perish; that the human soul is mortal; and that there is nothing to fear in death.

72 **Mithras**: Mithraism was a Persian mystery religion that was assimilated into Roman and Greek mythology; named after Mithras, god of light and truth. The religion was a major rival to Christianity, and was practiced widely up to the end of the fourth century AD.

72 **Isis**: another goddess after whom a mystery religion was founded. Egyptian deity of fertility, bringer of hope and new life.

72 **2 Maccabees**: the second of the two Maccabees in the Old Testament. They treat of the Jewish struggle for religious and political freedom against the Seleucid kings. The name of the books comes from their main figure, Maccabeus.

The Jewish martyr to whom Nietzsche refers was a man called Razis, one of the elders of Jerusalem (*v.* 2 M, 14:37–46). Convicted of Judaism, and about to be arrested and beaten by 500 soldiers, he fell upon his sword, wishing to die at his own hands rather than suffer an ignoble death at the hands of villains. But he missed, and so threw himself from a parapet, into the troops. Unfortunately, they drew back, and so he fell on empty space. Broken and bleeding, he tore out his entrails, taking them in his hands and throwing them at the crowd as he ran into it. Before he died, he called on Yahweh to give them back to him one day.

76 **Eros**: God of love, sprung from Zeus (according to Hesiod), or the

son of Ares (god of war) and Aphrodite (goddess of love). Often depicted as a handsome human man, the pinnacle of physical beauty.

76 **Aphrodite**: like Eros, enjoys a double tradition of birth: *Aphrodite Urania*, sprung from Uranus, represents sublime and heavenly love; *Aphrodite Pandemos* (for the common people), born of both sexes, goddess of physical aspects of love and guardian of prostitutes.

76 **Kobold**: a gnome that, in German folklore, was believed to live underground.

77 **Don Juan**: legendary Spanish nobleman featured in many works of literature and poetry: see Lord Byron's *Don Juan*. Generally a term used of a man who chases women.

77 **Plutarch** (*c.* AD 46–120): Greek prose writer and biographer, author of *Parallel Lives*, in which he compared life stories of Greek and Roman soldiers and statesmen.

77 **George Whitfield** (1714–70): British Methodist evangelist, suspended for his unorthodox methods and ideas.

83 **Prometheus**: cousin of Zeus and the son of a Titan. As punishment for bringing fire to mortals, Zeus had him bound by chains to a rock, and sent a vulture to consume his liver, which continually regenerated.

84 **Moses** (*c.* 13th century BC): Hebrew judge and lawgiver who led the Israelites out of Egypt and into the promised land of Canaan. Received the Ten Commandments on Mount Sinai. The Torah – the first five books of the Old Testament – is attributed to him.

84 **Passover**: in Exodus 12:23–27, the exemption of the Israelites from the slaughter of the first-born in Egypt. An annual religious and agricultural festival that celebrates the liberation of the Israelites from slavery in Egypt, and begins on the 14th day of the month of Nisan.

84 **Passover Lamb**: the sacrifice at the Passover feast. Also refers to Christ in 1 Cor. 5:7.

84 **Septuagint**: Greek translation of the Old Testament, including the Apocrypha. The name has as its root *septem*, seven, and refers to the 70 or so Jewish scholars who are said to have translated the Old Testament into Greek at Alexandria. Prepared for Greek-speaking Jews of Egypt who could not read Hebrew.

84 *Psalms* **96:10**: "So among the nations, 'Yaweh is King.' The world is set firm, it cannot be moved. He will judge the nations with justice" (New Jerusalem Bible).

91 *deus absconditus*: the "hidden/concealed god."

96 *In hoc signo vinces*: "in this sign you will conquer." The emperor Constantine is supposed to have seen a vision of the (Christian) cross, and to have heard or seen these words on the eve of his battle against the pagan emperor Maxentius in 312 AD. After he won, he converted to Christianity and encouraged others to do the same.

96 **Buddha** (*c.* 563 BC – 483 BC): meaning "enlightened one," the title

of Guatama Siddhartha, founder of Buddhism. After having lived the lives of both the hedonist and the ascetic, embraced the life of the Middle Way. He claimed that suffering, having a distinct cause, can be ended by following the Noble Eightfold Path, and arriving at nirvana, which is release from the cycle of rebirth and the end of all sensual cravings.

Book II

102 *O pudenda origo*: "O shameful origin."

103 La Rochefoucauld (1613–80): French writer whose *Moral Maxims* is a collection of short, highly cynical observations on life. He wrote, "Our virtues are mostly our vices in disguise."

109 Lord Byron (1788–1824): born George Gordon Byron, English Romantic poet often referred to as the "patron saint" of Romantic liberalism.

109 Napoleon (1769–1821): Emperor of the French from 1804 to 14 and 1814 to 15. He conquered most of Europe from 1803 in the Napoleonic Wars.

113 Calvin, John (1509–64): Genevan theologian and reformer whose *Institutes of the Christian Religion* presents a full statement of French Protestant belief. Calvin's main underlying question throughout his theology was how God's grace was possible, since humans were not worthy of redemption. He also believed that the Reformation was not installing something new but was merely "purifying" the church.

114 Don Quixote: character created by the Spanish novelist Miguel de Cervantes (1547–1616) in the book by the same name; Don Quixote sets out to revive the romance of knighthood and chivalry, mistaking windmills for giants, thinking every situation begs for rectification. Later, after being bested in a duel, he comes home forlorn and dies of disillusionment.

128 Oedipus: a character in plays of Sophocles and perhaps Greek drama's most tragic figure. Unwittingly killing his father and marrying his mother, he discovers that he is responsible for the plague that befalls his city, and consequently blinds himself and suffers self-exile.

130 *Moira* in Greek mythology: Greek word for "fate," or "lot, share." Not a person or deity, but merely a fact, the idea that the world is apportioned and that humans must therefore know their bounds. To act "beyond one's *moira*" is hubris. Even Zeus in the *Iliad* is bound to act in accordance with what is ordained.

130 Persephone (or *Kore*, "the Girl") and the underworld: in Greek mythology, daughter of Zeus and Demeter, who, when playing with a group of girls in a meadow, is spotted by Hades-Aidoneus, personification of the underworld. Enchanted by the girl, he causes the earth to open up and he rides out in a horse and chariot and steals away with her. She spends a third of her time in the underworld (in which time Demeter, in mourning, allows no harvest), and is given time each year on earth, the period in which Demeter allows the harvest: hence the appellations "daughter of the Goddess of the Corn" and "Mistress of the Dead."

131 Epictetus (*c.* AD 55–135): Stoic philosopher who himself wrote nothing but whose ideas were memorialized in *The Discourses of Epictetus* and the *Encheiridion*. He urged absolute trust in divine providence and indifference to external circumstances, i.e. those circumstances beyond one's control.

132 Voltaire (1694–1778): French writer of the eighteenth-century Enlightenment in whose *Candide* the character Dr. Pangloss pokes fun at Leibniz' notion that this was the best of all possible worlds. A great champion of freedom of religion, he fought ceaselessly against the tyranny of the Church. Nietzsche dedicated *Human, All Too Human* to Voltaire's memory.

132 Comte, Auguste (1798–1857): philosopher and sociologist, founder of Positivism and architect of a kind of non-theistic religion based on an abstract Supreme Being. His conception of "positive philosophy" is given full expression in his six-volume work *Course in Positive Philosophy* (1830–42). He imagined human societal development to go through the *theological, metaphysical,* and *positive* stages of existence, each necessary parts of growth in an inevitable and fixed pattern.

132 *On n'est bon que par la pitié: il faut donc qu'il y ait quelque pitié dans tous nos sentiments*: "People are good only out of pity. Therefore, there must be some pity in all our sentiments."

136 Indian philosophy and misery: Buddha, for example, perceived the tragedy and sorrow inherent in the impermanent world, and concentrated his efforts on relieving humans from sorrow. It is said, in fact, that he taught only two things: that there exists sorrow (the "first truth"), and that there is release from sorrow (the "second truth").

139 Stoicism: a philosophical tradition founded by Zeno (*d.* 261 BC), and whose last major figure was Marcus Aurelius (2nd century AD). Nietzsche refers to the Stoic ethical views (as opposed to their views on divinity): to be stoical was to face destiny with courage and with dignity, for the truly virtuous man accepts divine providence. In contrast with ancient Greek ethics, which stressed results, Stoics held that sometimes results were out of one's hands, so that in the end what truly matters is the *attempt* to be good.

142 *qualitas occultas*: "hidden quality."

144 Olympians: an allusion to the Greek deities, who lived on Mount Olympus. In the *Iliad*, they exhibited petty and ignoble traits, often appearing only as imperfect humans writ large.

Book III

154 refugium: "a refuge, place of rest, a way out."

157 Philoctetes: the central character of the Sophoclean tragedy of the same name. Philoctetes, in an expedition that sailed against Troy, was bitten by a snake. His cries of anguish and the abominable stench of the wound caused such misfortune among the crew that they, upon Odysseus' orders, marooned him on the deserted island of Lemnos, where he lived in agony for ten years, alone and crippled.

163 Contra Rousseau: the second part of the disjunctive here (which Nietzsche espouses) is opposed to the thesis of Rousseau that "man is naturally good, and only by institutions is he made bad" (*Discourse on Inequality*).

165 The four Socratic virtues: temperance, courage, wisdom and justice.

167 Bismarck, Otto von (1815–98): German politician and prime minister of Prussia 1862–90, and chancellor of the German Empire 1871–90. His vigorous expansionist policy led to wars in Denmark, Austria and France, and the eventual unification of Germany.

167 Carnot, Lazare N.M. (1753–1823): French soldier and politician. As a member of the National Convention in the French Revolution, he organized the armies of the Republic. He was minister of the interior in 1815 under Napoleon.

167 Niebuhr, Barthold G. (1776–1831): German historian who wrote the three-volume *History of Rome* (1811–32).

167 Ce qui importe, ce ne sont point les personnes: mais les choses: "What matters is not people but things."

168 Thucydides (c. 455 BC – 400 BC): often called the first true historian. Greek soldier and author of the *Peloponnesian War*. Famously described his task as warning future generations of how humans are likely to behave as long as human nature remains the same. Ruthlessly detailed in almost clinical fashion the relentless quest for power over others and expediency as the true measure of what should be done.

168 Sophocles (c. 496 BC – 406 BC): Greek tragedian. Of the 123 plays attributed to him, some of the more well known include *Antigone*, *Oedipus Tyrannus*, *Ajax* and *Elektra*.

168 Pericles (c. 495 BC – 429 BC): Athens' greatest statesman, in Thucydides' estimation. The Pericles of the "funeral oration" (*Peloponnesian War*) is a consummate imperialist, bent on extending Athenian power, though expressing this ambition with great delicacy and grace.

168 Hippocrates (c. 460 BC – 380 BC): Greek physician, commonly known as the "Father of Medicine."

168 Democritus (c. 460 BC – c. 370 BC): Greek philosopher and atomist, who held that everything exists by virtue of the chance collision of an infinite number of indivisible particles, which move forever through an infinite void.

168 *error veritate simplicior:* "error is simpler than truth."

169 **Paestum** (originally called Poseidonia): Italian city on the Etruscan seashore, founded *c.* 600 BC by Greek colonists. Home of three beautiful Doric stone temples erected in the sixth century BC, the zenith of the temple-building tradition.

169 **Pompeii**: city in Campania (near Paestum), situated on a small volcanic hill. It was destroyed in the eruption of Mt. Vesuvius in 79 AD. Site of the Doric Temple of the *Foro Triangolare* and Temple of Apollo. Pompeii was buried under a thick blanket of volcanic ashes and pumice, until excavation (begun in the eighteenth century) revealed a very well-preserved town filled with such things as amphitheatres and baths.

171 *homo pamphagus:* "an all-devouring man."

172 **Aeschylus** (525/4 BC – 456 BC): the first of classical Athens' tragedians, said to have written 90 plays. Among his works are the sole intact Greek trilogy, *Oresteia (Agamemnon, Choephori, Eumendies)*, *Seven Against Thebes*, and *Prometheus Bound*.

175 **Horace** (65 BC – 8 BC): Latin poet. Among his writings are the *Ars Poetica*, an essay in literary criticism (date uncertain) and the *Epistles* (20 BC – 17 BC), dialogues on philosophical and literary topics.

175 *Credat Judaeus Apella:* "Let Apella the Jew believe it." This is a quote from one of Horace's satires in which he sarcastically dismisses a claim someone has made to him.

189 *Gewaltmenschen:* "brutes."

190 **Schiller, J. C. F. von** (1759–1805): German philosopher, poet and dramatist, concerned with man's rational life and its relationship with art and beauty. Believed that aesthetics and not religion (*pace* Kant) was central to morality's role of shaping man's sensuous life. Among his writings are *On the Aesthetic Education of Man* and *Naive and Sentimental Poetry*.

190 **Humboldt, Wilhelm von** (1767–1835): German philologist, philosopher and diplomat, a pioneer of comparative linguistics. In his book *On the Dual* (1791), he effectively ended all attempts to find the origin of language by arguing that the older languages (e.g. Sanskrit) are syntactically more complex than more recent ones.

190 **Schleiermacher, Friedrich E. D.** (1768–1834): German theologian and philosopher, often considered the father of modern Protestant theology. Author of *Reden Über die Religion* (1799) and *Kurze Darstellung des Theologischen Studiums* (1811).

190 **Schelling, Friedrich W. J. von** (1775–1854): German philosopher and leading figure in the German Idealist movement. Among his works are *Ideen zu einer Philosophie der Natur* (1797).

191 **Corneille, Pierre** (1606–84): French playwright, whose great success came with his tragedies, which included *Médée* (1625) and *Le Cid* (1636 or 1637), among others. Considered by many the father of French classical tragedy, and one of France's premier tragic poets.

191 **Madame de Sévigné** (1626–96): French writer and lady of fashion, famous for her *Letters*, which described in great detail events of her daily life.

192 **Fénelon, François de Salignac** (1651–1715): French writer and ecclesiastic, condemned in 1699 for embracing the Quietist idea that one should accept damnation out of sheer devotion to God. His *Telemachus* (1699) was a sort of political manifesto, with its picture of an ideal commonwealth, and earned him banishment at the hands of Louis XIV.

192 **Madame de Guyon,** (Guyon, Jeanne-Marie de la Motte: 1648–1717): French mystic, preacher and practitioner of Quietism.

192 **French Quietists**: adherents of a school of mysticism that took the path of "true love," which is to say, the renunciation of hope and reward and the acceptance of damnation.

192 **Trappist monasteries**: the Trappists – so-called because their original house was in La Trappe in Normandy–was founded by Dominique de Raucé in 1664. The Order was marked by a particularly strict observance of the rules of the Cistercian Order (from which the Trappists splintered): they remained silent, did much manual labor and ate no meat. (It has since once again come under the governance of the Cistercian Order.)

192 **Huguenots**: another name for French Calvinists. Louis XIV unleashed his forces in acts of extreme cruelty and duplicity when the Huguenots would not conform to Catholicism. Fearing for their lives, 400,000 fled France, taking their well-known industrial skills with them.

192 **Port-Royal**: site of a Jansenist center, among whom is counted Blaise Pascal (1623–62). (Jansenism was a Christian teaching of Cornelius Jansen; it divided the Roman Catholic Church in France during the seventeenth century, as it stressed the predestination of St. Augustine of Hippo, *contra* the Jesuits.) The "Jansenist Gentlemen" of Port Royal established a number of schools there, stressing the sciences, as well as love for the child and close contact between students and teachers.

197 **Newton, Isaac** (1642–1727): English physicist and mathematician, who conceived the idea of universal gravitation in 1665 and showed that Kepler's three laws could each be derived from a single law of gravitation. Author of *Philosophiae Naturalis Principia Mathematica* (1687) and *Opticks* (1704).

199 **Odysseus**: in Homer, a brave, sagacious and cunning hero, son of

239

NOTES

Laertes (King of Ithica). He spends ten years returning home after
the sacking of Troy. Odysseus' mother, when visited by him in Hades,
calls him "ill-fated beyond all mortals" (*Odyssey*, XI, 216).

199 Themistocles (*c.* 524 BC – *c.* 460 BC): Athenian democratic statesman
and father of Athenian sea power. Chiefly responsible for Greek victory over the Persian Empire at the Battle of Salamis in 480 BC
because of his vehement insistence that Greece invest heavily in its
navy. Nietzsche's reference to "the dextrous Odysseus of the classical
age" probably stems from Themistocles' perceived duplicity and slick
demeanor (in the minds of many earlier writers).

201 The age of Louis XIV: 1643–1715, the reign of Louis XIV.

202 Sturm und Drang "storm and stress": an early German Romantic
movement in literature and music (*c.* late 1770s), the name of which
is taken from a play by Friedrich von Klinger, 1776. It is concerned
with the depiction of unbridled passions. Among its chief figures are
Goethe, Schiller and Herder.

206 *bestia triumphans*: "the triumphant beast."

207 *admirari id est philosophari*: "to marvel (wonder), that is to philoso-
phize." This is more than the mundane idea that curiosity makes one
think; rather, it evokes Plato and Aristotle, who thought marvelous
(and terrifying) phenomena of nature were an inspiration to reflective analysis.

Book IV

240 Ajax: in Sophocles' play by that name, he went mad with anger and
disillusionment, finally killing himself.

240 Tristan and Isolde: principal characters in a medieval tale of
romance, who, after drinking a love potion prepared for Isolde and
another, both die at their own hands, remaining forever in love. The
subject of an opera by Richard Wagner (1813–83), which remained
Nietzsche's favorite Wagnerian opera to the end of his life.

256 *dolce far niente*: literally, "sweet to do nothing," but here it essentially
means, "an evening of simply doing nothing."

259 panegyrist: one who praises highly in public as part of a formal eulogy,
as at a public festival.

268 Scylla and Charybdis: these two "creatures" live opposite each other
in caves (*v. Odyssey* XII, 101 ff.). The former is an immortal sea monster with six heads and twelve feet, while Charybdis is a sort of
whirlpool in which no ship can possibly survive.

272 Livingstone, David (1813–73): born in Blantyre, Strathclyde, a missionary and explorer. Author of *Missionary Travels* (1857).

285 *Chi non ha, non e*: "he who does not have (money) is not (anybody)."

298 *profanum vulgus*: "the common people."

298 *ad majorem dei gloriam*: "to the greater glory of God."

298 **Carlyle, Thomas** (1795–1881): Scottish man of letters, historian, and "hero-worshipper."

307 *Facta ficta*: "fictitious or phony deeds."

321 **Lemnos**: an island off the northeast Aegean Sea.

321 **Neoptolemus**: in Greek mythology, son of Achilles and Deidameia. According to Sophocles, after Achilles' death, he was sent to Troy, because the Greeks needed his presence in order to take the city (*Philoctetes*, 114f.; 345 ff.)

321 **propylaea**: in classical architecture, a monumental entrance or vestibule before one or more buildings.

325 **Wesley, John** (1703–91): English religious leader and ordained priest.

325 **Bohler, Peter** (dates unknown): met John Wesley in 1738, and had a considerable influence upon him.

327 *aqua fortis*: "strong water" (i.e. a deadly drink).

344 **Homer**: believed by the ancient Greeks to be the author of both the *Iliad* and the *Odyssey*. However, as the entry on "Homer" in the *Oxford Classical Dictionary* (2nd ed.) puts it, "Our ignorance of Homer's date, place, and life has led to scepticism about his existence."

347 **Pythagoreans**: followers of Pythagoras (6th century BC), a Greek philosopher and mathematician who founded a rather strange religious and moral school, open to both women and men, some of the practices of which included moral purification (strict silence and severe self-examination) and abstinence from beans and certain meats.

353 **Fichte** (1762–1814): German philosopher and "idealist" who studied theology and then philosophy at Jena, later becoming a zealous follower of Immanuel Kant.

364 **Atlas**: in mythology, a Titan, the guardian of the pillars of heaven (*Od.* I, 53) and, according to later writers, holds up the sky itself (in Hesiod and Aeschylus). Tricked Heracles into holding up the sky (whilst Atlas fetched the apples of Hesperides), until he was forced to assume the burden again.

367 **Cynics**: followers of the ideas of Diogenes of Sinope. A quasi-philosophical discipline that espoused rejection of all convention, practiced shamelessness, and tried to live on nothing.

415 *Remedium amoris*: "a remedy or cure for love": this is the title of one of Ovid's didactic poems, about how to fall out of love.

417 *credo quia absurdum est, credo quia absurdum sum:* "I believe because it is absurd, I believe because I am absurd."

Book V

423 ringing the angelus: the angelus is a bell rung as a call to recite a devotional prayer to commemorate the Annunciation, a Christian feast celebrating the angel Gabriel's announcement to the Virgin Mary of the Incarnation.

427 rococo horticulture: from the style of art, especially in architecture: "rococo" refers to a movement that began in early eighteenth century France. It was characterized by very elaborate, almost immoderately so, ornamentation such as foliage, animal figures, and scrolls.

427 embellir la nature: "to embellish/improve upon nature."

430 labors of Heracles (also Hercules): in Greek folklore, Heracles, a hero but not a god, suffered under 12 labors, one of which was to clean the stables of Augeas.

436 casuistical: of or relating to casuistry, a method for resolving problems of conscience, which includes asking oneself whether the act contemplated conflicts with a law.

440 vita contemplativa, vita practica: contemplative life, practical life.

450 Marcus Aurelius (AD 121–80): Roman Emperor from 161–80 and the last of antiquity's great Stoic philosophers. Author of the *Meditations,* a twelve-part book filled with reflections on life, death and right conduct.

459 vitam impendere vero: "to devote one's life to truth."

459 verum impendere vitae: "the truth hangs over [i.e. threatens] life."

460 Tiberius (I) (42 BC – AD 37): Emperor, son of Tiberius Claudius Nero and Livia Drusilla. Augustus was essentially forced to recognize Tiberius as his successor, as the two favorite candidates (Augustus' grandsons) had died. Augustus at that time then adopted Tiberius.

460 Augustus (63 BC – AD 14): also known early in his life as Octavianus. First Roman Emperor (27 BC – AD 14), and great-nephew of Julius Caesar, who adopted him as his son and heir. Became ruler of the entire Roman world and assumed the title of "Augustus" ("sacred," "exalted").

473 ubi pater sum, ibi patri: literally, "where I am a father, there is my fatherland"; in effect, a way of saying "my country is wherever I am with my family."

496 Panhellenic city: a reference to the city of Syracuse, which was then under the rule of Dionysius.

496 Mohammed (also Muhammad: c. 570–632): the founder of Islam, born in Mecca. Had visions, which he claimed were revelations from God, some 650 of which make up the Koran.

499 Procrustean bed of virtue: "Procrustean" refers to an arbitrary standard to which all must conform, without regard to individual circumstances. The term has its origin in a figure of Greek mythology, *Procrustes,* an awful Greek giant who, after overcoming his victim, would cause "much woe" by either hammering out or lopping off parts of the victim, so that he would fit perfectly into one of his two beds.

499 Diderot (1713–84): French encyclopedist and philosopher, published *Pensées philosophiques* (1746); for twenty years worked on the monumental, 28-volume *Encyclopédie, ou Dictionnaire Raisonné des Sciences, des Arts et des Métiers* (1751–72), an epic summary of human knowledge.

520 *gloria mundi*: "the glory of the world."

540 Michelangelo (1475–1564): Italian sculptor, painter and architect.

547 Alexander III of Macedonia ("the Great") (356 BC – 323 BC): son and successor of Philip II, pupil of Aristotle, and arguably the greatest military leader of antiquity. Nietzsche's reference to Alexander here as decisive is further buttressed by these common ancient characterizations: he was a "monster of celerity" in battle, often even losing control of his troops, so fiercely and singlemindedly did he pursue the enemy. (Yet he showed great patience in the siege of Tyre, painstakingly awaiting the right moment for attack.)

549 Alfred de Musset (1810–57): French writer, author of *Contes d'Espagne et d'Italie* (1830) and *Un Spectacle dans un fauteuil* (1832), among other works.

550 empyrean: the highest heights of heaven, paradise; the abode of God and the angels.

558 Pope, Alexander (1688–1744): English poet, author of *Pastorals* (1709) and the mock-heroic poem *The Rape of the Lock* (1712), among other works.

562 Odysseus' mother: see Homer's *Odyssey*, Book XI, wherein Odysseus visits Hades.

568 Phoenix: a legendary bird in ancient Egyptian mythology whose existence is marked by five or six centuries of life in the Arabian desert, then consumption in its own fire, after which it arises anew in an act of freshness and transformation – the phoenix being thereby an immortal bird.

Index

All references are by section, not page, number. "P" indicates preface section.

244

Cambridge texts in the history of philosophy

Titles published in the series thus far

Antoine Arnauld and Pierre Nicole *Logic or the Art of Thinking* (edited by Jill Vance Buroker)

Boyle *A Free Enquiry into the Vulgarly Received Notion of Nature* (edited by Edward B. Davis and Michael Hunter)

Conway *The Principles of the Most Ancient and Modern Philosophy* (edited by Allison P. Coudert and Taylor Corse)

Cudworth *A Treatise Concerning Eternal and Immutable Morality* with *A Treatise of Freewill* (edited by Sarah Hutton)

Descartes *Meditations on First Philosophy*, with selections from the *Objections and Replies* (edited with an introduction by John Cottingham)

Kant *Critique of Practical Reason* (edited by Mary Gregor with an introduction by Andrews Reath)

Kant *The Metaphysics of Morals* (edited by Mary Gregor with an introduction by Roger Sullivan)

Kant *Prolegomena to any Future Metaphysics* (edited by Gary Hatfield)

La Mettrie *Machine Man and Other Writings* (edited by Ann Thomson)

Leibniz *New Essays on Human Understanding* (edited by Peter Remnant and Jonathan Bennett)

Malebranche *Dialogues on Metaphysics and on Religion* (edited by Nicholas Jolley and David Scott)

Malebranche *The Search after Truth* (edited by Thomas M. Lennon and Paul J. Olscamp)

Mendelssohn *Philosophical Writings* (edited by Daniel O. Dahlstrom)

Nietzsche *Daybreak* (edited by Maudemarie Clark and Brian Leiter, translated by R. J. Hollingdale)

Nietzsche *Human, All Too Human* (translated by R. J. Hollingdale with an introduction by Richard Schacht)

Nietzsche *Untimely Meditations* (edited by Daniel Breazeale, translated by R. J. Hollingdale)

Schleiermacher *On Religion: Speeches to its Cultured Despisers* (edited by Richard Crouter)